INDIA IN THE CRISIS

INDIA IN THE CRISIS

BRIJ NARAIN

GYAN

Published by

GYAN

Gyan Publishing House
5, Ansari Road
Daryaganj, New Delhi-110002
Phone: 011-47034999, 9811692060
E-mail: books@gyanbooks.com

Distribution Network
gyanbooks.com
India, USA, Canada, UK, Australia

ISBN: 978-93-7169-744-6 (PB)

First Published, 1934

2nd Impression 2025

Printed at: Gyan Press, Delhi.

INDIA IN THE CRISIS

Author: BRIJ NARAIN

India in the Crisis

By

BRIJ NARAIN
Professor of Economics
Sanatana Dharma College, Lahore

ALLAHABAD
THE INDIAN PRESS, LTD.
1934

PREFACE

I have written this book not without serious misgiving. About two years ago I wrote a short account of the trade depression in Urdu for the benefit of the business community. The business community completely ignored the book. This is my second attempt to draw the attention of the Indian public to vital problems arising out of the crisis, which affect all of us, whatever our faith, and which require a solution. The English reading public in India is microscopically small—it consists largely of University students who, under the guidance of examiners, take more interest in ancient things like *damdupat* and the origin of the caste system than in what is happening around them. As for the rest, they find the Communal Award and such issues as 'Music before Mosques' or 'Azan and Arti' more exciting than the disruption of old economic systems and the birth of new.

I am glad to take this opportunity of thanking Prof. Chiranjiva Lal Mathur of the Dyal Singh College, Lahore, and Prof. Krishn Datta of the Hailey College of Commerce, Lahore, for kindly reading a great part of the manuscript and criticising it.

Brij Narain

Lahore
Sept. 9, 1934

CONTENTS

Part I—India in the Crisis

PART I

INDIA IN THE CRISIS

CHAPTER I

AGRICULTURE

I

While the trade depression has made the whole world poor, India has probably suffered more than any other country. The numbers dependent on agriculture in our country are excessive, and secondly, our agricultural organization is not easily adjustable to a fall of prices.

The *Farm Accounts in the Punjab* provide valuable material for the study of Punjab agriculture during the depression. So far as the present writer is aware, such Accounts are not available for farming in other parts of India. The value of *Farm Accounts in the Punjab* consists in the accurate data that they furnish in regard to income and expenditure of the farms selected for study. But these Accounts also enable us to form some idea of the heavy losses suffered by cultivators in the Punjab on account of the fall of prices. As agriculture in many parts of India is not more prosperous than in the Punjab, agriculturally the most advanced Province of British India, the Punjab Farm Accounts may be regarded as of more than Provincial interest.

Falls of Prices

The following table shows the prices of the more important agricultural commodities from 1926-27 to 1931-32.

TABLE I

Wholesale Harvest Prices of some Important Agricultural Commodities in the Punjab from 1926-27 to 1931-32. (Farm Accounts in the Punjab, 1931-32 Introduction, p. i.)

Year	Wheat		Gram		Rapeseed		Gur		Cotton Desi		Cotton American	
	Rs.	a.	Rs.	a.	Rs.	a.	Rs.	a.	Rs.	a.	Rs.	a.
1926-27	4	8	3	14	7	7	5	15	7	14	9	6
1927-28	4	6	3	13	7	3	5	6	10	13	13	12
1928-29	4	6	4	12	7	0	6	2	10	0	13	2
1929-30	3	2	3	12	5	12	6	5	6	15	8	15
1930-31	1	9	1	14	3	13	4	2	4	7	5	9
1931-32	2	1	1	13	3	8	3	13	5	7	6	10

Taking the price of each commodity in 1928-29 as 100, the percentage fall in 1930-31 was as follows:

	Fall of price in 1930-31, 1928-29=100 per cent
Wheat	64
Gram	61
Rapeseed	46
Gur	33
Cotton:	
Desi	56
American	58

Wheat and cotton are the two most important money crops of the Punjab. It can be easily imagined that the heavy fall in their prices suddenly impoverished the whole of rural Punjab.

The fluctuations in the net income per acre of various holdings from 1928-29 to 1931-32 are shown by the following table.

Table II

Net Income per acre of the cultivators if the whole Land had belonged to them (Farm Accounts in the Punjab, 1931-32, p. xi).

Holding Dist.	and area	1928-29	1929-30	1930-31	1931-32
		Rs. a. p.	Rs. a. p.	Rs. a. p.	Rs. a. p.
Lyallpur	802·5 acres	54 3 0	44 2 10	11 8 2	24 5 5
,,	27·3 ,,	33 14 6	29 6 0	4 14 8	20 8 2
,,	27·6 ,,	16 15 11	12 6 11	4 1 9	12 5 10
Sargodah	52·6 ,,	35 3 7	12 7 10	6 12 9	10 1 11
Montgomery	48·6 ,,	42 11 7	32 0 9	14 8 1	18 6 1
Amritsar	20·3 ,,	61 5 10	24 15 9	11 11 9	5 7 6
,,	18·5 ,,	65 12 4	30 13 4	4 5 10	—0 1 11
,,	16·5 ,,	..	..	24 1 5	22 15 0
Rohtak	11·2 ,,	16 15 11	—3 9 7	2 7 10	8 0 8
,,	10·6 ,,	39 14 6	36 10 6	27 2 6	23 14 5
,,	22·1 ,,	35 6 2	19 11 3	10 5 3	20 3 3
Multan	15·3 ,,	15 0 9	3 15 0	10 5 11	12 3 3
,,	34·5 ,,	14 8 4	18 11 3	11 4 7	8 1 6
,,	29.5 ,,	..	..	3 2 3	1 9
Jullunder	49·4 ,,	43 10 4	33 4 8	17 4 4	17 5 8
,,	20·6 ,,	25 9 7	—2 11 10	—6 8 0	1 11 2
,,	9·8 ,,	44 10 8	24 8 0	16 7 3	25 3 7

Holding Dist. and area		1928-29	1929-30	1930-31	1931-32
		Rs. a. p.	Rs. a. p.	Rs. a. p.	Rs. a. p.
Hoshiarpur	8·4 acres	20 7 7	31 7 7	12 10 4	17 6 4
Ludhiana	70·1 ,,	21 3 2	10 6 7	3 0 1	5 6 10
,,	15·4 ,,	..	20 6 1	4 11 4	21 12 8
Jhelum	27·7 ,,	..	..	8 4 3	19 6 5
,,	20·2 ,,	..	..	—5 3 1	15 10 7
,,	26·0 ,,	..	..	—2 0 5	—2 3 11

Of the 23 holdings mentioned in the table, 3 holdings showed loss in 1930-31 while the income of 9 other holdings was less than Rs. 10 per acre.

For general purposes, the table given below, also borrowed from the Farm Accounts for 1931-32, is more useful:

Table III

Average net income per acre of the cultivators of various Districts, if the whole land had belonged to them, (Farm Accounts in the Punjab, 1931-32, p. xiii).

District and area		1928-29	1929-30	1930-31	1931-32
		Rs. a. p.	Rs. a. p.	Rs. a. p.	Rs. a. p.
Lyallpur	857·6 acres	53 14 3	44 6 7	11 14 11	23 13 3
Sargodah	52·6 ,,	35 3 7	12 7 10	6 12 9	10 1 11
Montgomery	48·6 ,,	42 11 7	32 0 9	14 8 1	18 6 1
Amritsar	55·5 ,,	64 5 5	27 12 0	14 7 8	8 13 2
Rohtak	44·1 ,,	31 0 0	18 0 3	13 1 5	18 0 0

District and area		1928-29	1929-30	1930-31	1931-32
		Rs. a. p.	Rs. a. p.	Rs. a. p.	Rs. a. p.
Multan	79·5 acres	14 11 6	13 9 9	7 14 1	6 7 5
Jullunder	80·2 „	38 12 0	23 13 6	11 12 9	14 4 6
Hoshiarpur	8·4 „	20 7 7	31 7 7	12 10 4	17 6 4
Ludhiana	85·5 „	21 3 3	12 4 4	3 7 2	8 6 5
Jhelum	74·1 „	..	..	0 13 5	10 12 8
AVERAGES.					
Canal Colonies	950·2 acres	53 0 2	42 15 2	11 11 2	22 12 9
Well-irrigated	427·6 „	32 2 0	18 7 6	7 12 10	10 12 6
Total	1,386·8 „	47 7 8	36 12 9	10 9 2	19 1 6
AVERAGES, EXCLUDING RISALEWALA					
Canal Colonies (a)		33 11 4	24 3 0	7 14 7	14 14 5
Total (b)		32 8 4	20 1 3	7 13 4	11 14 2

The average net income, excluding Risalewala is separately shown in this table. This is because the Risalewala Farm is not typical of the average holding in the Punjab. It is a Government farm of about 800 acres managed by the Government Agricultural Department.

Excluding Risalewala, the average net income per acre for the ten districts fell from Rs. 32-8-4 in 1928-29 to Rs. 7-13-4 in 1931-32.

It should be noted that in calculating the net income, remuneration for the labour of the cultivator and of his family was not included.

Further, the holdings are all irrigated (canal or well-irrigation) and are situated in the relatively prosperous districts of the Punjab. If *barani* holdings in the poorer districts such as Hissar, Gurgaon, Mianwali and Campbellpur were included, the average net income in 1930-31 would fall from about Rs. 8 to Rs. 4 or 5 per acre.

An income of even 4 or 5 rupees per acre might be sufficient to live upon if the cultivator had a good deal of land, say 50 acres. What is the average amount of land per cultivator in the Punjab and other Provinces?

The following table shows the area actually sown in the major Provinces in 1930-31 and the number of earners both male and female, whose principal occupation was cultivation. Working dependents and those who followed cultivation as a subsidiary occupation have been excluded.

TABLE IV

Sub-order 1 (a) Cultivation[1]

Total earners principal occupation

Provinces	Males	Females	Total	Net area actually sown in 1930-31. Acres.[2]	Net area per cultivator, taking males and females tog. Acres.
Bengal ..	8,393,877	632,152	9,026,029	23,460,300	2·6
Bihar and Orissa	8,310,190	3,176,200	11,486,390	24,470,900	2·1
Bombay ..	3,450,907	1,023,251	4,474,158	32,620,701	7·3
Central Provinces & Berar ..	3,204,436	1,884,331	5,088,767	25,364,376	5·0
Madras ..	7,774,536	2,939,302	10,713,838	34,222,604	3·2
Punjab ..	3,541,523	172,409	3,713,932	26,683,664	7·2
U. P. ..	11,714,505	2,612,769	14,327,274	35,542,446	2·5

[1] Statistical Abstract for 1930-31.
[2] Census of India, Volume I, Part II, page 221.

The area actually sown in the Punjab in 1930-31 was on an average 7·2 acres per cultivator. Assuming that on an average net income per acre sown, irrigated or unirrigated, was Rs. 7-13-4, which is the average for irrigated holdings in the *Farm Accounts* for 1930-31, the total net income of a cultivator of 7·2 acres (assuming that the whole land belonged to him) was about 57 rupees. In 1931-32 this income rose to about 86 rupees. As we have said above, the inclusion of *barani* holdings would considerably lower these figures. We may assume, for the sake of argument, that on an average each acre sown in the Punjab in 1930-31 and 1931-32 yielded a net income as high as the average for irrigated acres. But actually this is impossible.

The terrible meaning of these figures will be realized when it is remembered that excepting Bombay (where land per cultivator is equal to that in the Punjab) in other Provinces of British India the cultivator has less land than in the Punjab. In Bengal, the United Provinces, and Bihar and Orissa, the net area sown per cultivator in 1930-31 was less than 3 acres, and in the Central Provinces and Berar it was 5 acres. The cultivator in other Provinces is not more prosperous than the Punjab cultivator. And the Punjab cultivator is incredibly poor.

Inelastic Expenditure

Net income is the difference between gross income and expenditure. A study of farmers' expenditure shows that while, on account of the fall of prices, gross income fell heavily, expenditure fell to a far smaller extent.

As an illustration we may study the income and expenditure of a farm of about 28 acres situated at a distance of about 12 miles from Lyallpur.

TABLE V

Farm of 28 acres (Lyallpur District). .Canal-irrigated

	Total			Per Acre		
	Gross Income	Expenditure	Net Income	Gross Income	Expenditure	Net Income
	Rs. a. p.	Rs. a. p.	Rs. a. p.	Rs. a. p.	Rs. a. p.	Rs. a. p.
1925-26	2837 12 0	973 5 9	1864 6 3	101 5 8	34 12 3	66 9 5
1926-27	2341 1 10	946 0 10	1395 1 0	83 9 10	33 12 8	49 13 2
1927-28	1094 7 10	915 1 9	179 6 1	39 6 4	32 14 11	6 7 5
1928-29	1876 8 2	927 3 11	949 4 3	67 0 4	33 1 10	33 14 6
1929-30	1793 4 5	970 11 4	822 9 1	64 0 9	34 10 9	29 6 0
1930-31	976 4 2	841 15 7	134 4 7	35 11 11	30 13 3	4 14 8
1931-32	1268 12 4	708 9 6	560 2 10	46 7 8	25 15 1	20 8 2

In 1930-31, the gross income per acre of this farm, as compared with 1925-26, fell 65 per cent, and as compared with 1929-30, 44 per cent. The decrease in expenditure was 12 per cent as compared with 1925-26, and 11 per cent as compared with 1929-30.

The items of expenditure are shown in the table given below:

TABLE VI

Expenditure

	1925-26			1926-27			1927-28			1928-29			1929-30			1930-31			1931-32		
	Rs.	a.	p.	Rs.	a.	p.	Rs.	a.	p.	Rs.	a.	p.	Rs.	a.	p.	Rs.	a.	p.	Rs.	a.	p.
Land Revenue and water-rates	395	11	6	430	6	0	372	2	0	416	8	6	414	9	3	336	9	6	325	8	9
Seed ..	56	10	3	80	10	2	63	12	10	99	11	3	84	8	3	50	6	0	56	2	3
Upkeep of bullocks ..	350	11	0	358	1	1	434	4	6	343	4	6	353	13	8	379	5	8	253	11	8
Hervesting charges ..	50	4	0	16	14	0	10	8	9	8	13	6	39	14	3	26	3	9	9	12	3
Winnowing charges ..	75	1	0	39	6	8	10	14	1	37	7	11	26	6	2	10	13	6	21	12	8
Kamins ..	45	0	0	20	10	11	23	7	7	21	6	3	17	10	11	6	14	6	11	5	7
Implements ..													29	12	10	27	0	0	25	12	4
Misc. ..													4	0	0	4	10	8	4	8	0
Total ..	973	5	9	946	0	10	915	1	9	927	3	11	970	11	4	841	15	7	708	9	6

The heaviest items of expenditure are Government dues (land revenue and the water rates) and upkeep of bullocks. The proportion of different items of expenditure to the total expenditure is shown below:

TABLE VII

	1925-26 p. c.	1929-30 p. c.	1930-31 p. c.	1931-32 p. c.
Land Revenue and water rates	41	43	40	46
Seed	6	9	6	8
Upkeep of bullocks ..	36	36	45	36
Hired labour (kamins and winnowing and harvesting charges) ..	17	9	5	6
Implements and Misc. ..	..	3	4	4
Total ..	100	100	100	100

In the year 1930-31, the worst year of the depression, of the total expenditure of the farm amounting to Rs. 841-15-7, Rs. 206-5-6 is accounted for by the land-revenue (24·5 per cent) and Rs. 130-4-0 by the water rates (15·5 per cent). The upkeep of bullocks cost Rs. 379-5-8. The cultivator (tenant) maintained two pairs of working bullocks. One of these bullocks, worth Rs. 40 died, and another was bought for Rs. 120 to replace it. The death of the bullock unduly raised the cost of cultivation under this head. The upkeep of bullocks cost Rs. 13-14-3 per acre in 1930-31 as compared with Rs. 12-10-2 in 1929-30, and Rs. 9-4-8 in 1931-32.

It will be noted that in 1930-31 the cost of hired labour was comparatively insignificant. Four able-bodied male members of the family worked on the holding, and no permanent labour was employed. Casual labour was employed for harvesting some of the crops. Payments were made to casual labourers in kind, whose value in rupees is shown in the table given above.

Similarly in 1931-32, no permanent labour was employed, and the casual labour employed was paid wages in kind. The Farm Accounts for 1931-32 says (p. 188):

"Four members of the tenant's family worked on the farm and were assisted by casual labour for the harvesting of certain crops. Permanent labour was not employed this year, as the members of the family were quite sufficient to carry on the cultivation work. The picking of cotton was done by women labourers at one-twelfth share of the total produce. The rate of payment in the case of *Jhoka* was one seer per maund of *Shakkar* produced. The rest of the crops were harvested entirely by the tenant without any help from outside. The winnowing of wheat and gram was done by the labourers at the rate of two seers per maund".

It is known to every one in India that the Indian cultivator employs hired labour to a very small extent, and that wages are paid to hired workers in kind. Still it was necessary to draw attention to these facts, as their importance is not realised by foreign experts whose assistance is invoked by the Government of India to solve our economic problems. The Hilton Young Currency Commission of 1925, whose report used to be described as 'epoch-making', devoted some attention to the adjustment of agricultural wages to the 18d. gold rate. They noted that the world-wide effect of the war was "to leave the prices of agricultural produce at a lower level in relation to manufactured articles". That meant loss to India. "But it is a loss", wrote the Commission, "which she shares with all other agricultural countries and which cannot be made good by any monetary policy" (para 192). This was the reply of the Commission to the criticism that the fixation of exchange at a high level might hinder exports. Index numbers of wages in rural areas were compiled by the Bombay labour office for the use of the Commission. These index numbers indicated "a general tendency to improvement in the wages of the labourer", and the Commission expected this tendency "to facilitate adjustment to falling prices, which indeed operate as a check to the rising tide of wages". And they added: "A similar phenomenon has been observed in the case of Government services, where the increase in the value of the rupee has enabled Government to refuse increase of pay which it might otherwise have been difficult to resist" (para 192).

It is evident that our foreign experts supposed that agricultural wages formed a considerable proportion of the cost of production of food-stuffs and raw materials. Wages had risen; if they were reduced, cost of production would fall. Costs would thus be adjusted to falling prices and the Indian grower would have no difficulty in competing with his foreign rivals in spite of the 18d. gold rate.

Our farmers are in difficulty precisely because their costs do not become adjusted to falling prices—or because the costs are inelastic. Wages paid in kind are automatically adjusted to falling prices, but, as we have seen, the wages that the cultivator pays form an inconsiderable proportion of his costs. Government dues form the most considerable proportion, and they are rigidly collected, irrespective of the fact whether the cultivator on his year's cultivation makes any profit or suffers a loss. In the year 1931-32, the land revenue paid by this farm of about 28 acres in the Lyallpur District was Rs. 204-6-9, or 28·8 per cent of total expenditure (Rs. 708-9-6), and the water-rates amounted to Rs. 121-2-0 or 17 per cent of total expenditure. The Government dues thus accounted for about 46 per cent, or something less than half of total expenditure. It seems a little absurd, in a discussion of adjustment of costs to falling prices, to draw attention to the need for reducing wages, when wages are of little importance, and to forget the really big items of expenditure which are practically irreducible.

It is clear that the problem of adjusting costs to falling prices in Indian agriculture is that of reducing Government dues, and the cost of upkeep of bullocks. Failing reduction in these two items, the adjustment must take place by a heavy decrease in the remuneration of the cultivator and his family. The Farm Accounts show that such indeed has been the process of adjustment to falling prices during the depression.

Remissions of Government dues have been granted on account of poor crops and the fall of prices. Complaints on account of the inadequacy of the remissions are loud and general. That even after the remissions, the land revenue and the water rates form a considerable proportion of total expenditure, may be shown by an example.

The total expenditure of a holding of 52¾ acres in Sargodha in 1930-31 (see *Farm Accounts* for that year) was Rs. 1,002-2-7. The amount due on account of the land revenue and water-rates was Rs. 409-15-9, but a remission of Rs. 74-4-9 was granted. Allowing for the remission, the proportion of these charges to total expenditure was 33·5 per cent. In 1931-32 the remission amounted to Rs. 73-4-6 out of a total of Rs. 422-3-9, which was the amount due. The proportion of Government dues actually paid to total expenditure was 35·9 per cent in 1931-32.

II

The Land Revenue

We have seen that of the total costs in agriculture Government dues in India form a very considerable item. We have also seen that no adjustment of costs to the fall of prices is possible unless Government dues are heavily reduced.

The land revenue has been paid in India from time immemorial. What is the nature of the land revenue as it is levied at present?

Tax or Rent?

The nature of the land revenue has formed the subject of lengthy discussion.

In a minute written in 1875 Sir H. Maine answered the question whether the land revenue was or was not rent in the negative. It seemed to him incredible that since the beginning of history any Government should have taken the full economic rent of the land cultivated by its subjects. To do this it would be necessary for the Government to "put up the soil in parcels to competition", without recognizing any hereditary rights of property. "No evidence", said Sir H. Maine, "of any such system exists; some preferential rights, whether they can or cannot be called ownership, have always been acknowledged".

Such preferential rights which may be described as ownership, we may add, were recognised by the Moghul Kings. In the *Ain-i-Akbari*, Abul Fazal refers to خداوندان مال who held their lands by ancestral descent:

پیداست در هر آباد بوم خداوندان مال فراوان باشند و
زمینهائے کشت و کار پدر به پدر دارند;

"It is well known that in inhabited parts of the country there are numerous owners of property, who hold cultivable lands by ancestral descent" (Persian Text, A. S. B., vol. I. p. 290).

If then rights of property were recognized in India in pre-British days, how did the land revenue come to be looked upon as rent by the British Government? The burden of the land revenue under Indian rule was heavy—the State demand sometimes absorbed nearly the whole of the net income from cultivation. Rent and State ownership, according to Sir H. Maine, "did certainly express to an English ear, better than any others, the nature of the right which was exercised by the Indian Governments. The morality current in England did not forbid the exaction of an extreme rent from a tenant, just as the morality current in India did not forbid the exaction of excessive contributions from a subject in virtue of the land which he occupied." Under Indian rulers, then, the land revenue was a tax, but it was so heavy as to be equal to an extreme rent. Our British rulers mistook it for rent.

In a minute, also written in 1875, Sir Louis Mallet emphasized the importance of distinguishing between rent and revenue. This was not a question of words to the cultivator. Sir Louis Mallet protested against the policy of resisting and removing taxes such as income-tax and customs, and adding to the charges laid on the land in order to provide the sums needed for public works, education, health, famine, and other beneficent objects. He described that policy as 'communistic'. "I shall rejoice to see a limit placed on future assessments", he said, "with a view to which the renunciation of the theory of State landlordism would be the most effectual step".

Under which theory can the State demand more revenue from the cultivator? Under the rent theory, Lord Salisbury (Secretary of State for India, who took a share in this controversy in 1875), pointed out, the State would be obliged to leave wages and profits to the cultivator—it could take only the surplus produce of the soil. Under the tax-theory, on the other hand, the State might take whatever it pleased: the cultivator's payments would be limited only by the power of mercy of the Government. "It speaks boldly for the character of British rule" added his Lordship, "that the advocates of the Ryot call for the application of the tax-theory". He agreed with Sir Louis Mallet that the "nondescript land dues should tend to the form of revenue rather than that of rent."

The occasion which gave rise to this instructive discussion 60 years ago was a difference of opinion between the Governor of Madras and his Council regarding the power of the Local Government to increase the assessment.

The question was re-discussed in detail by the Indian Taxation Enquiry Committee of 1924-25. On the question whether, the State claimed exclusive proprietary rights over the land under Hindu and Mohammadan rule, the Committee quotes from the judgment of the Bombay High Court in a case from Kanara disposed of in 1875 (p. 61).

"This review of the authorities leads us to the conclusion arrived at also (after careful discussion of the question) by Prof. H. H. Wilson, that the proprietary right of the sovereign derives no warrant from the ancient laws or institutions of the Hindus and is not recognized by Hindu lawyers as exclusive or incompatible with individual ownership".

Colonel Galloway, a recognized authority on the subject of Indian land tenures under Mohammadan rule, says:

"The soil was the property of the cultivator as much as it could be. Law gave no power, policy gave no motive to remove him, so long as he paid his taxes. When he did not, his lands could be attached; and so can those of the first *peer*, holding by the firmest tenure of the English law. The right of the Indian husbandman is the right of possession and of transfer; and the rate of his land-tax was fixed; often indeed the amount. In what respect, then, is his right of property inferior to that of the English landholder?" (Report of Taxation Enquiry Committee, p. 62).

The Taxation Enquiry Committee concluded:

"On these two points the Committee are unanimously of opinion that, under both Hindu and Mohammadan rule, the State never claimed the absolute or exclusive ownership of the land and definitely recognised the existence of private property in it" (p. 62).

Thus the land revenue is not of the nature of rent. It is a tax. Let it be a tax on things and not on persons, but it is a tax all the same.

As a tax the land revenue is of a very peculiar nature. It is different from the land-tax of any other country. In other countries, as the Taxation Enquiry Committee pointed out, the land tax is levied at a definite rate upon a definite basis of assessment. As we shall presently see, the incidence of our land tax on different holdings varies very greatly. In one case the land revenue may take only a small fraction of the 'net income' from cultivation; in another case it may absorb the whole of the 'net income', and even exceed it. There is no definite basis of assessment: it may be rentals or net assets. "The rentals may be customary, controlled or assumed. The net assets may include or exclude the subsistence of the cultivator" (p. 77). No definite principles govern the rate of assessment imposed: it may depend on the will of the Local Government, or the view of the settlement officer of the economic conditions of the tract or of the District at the time of settlement, or on the conditions of tenancy.

The Committee also drew attention to other serious defects of the land revenue system. The land revenue, the Committee said, "viewed as a scheme of taxation, is not only not progressive, but actually tends in the opposite direction". The land revenue imposes heavier burdens on the poorer landowners. But how can a tax on things be made progressive? The Committee referred to the creation "of a very large number of uneconomic holdings, the holders of which pay land revenue which would be inconsiderable if cultivation were intensive or on a large scale, but rests as a heavy burden upon a small and impoverished holder" (p. 78).

Small and impoverished holders of ten years ago, when the Committee reported, have become more impoverished now, prices having fallen.

In European countries and Japan in addition to a light land-tax there are death duties and a tax on agricultural income. Land taxation is thus made progressive on the whole. These sources of revenue are not utilised here, with the result that the burden is shifted "more and more on to the less prosperous cultivators".

The land revenue is an important source of revenue in the Provinces. In European countries there is a tendency to use the land-tax more and more for local purposes. In India it is a tax utilised for general purposes. "Only a very small fraction of the tax collected from the cultivator is actually used for rural development, and the illiterate ryot is therefore unable to recognise the benefits which he derives from the direct tax that he pays" (p. 79).

The land revenue being a tax *in rem* levied at a flat rate, it can not be graduated, nor exemption granted to particular lands because of the circumstances of the persons who cultivate them. "The real relief of the poorest cultivator in these

2

circumstances", wrote the Committee, "is to be found in a better system of rural economy generally rather than in a change of the land revenue system" (p. 88). Or, as we may say in the words of another high authority, the question of relief of agriculture cannot be dissociated from the whole problem of *rural betterment* or village improvement (*The Agricultural Situation in 1931-32*, note on measures of Government farm relief in India, p. 181). Village improvement has been already taken in hand. The land revenue will not be felt as a burden by the smallest holder when the supply of water in the villages for drinking and other domestic purposes improves, roads and wells are cleaned, the standard of general sanitation rises, and the panchayats begin to take a more serious view of their duties!

The lightening of tax-burdens through village improvement or rural reconstruction may take centuries. Village improvement started many years ago—it has not led to any perceptible improvement in the taxable capacity of the peasant.

The Taxation Enquiry Committee made two definite suggestions. First, the standard rate of assessment was not to exceed 25 per cent of annual value. This recommendation has been accepted by the Punjab Government and, at the same time, it has been laid down that assessments shall be revised only once in 40 years. As regards the basis of assessment the Committee said: "What the Committee would recommend is that for the future the basis of the settlement should be annual value, a term by which they mean the gross produce less cost of production, including the value of the labour actually expended by the farmer and his family on the holding, and the return for enterprise. . . ." (p. 85).

The annual value is thus to be determined by deducting from the value of the gross produce the farmer's wages and profits and other elements of cost of production. Of this annual value, 25 per cent was to be the State's share. Annual value in this sense would represent a real surplus. If after deducting the wages of the farmer and his family for the labour expended by them, the wages of hired labour, cost of seed, upkeep of bullocks, and the cost of implements, and making allowance on account of 'the return for enterprise', the peasant was left with, say 4 rupees per acre, let the State take one rupee.

What is the actual state of things? Let us leave out "the return for enterprise" altogether. Let us also entirely ignore the wages of the farmer and his family for the labour expended by them on the holding. Deducting from the value of the gross produce all other elements of cost of production, what is the proportion of the land revenue to 'net income' from cultivation? It must not be forgotten that we are using 'net income' in a very peculiar sense.

The *Farm Accounts*, again, are of material help in answering this question. The most interesting figures are for the year 1930-31. The table given below is based on data furnished by *The Farm Accounts in the Punjab, 1930-31.*

TABLE VIII

Table showing the Proportion of the Land Revenue to Gross and Net Income per Acre for various holdings in 1930-31, based on Farm Accounts in the Punjab for 1930-31.

Dist. and Holding	Net Income per acre	Land Revenue per acre	Proportion of L. R. to Net Income	Proportion of L. R. to Gross Income
Well-irrigated holdings	Rs. a. p.	Rs. a. p.	Per cent	Per cent
Jullundar A ..	13 12 9	3 3 8	23·4	6·0
,, B ..	18 12 3	2 5 0	12·3	6·6
,, C ..	—5 8 6	2 14 8	..	7·7

NOTE.—Minus (—) signifies net loss.

Dist. and holding	Net Income per acre	Land Revenue per acre	Proportion of L. R. to Net Income	Proportion of L. R. to Gross Income
Well-irrigated holdings	Rs. a. p.	Rs. a. p.	Per cent	Per cent
Ludhiana A ..	2 7 11	1 13 7	74·2	9·1
,, B ..	—1 11 9	2 0 6	..	5.6
Hoshiarpur A ..	11 12 10	3 1 3	26·1	6·7
,, B ..	21 8 8	4 2 1	19·2	6·6
Amritsar A ..	—0 0 7	1 14 0	..	6·4
,, B ..	10 2 2	2 3 2	21·7	4·4
,, C ..	1 2 5	1 1 9	96·7	3·0
Multan A ..	4 13 10	1 9 3	32·5	7·3
,, B ..	11 4 5	1 12 3	15·7	6·1
,, C ..	3 15 8	0 13 5	21·0	5·5
Rohtak A ..	—2 0 11	2 5 0	..	6·1
,, B ..	23 3 2	3 5 8	14·5	5·6
,, C ..	8 12 10	3 6 4	38·5	8·0
Jhelum A ..	9 15 7	1 11 4	17·1	6·3
,, B ..	—3 6 11	1 12 2	..	7·5
,, C ..	—0 10 0	1 6 5	..	11·5
Canal irrigated holdings				
Lyallpur, Batai ..	10 8 5	5 9 9	53·3	15·0
,, Siri ..	8 9 5	4 7 8	52·2	15·2
,, Risalewala	18 8 11	7 0 9	37·9	13·8
Montgomery, Batai	11 3 10	2 2 2	19·0	5·3
Sargodah, Siri ..	6 10 6	3 4 5	49·1	15·3

The proportion of the land revenue to 'net income', in the case of canal irrigated holdings is found to vary between 19·0 and 53·3 per cent. In the case of 6 well-irrigated holdings, the land revenue was paid though there was no 'net income' at all. In the other 13 cases, the proportion varied between 12·3 per cent and 96·7 per cent.

Let us next consider the proportion of the land revenue to annual value in a more accurate sense, that is the surplus left after deducting, from the value of gross produce, cost of production including the wages of the farmer and his family for their work on the holding. For this study we select two irrigated holdings mentioned in the Table given above.

We have first to settle the rate of remuneration for the farmer and his family. The standard would be indicated by the payment to permanent labourers employed by the farmer; it would be reasonable to allow the farmer a little more. Rs. 100 plus food and clothing were paid to each of two permanent labourers employed by the landlord of holding A, Jullundar (*Farm Accounts, 1930-31*, p. 25). A permanent labourer employed by the cultivator of holding B, Amritsar, was paid Rs. 100 plus food, clothes and shoes; his total cost came to Rs. 145-8-0 (p. 101). A remuneration of Rs. 150 to each able-bodied member of the farmer's family is therefore not an overestimate.

Let us now take the farm of 27¼ acres in the Lyallpur District which was farmed by Batai cultivation in 1930-31. The land revenue paid represented 15 per cent of gross income and 53·3 per cent of 'net income' without making any allowance for the wages of the cultivator. Four able-bodied male members of the peasant's family worked on the holding. We ignore female members of the family who may have rendered assistance. The wages of the 4 able-bodied workers would amount to Rs. 600. The gross income of the farm was Rs. 976-4-2; cost of production (excluding the land revenue) was Rs. 635-10-1. Adding wages, Rs. 600, the total cost increases to Rs. 1,235-10-1, or is found to exceed the gross income. The land revenue amounted to Rs. 206-5-6.

In Table VIII the lowest proportion of the land revenue to 'net income' in our peculiar sense is that for Rohtak B, 14·5 per cent. The proportion of land revenue to gross income in this case was 5·6 per cent. Three able-bodied men worked on this farm. The total expenditure, excluding the land revenue (Rs. 28-6-3) amounted to Rs. 475-5-7. The addition of Rs. 450 on account of wages raises the cost of production to Rs. 896-11-4, while the gross income was estimated at Rs. 708-0-10.

The information about the number of able-bodied men working on farms (apart from hired labour) is not available for all the farms. Where it is available, the result in all cases but one of including the wages of able-bodied workers in the cost of production is to turn 'net income' into a net loss. The exception is Jullunder Holding A, where gross income exceeded cost of cultivation by Rs. 94-9-11, which may be called the real net income of the farm in 1930-31. The land revenue in this case amounted to Rs. 127-9-3, or exceeded real net income.

TABLE IX

Farm Accounts 1930-31

			Gross income	Expenditure including wages of farmer and working members of his family	Net income	Land revenue
			Rs. a. p.	Rs. a. p.		Rs. a. p.
Jullunder	B	..	366 0 4	620 0 7 (3)	..	24 2 9
Ludhiana	A	..	1,019 13 10	1,210 0 0 (2)	..	94 5 9
Hoshiarpur	A	..	414 5 6	439 10 10 (1)	..	26 4 0
Amritsar	B	..	972 12 6	1,087 10 7 (2)	..	32 2 0
,,	C	..	429 3 3	577 4 6 (1)	..	1 7 3
Multan	C	..	432 12 8	791 5 9 (3)	..	25 0 3
Rohtak	B	..	708 0 10	896 11 4 (3)	..	28 10 3
,,	C	..	681 3 5	1,139 14 3 (4)	..	54 8 6
Jhelum	A	..	717 15 2	923 1 3 (3)	..	47 8 0

NOTE:—The figures in brackets stand for the number of able-bodied workers whose wages have been added at Rs. 150 for each worker.

Nine out of 13 well-irrigated farms which show a positive 'net income' in table VIII are thus accounted for.

It will be admitted that in order to find annual value, or real net income, the wages of the working members of the farmer's family must be deducted from the gross income. Is Rs. 150 per able-bodied worker an excessive amount?

In his "Studies in the Cost of Production of Crops in the Punjab" (1934) Prof. Kartar Singh takes 5 annas per day as the average wage for manual labour. The average daily earnings of tenants on the Risalewala Farm varied between 9 pies in 1930-31 and As. 8-10 in 1928-29; the average for the five years 1927-28 to 1931-32 is 5 annas, equal to Rs. 114-1-0 per year. The difference between Rs. 114 and Rs. 150 is not negligible, and I may state why the latter figure must be preferred.

Labour costs do not mean costs which are just sufficient to keep a worker's body and soul together. Wages required to maintain the labourer and his family on a reasonably high level of efficiency and comfort are true costs. A tenant may earn very little because of the tyrannous system which compels him to pay half the gross produce of the land as hire for the use of land. When prices fall, while he still continues to pay the same half-batai as before, his earnings may be reduced to practically nothing. The average earnings of the Risalewala tenants for the five years 1927-28 to 1931-32 were low on account of the heavy fall in their earnings in 1930-31 and 1931-32.

A more reliable, though not entirely satisfactory standard would be wages actually paid to permanent labourers employed by landlords. Even these wages may be unduly low. In fact they are not much more than subsistence wages. But it is reasonable to suppose that a man who works on his own account would expect to earn at least as much as he would earn if he were working for another. If a hired employee is engaged on Rs. 100, plus food, clothes and shoes (equal to about Rs. 150) this is also the minimum rate of wages for the able-bodied male members of the farmer's family who work on the farm. This is the minimum—in fact they would expect to earn something more, in addition to wages, as return for enterprise.

In estimating the taxable capacity of a person labour costs must be conceived in a liberal sense. Wages must be sufficient to provide food, clothing and shelter for the worker and his family. In addition the worker must have a little money for travelling, ceremonies, conventional necessaries and comforts, education, medicines and amusements. All this expenditure may be regarded as necessary, whether any one lives in a town or a village; any curtailment of necessary expenditure must result in a loss of health, strength, and efficiency of both the present and future generation of workers.

The foregoing discussion shows that in the year 1930-31 the land revenue was not the share of the State in any 'profits of cultivation'. It was a heavy tax on the subsistence of the worker. *The land revenue has been defined as a tax on things. It is really a tax on subsistence.*

The Farm Accounts for 1930-31 shows the proportion of the land revenue to the value of gross produce. As we have seen, this proportion is of no use at all. The State's demand, even when it is as low as 5 per cent of the gross produce, as we have seen, may impose a heavy tax on the wages of the farmer.

The cultivator under Akbar paid the land revenue at the rate of $33^1/_3$ per cent of the value of gross produce, and still lived to till the land. If the rate of assessment in terms of gross produce were today equal to that under Akbar, the whole country would become a desert. But there is abundant evidence to show that India, in spite of the high rate of the land tax, was a land of plenty under the Moghuls.

Conditions, then, were different. From the point of view of the cultivator, conditions, today, in spite of the opening of the world markets and the development of canal irrigation, are worse, not better than they were 300 years ago. The references to land in the works of contemporary writers show that there was no lack of good cultivable land under the Moghul Kings. Probably the average yield of the land was also higher. This is suggested by certain figures of yield given in the *Ain-i-Akbari.* Even if there has been no deterioration of the soil, the extension of cultivation must have lowered the average yield per acre on account of the addition of inferior soils. Finally, the pressure of population on the soil has increased during the past 40 years not only as the result of the growth of numbers, but the decline of industries.

Such heavy taxation of land, as in India, is unknown in any civilised country. According to a publication of the League of Nations (*The Relation of Labour Cost to Total Costs of Production in Agriculture, Geneva,* 1926), of the net output of farms costed in Denmark, the taxes amounted to 5·1 per cent in 1923-24, and 4·9 per cent in 1924-25 (p. 26). The total net return in French agriculture in the year 1924 was estimated at 34,432 million francs, of which sum taxes accounted for only 1,583 million francs or 4·6 per cent. These taxes, it is expressly stated, "include all classes of taxes paid by the farming population" (p. 28).

The land revenue and the water rates (net receipts) provide more than 60 per cent of the total revenue of the Punjab Government. The main burden of our top-heavy Provincial administration rests on the land. And this is the chief reason why it is so difficult to grant relief to agriculture.

	1928-29 Lakhs	1929-30 Lakhs	1930-31 Lakhs	1931-32 Lakhs
Land revenue, gross	454	457	459	371
Deduct revenue credited to irrigation	176	199	190	170
Land revenue ..	278	258	269	202
Irrigation ..	374	394	362	411
Total ..	652	652	631	613

As compared with 1928-29, or 1929-30, the decrease in the revenue under the two heads combined, as shown above, was 6·3 per cent in 1930-31 and 9 per cent in 1931-32. The fall of prices ruined the cultivator, but his taxable capacity remained practically unchanged!

It will be admitted that in the case of the small holder the capacity to pay the land revenue is *nil.* Is it possible or practicable to exempt the small holder from the payment of the land revenue?

The question was considered by the Taxation Enquiry Committee, and their answer was in the negative. To grant exemption to uneconomic holdings would be to put a premium on fractionisation of the economic holdings (Report, p. 78). Fractionisation already exists and tends to increase. The land revenue is not a force holding fractionisation in check. The real difficulty is of another kind. Nothing can be done for the poor land-holder because his exemption would mean a heavy loss of revenue, which cannot be replaced from other sources. The Taxation Enquiry Committee also referred to another danger. Suppose the burden of the relief granted to the poor land-holder fell on industry. *Pro tanto*—industrial development would be retarded, which would curtail the demand for labour. "In the result the position of the poorest holders who remained on the land would be no better than before, while their chances of alternative employment would be diminished" (p. 79). It is thus shown that in the interests of the poor holder himself, no relief should be granted to him!

That some, and, perhaps, substantial relief can be granted to the poor holder by reducing the cost of administration has never occurred to official committees and official writers. This aspect of the question is not discussed in the Report of the Taxation Enquiry Committee.

There would be more money for the Provinces if Central expenditure could be heavily reduced. In the Provinces, if the machinery of administration were simplified, and the scale of official salaries adjusted to the economic condition of the country, a large saving might be effected.

The Land-revenue and Prices of Agricultural Produce

A tax on economic rent, conceived as a surplus above cost, cannot be shifted, as economic rent (it is argued) does not enter cost of production. But wages form part of cost of production. A tax on wages would increase cost and lead to a rise of prices.

Similarly a tax on profits, regarded as a necessary return to business enterprise, would tend to raise prices. If taxation encroached on wages and profits in a manufacturing industry, labour and capital would leave the industry, production would contract, and, demand remaining the same, the price of the product would be forced to rise.

The case of agriculture, as it is practised in India, is, however, different. The land revenue, encroaches on wages and profits, and yet there is no rise of prices in consequence. The *only effect of the land-tax is to lower the standard of living of the cultivator.*

This is because enormous numbers depend on cultivation, and they have no alternative means of livelihood. The cultivator may grow more of one crop and less of another, but he cannot leave his occupation.

III

Water-Rates

So far we have discussed the nature of the land revenue. What is the nature of the water-rates?

The water-rates are very largely a tax. They are not merely a price paid for the use of water.

When a service is a Government monopoly, and when the charge made for the service much exceeds the total cost, th charge is a tax.

TABLE X

Irrigation receipts in the Punjab, in lakhs

	1928-29	1929-30	1930-31	1931-32
	Rs.	Rs.	Rs.	Rs.
Gross receipts including indirect credits (land revenue due to irrigation)	588	653	614	576
Less working expenses	215	263	254	168
Net receipts	373	399	360	408
Add receipts from works for which no capital accounts are kept	1	4	1	3
Total net receipts	374	394	362	411
Expenditure :				
Interest on Debt	121	126	130	133
Miscellaneous	15	10	11	16
Total Expenditure	136	136	142	148

After meeting the interest on debt and paying the working expenses, the Punjab canals yield a considerable surplus:

	Irrigation 'surplus', lakhs
1928-29	238
1929-30	258
1930-31	220
1931-32	293

This 'surplus' comes from the pockets of farmers, and it is utilised for general purposes. It may be noted that the 'surplus' exceeded 2 crores in 1930-31 and was equal to about 3 crores in 1931-32—in other words, at a time when the fall of prices had rendered cultivation unremunerative over large parts of the country, the farmer continued to pay the water-rates on a scale much higher than the actual cost of the service.

It has been argued that since canal water is a free gift of God meant for the benefit of the whole population, the price for the use of water for irrigation purposes may be determined by considerations other than those relating to cost of the service[8]:

"Now what are the principles on which this price should be fixed? It may be fixed in relation to the increase that is brought about in the produce by using this water. It may be fixed in relation to what the cultivator would have spent if no canals existed, and he had been compelled to make his own arrangements for the supply of an equal amount of water. The State, representing the general population, is therefore entitled to get a fair share of the cultivator's increased prosperity in return for the water supplied from the canals belonging to the nation. The income from the 'Abiana' revenue must therefore be for the benefit of the people at large".

The argument deserves careful examination for it enjoys official support.

Following the same line of argument the Taxation Enquiry Committee wrote in 1924-25:

"The Government, by making irrigation available to a particular piece of land, especially if it guarantees to continue to do so, gives a potential increase both to the annual and to the capital value of the land. There would of course be no actual increase in the latter if the whole of the increase in the annual value were taken in the shape of payment for water. But in actual practice what is taken is generally quite a small fraction of this increase. Consequently, the result of the action of the Government in guaranteeing the

[8] Prof. Gulshan Rai of the Sanatana Dharma College, Lahore, in the Civil and Military Gazette of Lahore, dated May 5, 1934.

supply of water is to give a large unearned increment to the owner of the land, whether he is a cultivator or a rent receiver, and it is a generally accepted theory of taxation that there is no source of income from which a considerable share may be taken for purposes of the State so appropriately as from an unearned increment or windfall of this kind" (para 131).

The minimum charge for water, except in special cases, would be equal to the cost of service, that is the cost of maintaining the irrigation works plus interest on capital cost. The maximum charge may be so fixed as to appropriate the whole of the increase in the return from the land resulting from the use of canal water. "The normal", the Taxation Enquiry Committee recommended, "should be a moderate share of the value of the water to the cultivator" (p. 112).

This may seem to be a reasonable view, but the working of this principle in actual practice is open to serious objections.

The normal charge devised to take from the cultivator 'a moderate share of the value of water' in the days of prosperity, may continue to be levied even when cultivation becomes unremunerative, as it did in the Punjab in the year 1930-31. The gross amount of irrigation revenue realised in that year amounted to 6,14 lakhs. Can it be pretended that this charge was 'a moderate share of the value of water' to the cultivator in that year?

Apart from the difficulty of reducing the charge in accordance with fluctuations in agricultural conditions, the principle of determining its amount with reference to the value of water to the cultivator, and not to the cost of service, is entirely wrong.

The service rendered by the State in supplying canal water to the cultivator is in essence of the same nature as the service rendered by the Lahore Municipality in supplying water for drinking purposes, or by the Government N. W.

Railway in carrying passengers and goods, or by the Government Post and Telegraph Departments in providing these means of communication.

The Municipal charges for water are not fixed with reference to the value of water to the consumer. The value of pure water for drinking purposes is so great that even if the Lahore Municipal Committee doubled or quadrupled the charge for water, the price would be still less than the value of the water. It might be argued that this water is not used for productive purposes; canal water is used to grow crops. But an abundant provision of water fit for drinking and other purposes is necessary in the interests of health. If the Lahore Municipal water-supply failed, the people of Lahore would be forced to use well-water again, which would react on their health, and therefore productive efficiency. Indirectly the value of municipal water in augmenting efficiency and production is enormous. Directly, the value of consumer's surplus resulting from the provision of municipal water at cheap rates is inestimable.

Rapid means of communication and transportation directly add to the wealth of the country. Railway engines and wagons are not free goods; nor are canal weirs free gifts of nature. The Government Irrigation Department sells water; the Government North Western Railway sells transportation. If the Canals did not exist, cultivation in canal-irrigated areas would become impossible. If the railways disappeared, the whole economic life of the country would be disorganized. Where canal irrigation has only replaced well-irrigation, the cultivator would have to spend much more on well-water, if the canal ceased to flow. If there was no railway connecting Amritsar and Rawalpindi, the cost of sending goods in *gaddas* would be much heavier than the present railway charge, apart from the question of slowness, as compared with the railway, of a *gadda* service, and the risk of loss to which the goods so sent would be exposed. The cost of sending a letter from Peshawar to any part of India is inappreciable. Suppose one were obliged to make one's own arrangements, through runners, for sending a letter to Madras. What would the cost be?

The services provided by railways, and well-organised post and telegraph departments, from the point of view of production and national wealth, are of the highest value. The charges for these services, however, are not based on considerations of increase in national wealth which accrues from them, but simply the cost of service on the whole, including interest on capital. We are not arguing that Government should not share in the increase in national wealth which may arise from specific services, rendered by the Government. But the Government should take its share in the form of direct taxation, not in the form of prices charged for the service. The advantage of a direct tax on income is that it can be graduated. It has also an exemption limit, or no tax is levied where taxable capacity does not exist. Exemption and graduation are the means employed to adjust the burden of the income tax to the capacity of the tax-payer.

The water-rates are unquestionably a tax. The cultivator, however, is not taxed openly, but surreptitiously—the tax is disguised as price; secondly, when payment is made thus, the tax tends to rest more heavily on the poorer cultivators.

IV

Landlord and Tenant

In the discussion of agricultural income we have so far ignored the question of proprietorship, or rent of land. But it is an important question. Even in the Punjab, which is called the land of peasant proprietors, 60 per cent of the land is cultivated by tenants paying rents in cash or kind. The predominant form of rent in the Punjab is 'Batai' or 'wandai', which means 'division'. 'Batai' or 'wandai', is a share of the gross produce paid to the landlord as rent.

Batai is known in Europe as Metayage in France, Teilbau (share-cultivation) in Germany and Mezzadria in Italy. Mezzadro, like our batai tenant, is a cultivator who undertakes to pay a certain proportion of the crop to the landlord as rent. This form of rent is of considerable importance in certain parts of Italy. According to an official enquiry made many years ago, there were in 1911, 2 million batai tenants in Italy as compared with about 1½ million in 1871. The official enquiry also showed that the condition of these tenant cultivators paying rent in kind was better than that of other classes of cultivators.[4]

In the Punjab, in the case of canal-irrigated lands, the landlord, as a rule, provides only land; the tenant provides the rest. The tenant and the landlord generally share the land-revenue and the water-rates equally. The whole cost of seed and upkeep of plough-bullocks is paid by the tenant. He also provides the implements. But the expenses of harvesting and winnowing and the dues of the kamins are deducted from the common heap before division is made.

The rate of batai in the canal colonies is generally half and half. But in the case of well-irrigation it varies in different Districts, and in different parts of the same District. The rate of batai depends on custom, and the custom may be different in regard to the division of grain and straw. In the Report on the Land Revenue Settlement of the Montgomery District in the Multan Division (1878) much interesting information is given about rents in kind and the customary dues of kamins (p. 130 *et seq*). The share of the produce paid by the tenant varied in different parts of the District. In Montgomery it was as high as half in places; in Dipalpur it fell as low as one-seventh. "The usual rates", says the Settlement Officer, "seem to be half, two-fifths and one-third on sailaba lands on the Ravi; and one-third, one-fourth and one-fifth on well-irrigated lands". Sometimes

[4] HWB. Vol. VIII, Teilbau.

the rate of batai varied in the case of wells situated close together, similar in every respect and owned, practically speaking, by the same persons. "No explanation of this anomaly could be given", says the Settlement officer, "except that it was the custom for one well to pay so much, and for the other to pay so much" (p. 131).

According to the Report on the second regular settlement of the Jhelum District (1883) the landlord's share in Tahsil Talagung varied from one-fourth to one-half, but the most common rates for unirrigated lands, which were then small in extent, were one-third and two-fifths.

The variation at the present time in the rates of batai for well-irrigated lands may be illustrated from examples given in the Farm Accounts in the Punjab for 1931-32. The cultivator of B holding in the Jullundar District worked on half-batai conditions; the cultivator of B holding in the Multan District two-fifths of the total produce, except green fodder and bhusa. The landlord paid half the cost of harvesting, winnowing, watchman and weighman, full charges of land revenue, interest and depreciation on the Persian wheel, a part of cleaning charges of the well, barley seed for one *kanal* and cleaning of a canal. The tenant paid all other charges and received three-fifths share (p. 124). The cultivator of holding C in the same District paid half-batai. The land was irrigated by an inundation canal in summer and by a well in winter. The landlord paid the cost of cleaning the well and interest and depreciation on the Persian wheel put on the well; that of replacing mahl and buckets was borne by the tenant. The cultivators of the three holdings in the Jhelum District paid half-batai, excepting bhusa and rabi fodders of which the landlord took one-third share. The landlords paid the land revenue and bore a part of the expenses on Persian wheels and kamins, while the tenants met the whole cost of the upkeep of bullocks, seeds and implements.

At the present time canal-irrigation is far more important than well-irrigation in the Punjab, and in our discussion of batai we shall confine our attention to canal-irrigated holdings.

We have seen that the batai tenant must provide his own plough cattle, seed and implements. The European metayer is better off in this respect. For generally the owner or proprietor provides the *Inventar* (stock). In fact this is an advantage claimed for metayage: "A further economic advantage is that Teilbau (share-cultivation) gives peasants lacking capital an opportunity to undertake economic work on their own account and at their own risk; and the proprietor is enabled to share in the increase of production while remaining the master of his property."[5]

The systematic study of batai cultivation began in the Punjab in 1926 and the first fruit of this study was "Some Aspects of Batai cultivation in the Lyallpur District of the Punjab" by Prof. H. R. Stewart of the Agricultural College, Lyallpur. The area selected for the investigation was 232 acres, belonging to one landlord, who had given it in 1923-24 on batai to 18 tenants. Two of these tenants cultivated approximately one square; each of the others had only one plough and cultivated half a square. The object of the investigation was to determine (1) the income from an holding farmed on the batai system, (2) shares of the landlord and the tenant in the net income, (3) the various items of expenditure and how they were shared between the landlord and the tenant and (4) the time spent by the average tenant in the cultivation of his holding.

Since 1925-26 the Farm Accounts, which include several studies of batai cultivation, have been published regularly every year. They are of the greatest value in furnishing accurate answers to the questions stated above.

In the case of the area of 232 acres mentioned above,

[5] HWB. Vol. VIII, Teilbau.

farmed on the batai system in 1923-24, the man labour performed on an average was 170 days; the Government dues amounted to Rs.11 per acre, which was shared equally between landlord and tenant; other expenses (seed and upkeep of bullocks) were borne wholly by the tenants. The dues paid to kamins were deducted from the common heap before division between landlord and tenant. The gross income per acre of landlord and tenant was equal, but the tenant's net income was much less than that of the landlord. "Whilst the tenant profits on an average to the extent of Rs.19 per acre in return for his labours", says Mr. Stewart, "the landlord reaps Rs.30." And he adds: "It is not the object of this paper to criticise the contrast but to determine it" (p. 7).

It is obvious that when the major portion of the expenses is paid by the tenant out of his share of the gross produce, the landlord paying only half the Government dues, the landlord's share of the net income (calculated without making any allowance for wages of the worker and profits of enterprise) would exceed 60 per cent in a normal year. In a bad year, the tenant will earn still less, or he may earn nothing at all. When the tenant instead of earning anything suffers a net loss, he may be regarded as having worked, with his family, entirely for the benefit of the landlord.

If an average is taken of the shares of landlord and tenant in the net income from land farmed on the batai system, as shown in the Farm Accounts for the year 1923-24 and from 1925-26 to 1930-31, the price paid for the use of land is found to be about 82 per cent of the total net income. This includes good, bad and indifferent years.

The figures for 1930-31 and 1931-32 are given below:

Area and District	Landlord	Tenant	Total	Net Income per acre: landlord's share as percentage of total income per cent.
1930-31	Rs. as. p.	Rs. as. p.	Rs. as. p.	
27¼ acres, Lyallpur	10 14 6	5 15 10	4 4 8	221·7
802·5 „ „	16 11 1	1 13 10	18 8 11	90·0
25 acres Montgomery	12 13 4	3 11 8	9 1 8	140·9
1931-32				
27¼ acres, Lyallpur	16 7 9	4 0 5	20 8 2	80·5
802·6 „ „	16 8 10	8 4 3	24 13 1	67·0
48¾ „ Montgomery	12 4 5	5 13 7	18 2 0	67·9

The large farm of about 803 acres is the Risalewala Government farm. The Risalewala tenants did not pay any land revenue, but the full water rates at Rs.4-7-11 per acre. If it were private property, the farm would have paid Rs.7-0-9 per acre on account of the land revenue (including local rates, 12½ per cent and lambardari fee amounting to 5 per cent of the land revenue). The average net income for the family and per adult man on the farm is shown below (Farm Accounts for 1931-32, p. 206):

	Average net income for the family		Average net income per adult man	
	Per day	Per day Worked	Per day	Per day Worked
	Rs. as. p.	Rs. as. p.	Rs. as. p.	Rs. as. p.
1927-28	0 14 0	2 1 4	0 6 8	0 15 10
1928-29	1 2 6	2 7 4	0 8 10	1 2 8
1929-30	0 13 1	1 12 4	0 5 9	0 12 8
1930-31	0 1 8	0 3 7	0 0 9	1 1 7
1931-32	0 7 3	0 14 5	0 3 0	0 6 7

It is seen that the net income per day of an adult man steadily fell from about 9 annas in 1928-29 to about 9 pies in 1930-31. It rose in 1931-32 but was still about one-third of the figure for 1928-29.

Taking the three farms cultivated on the batai system, on an average the landlord's share amounted to 71·8 per cent in 1931-32 and 150·8 per cent in 1930-31.

Prof. Stewart does not comment on the contrast between the income of the worker and the non-worker, nor does Prof. Kartar Singh. They deserve our thanks for determining the contrast. But the figures are an indictment of the whole system under which the greater portion of the land of the Punjab is cultivated. It is a system which rewards idleness and penalizes honest labour.

Landlord Rights

We have seen above that under Hindu and Mohammadan Kings the State was not the universal landlord. It recognised rights of property in land. In the Report on the Revised Settlement of the Montgomery District (1871-76) it is stated (p. 211):

"It must always be remembered that under native rule no such thing as absolute proprietary right was recognised. The missing class was not the hereditary tenant but the proprietor".

The proprietor, however, existed. Commenting on this view, E. B. Steedman, Settlement Officer, says in his Report on the Revised Settlement of the Jhang District (1874-1880):

"It is difficult, perhaps impossible, to define with any accuracy to what extent the rights of property in land did exist, but they were certainly not extinct. The ruling power was not an all-powerful landlord, and all the subjects, except those enjoying special privileges, merely tenants-at-will. That some rights of transfer and mortgage were possessed and exercised during the reigns of the later Syal Khans, is abundantly proved. Many undoubted genuine deeds have been produced in land cases during this Settlement" (p. 64).

Proprietorship in the Punjab under the Sikhs meant cultivating proprietorship. The land revenue demand was heavy. There was therefore a tendency to ignore non-cultivating proprietors and to recognise the cultivator as proprietor. The State might grant jagirs for services rendered to the State, or to holy men. But the revenue which privileged persons enjoyed was not an additional charge on the cultivator; it was a remission of revenue due to the State. Generally speaking, then, only two parties shared in the produce of the land: the State and the cultivator.

Under Akbar there were no intermediaries because Akbar wanted all the revenue for the State, except that portion of it which jagirdars and others were permitted to enjoy on behalf of the State. And such was the position under Sikh rule. In the territories governed by Diwan Sawan Mal any one who broke up new land, or began to work a deserted well, became the proprietor of that land and liable to pay the land revenue. "In practice", writes Mr. E. B. Steedman (loc. cit. p. 69), "the Diwan held that no man had any right to any land that he could not cultivate, and grants of waste land were given to any body who could bring it under cultivation. Not only did this take place, but many persons who had formerly been tenants-at-will found themselves invested with the doubtful privilege of paying direct to the State. The proprietors dropped out because there was no room for them".

The privilege of paying direct to the State was doubtful because the State's demand was heavy.

"The State", continues Mr. Steedman, "took every thing it could from the cultivator, and the idea of a middleman intercepting part of the collection was not for a moment entertained".

The new proprietors belonged to every class. "Nothing", Mr. Steedman tells us, "was sacred to Sawan Mal. Churas and kamins were in his eyes just as good proprietors, probably better than Syals and Beloches. There were then no boundaries. The Syals retained what they could cultivate.

The waste was occupied by Sawan Mal's colonists" (Loc. cit. p. 69).

The old proprietors may not have dropped out completely, but it is clear that under such conditions they could not prosper. A new class of proprietors arose, those who cultivated the land. That may probably account for the comparatively large number of peasant proprietors in the Punjab.

The existence of intermediaries today, who have nothing to do with the cultivation of the land and who live on the fruits of others' toil, is largely due to the British Government. The Report on the First Regular Settlement of the Muzaffargarh District (1873—1880) by Edward O'Brien, Settlement Officer, gives an interesting instance of superior proprietors being formed by the direct action of the British Government. A number of Pathans had settled in the Muzaffargarh District under the Afghan governors of Multan. They enjoyed grain allowances, called *kasur,* which were not a tax on cultivators but were paid out of the Government's share of the produce. The Sikhs took Multan in 1818 and the Pathans fled. In 1848 they returned to help Major Edwards in his operations against Mul Raj. For their services the Pathans claimed restoration. Their claim was conceded and they obtained decrees for *kasur* in various villages under the rules issued by the British Government. The old *kasur* was a deduction from the revenue; the new *kasur* meant the imposition of an additional grain cess on the cultivators. The Deputy Commissioner reported in 1853 that the new *kasur* had "paralyzed the industry of the cultivators" (p. 93). He protested again in 1859 instancing villages that had been ruined by that policy. "The result was", says the Settlement Officer, "that in some villages the Pathans succeeded in ousting altogether the inferior proprietors [Sawan Mal's cultivating proprietors]; in others they reduced them to the position of tenants-at-will". In still other cases the Pathans settled down as superior proprietors with the right, enforceable by law, to exact *kasur.*

These are unpleasant facts, but they are of some importance as showing the origin of landlord rights in particular cases, and also how cultivating proprietors may disappear altogether, or be turned into tenants-at-will.

The State having called useless intermediaries into existence, may at least limit their demands.

The landlords, under the existing constitution, dominate the Provincial Councils. This is particularly true in the Punjab. What is their contribution to the country? Those who cultivate 60 per cent of the land of the Province live in poverty and want. And they have no voice in the administration of the country.

Government Measures of Farm Relief

The depression in agriculture has affected all countries, and almost every where the Government has intervened to assist agriculture both directly and indirectly.

Government measures of relief in 40 different countries are summarized in *The Agricultural Situation in 1931-32*, issued by the International Institution of Agriculture at Rome (1933).

We first turn to the note on India. This is also the most interesting. The note begins: "The publication of the Report of the Indian Central Banking Enquiry Committee in 1931 is of importance as indicating certain lines laid down in regard to relief of agriculture". The author of this note might have added that the Banking Enquiry Committee was appointed in July 1929, or before the disastrous fall of prices began, and that its work had nothing to do with the problems arising out of the depression. After summarising the recommendations of the Banking Enquiry Committee in regard to land mortgage banks, marketing of crops and the establishment in each Province of a Provincial Board of Economic Enquiry, the writer says: "The general question of measures in relief of agriculture is one that cannot be dissociated in any country, and less than ever in India, from the whole problem of *rural betterment*, or village improvement". The people of India, it is pointed out, live in villages, of which India has 500,000. They are poor, and live under insanitary conditions. Consequently the standards of health, physical efficiency and work capacity are low. Provincial Health Departments deal with questions of health; village *panchayats* are entrusted with such essential duties as the supply of water for drinking and other domestic purposes etc. The writer is disappointed with the work of the *panchayats*. The failure of *panchayats* is sometimes due to the absence of leadership, "the educated element, except for the village school-master [i.e., where there is a village school], being scarcely represented in the typical Indian village" (p. 181). It is, however, satisfactory to note that the work of officials in regard to village improvement and villages reconstruction, "has effected much already". It may be expected to effect much more in the years to come.

Such is the account given in "*The Agricultural Situation in 1931-32*" of Government measures of farm relief in India. The account is, on the whole, truthful. Apart from inadequate remissions of the land revenue and water-rates, very little has so far been done to assist the peasant in meeting the crises. The problem of relief of indebtedness is, however, being considered in several Provinces. Attention is drawn to the Punjab Bill for the relief of indebtedness in Appendix A.

Government Measures of Farm Relief in other Countries

In Australia a Wheat Bounty Act was passed in October 1931 according to which payment is made to wheat growers at a flat rate of 4½d. a bushel on all wheat grown in Australia, irrespective of selling price. The grower, and the buyer of wheat, or receiver, state on a prescribed form the quantity of grain sold or delivered for sale, and the form then forwarded to the Department of Markets, which sends a cheque to the farmer for the amount.

Further, a sum of £2,500,000 was set apart for use as loan to the States for the assistance of farmers. In Tasmania short-dated loans are made to farmers on approved security by the Rural Credits Section of the Agricultural Bank for the purchase of machinery, stock, plants, manure etc. The rate of interest is 6 per cent, and the period of the loan a maximum of 10 years.

In BULGARIA an Act was passed in April 1932 according to which all debts not exceeding 200,000 levas (about £500) due by agricultural producers possessing not more than 25 hectares (about 62 acres) can be reduced as much as 50 per cent. This applies to all debts contracted before January 1, 1931. Besides the reduction of the debt, an agricultural producer may have the period of repayment prolonged up to ten years, according to the amount of the loan. The debt is paid by annual instalments, with 7 per cent interest. Under this law the following property of the farmer is exempt from distraint: (1) food required up to the time of the new harvest, both for the family and for live-stock, (2) seed, (3) agricultural equipment up to the value of 25,000 levas (£60), (4) land up to 5 hectares (about 7½ acres), (5) a given number of sheep, pigs, goats, hives of bees, 1 pair of work animals, and 1 buffalo. The law is not applicable to debts due to the State banks. It is also interesting to note that the Bulgarian Government prepared a bill in June 1932 for the reform of the land tax. The land tax has not been completely suppressed, but exemption has been granted to small and medium-sized agricultural holdings, and particularly to holdings devoted to the cultivation of tobacco and vines.

In DENMARK loans are made by the State from a special loan fund to owners of farms for the attainment of voluntary agreement, or compulsory agreement without bankruptcy. In order to obtain a loan 'the dividend' to be paid to the creditors may not, in the agreement, be paid at more than 35 per cent of their claims. If nothing more was paid to creditors, debt-reduction would amount to 65 per cent.

In addition to this 35 per cent, however, the creditors may receive a further 35 per cent under certain conditions. If during a period of 5 years after the agreement the average weekly quotations for butter and bacon rise to at least 35 per cent above the average of the latter half of 1931, the additional 35 per cent, secured by a mortgage, will be paid, otherwise the payment will be proportionately reduced. If the prices of the two products do not rise at all nothing further is to be paid.

A sum of 30 million crowns (about £1,500,000) was allocated for distribution among owners and tenants in order to lighten the burden of taxes and interest on mortgages. The aid granted did not exceed 2,000 crowns in any individual case (about £100). The amount is to be refunded by instalments, beginning July 11, 1937, but only if the prices of butter and bacon during the years 1932—36 rise at least 30 per cent above the average for the latter half of 1931. About 135,000 farmers, i.e., 67 per cent of all the farmers in Denmark, were found entitled to the subvention under this law.

In EGYPT Government measures of farm relief have three objects: (1) to prolong the credits previously granted; (2) to intensify the work of the Agricultural Credit of Egypt; and (3) to safeguard agricultural property by stopping, as far as possible, forced sales and expropriation of land. It is claimed that the intervention of the State has saved the creditors as well as the debtors.

In ESTONIA facilities have been offered to farmers for the conversion of their short term debts to the extent of 60 per cent of the value of the immovable property into long term loans for a maximum period of 20 years at a lower rate of interest.

In FINLAND the Central Bank for Agricultural Credit Societies raised both foreign and domestic loans in 1930 to make advances to farmers for the consolidation of their short-term credits. Further, the Rural Property Bank was reorganised to grant such consolidation loans in the form of bonds of the Bank at their nominal value (up to 70 per cent of the value of the real estate and up to 30 per cent of the value of movable property and forests). The bonds are guaranteed by the State and the rate of interest is 7½ per cent. The creditors are obliged to accept the bonds of the Bank at their nominal value as repayment of capital and interest on the debts for whose consolidation the loan was granted by the Bank, unless they agree to leave the capital outstanding as a permanent loan until the end of 1935 against an approved rate of interest.

In East Prussia, first an attempt is made to bring about a voluntary agreement between the occupier of the farm and his creditors. If that fails, the method of dealing with the debt is determined by competent authority. If the postponement of debt cannot be arranged, the arrears of interest may be remitted and the rates of interest reduced. If even this fails to give adequate relief, or to place the farm on a sound footing, the capital debts may be reduced but only if, in the sale by auction following on bankruptcy, the capital sum would be entirely or for the most part lost. The consent of the creditor is required if the capital debt is to be reduced by more than half, or the rate of interest lowered to less than 4½ per cent.

In accordance with special regulations issued in March 1932 the creditor was obliged to accept to a certain extent the special bonds issued for assistance to Eastern Germany. These bonds are issued by the Deutsche Rentenbank up to 500 millions of reichsmarks at 4½ per cent interest. Some of these are redeemable in 1935 and the rest in 1938. The interest on the bonds is paid out of the interest and amortization of the mortgages specially placed, up to an amount equal to that of the bonds issued, on the properties to be relieved of indebtedness. The net available profits realised by the Rentenbank and contributions from industry are also used for the payment of interest.

An Act was passed in Hungary in 1931 whose object was to find means of bringing about agreements between creditors and debtors regarding suitable reduction of debts, and the conditions for the settlement of the debts thus reduced. The Hungarian Financial Syndicate was entrusted with the work of completing the settlement of agricultural debts.

In LATVIA agricultural credit is granted principally by State credit institutions. On several occasions the rates of interest have been lowered and also the instalments of repayment. The Government has also transferred the short-term credits to the State Agricultural Bank to be converted into long-term credits. Measures were also under consideration to prevent forced sales of agricultural properties.

Agricultural indebtedness in POLAND is estimated at 160 zlotys per hectare (equal to about £2½ per acre). This indebtedness represents about 25 per cent of the value of the land in the case of small farms, and about 40 per cent for large farms. The rates of interest charged by creditors are high, even as high as 24 and 36 per cent. The debt charges constitute the most important part of the costs of production in Poland. Various measures have been enacted with the object of giving relief to debtors. These relate to forced sales of agricultural property, to the administration of properties distrained upon (the object being to render methods of distraint less vigorous) and to repayment of burdensome debts. The State protects farmers whose financial position has been weakened by the crisis against hard treatment, and particularly against usury. It is hoped that by facilitating the payment of debts, the farmers would be enabled to emerge from the crisis.

In RUMANIA debts to co-operative credit societies have been reduced 25 per cent. The reduction in private debts of owners of properties up to 10 hectares (about 25 acres) amounts to 50 per cent—only 50 per cent of the debt is to be paid with interest at 4 per cent, the repayment extending over a period of 30 years.

In the case of owners of large and medium sized estates, possessing more than 10 hectares, the accumulated interest may be remitted. "The debtors undertake to pay, within 6 months, 10 per cent of the debts and, in this case, they benefit by the reduction of accumulated interest; the reduction will be 10 per cent for the year 1931, rising progressively to 50 per cent for debts contracted in 1927 or earlier" (p. 212).

The Spanish Government has granted loans to municipalities through the National Insurance Institute to enable them to make advances to small land-owners and tenant-farmers. The amount of the advances is determined by the Municipality after ascertaining the real needs of the farmer. The interest payable is 5 per cent.

The information given above (borrowed from *The Agricultural Situation in 1931-32*, Chapter III) is of great interest. It shows, in the first place, the wide extent of agricultural distress at the present time, and secondly how, in different countries, both large and small, measures have been devised by Government to lighten the burden of rural indebtedness.

Rural Indebtedness in India

The Central Banking Enquiry Committee estimated the rural indebtedness of India at about 900 crores. The figures for the different Provinces, as given by the Committee, are reproduced below:

	Total Rural Indebtedness
Assam	22 crores
Bengal	100 ,,
Bihar and Orissa	155 ,,
Bombay	81 ,,
Burma	50—60 ,,
Central Areas	18 ,,
Central Provinces	36 ,,
Coorg	35—55 lakhs
Madras	150 crores
Punjab	135 ,,
United Provinces	124 ,,

These estimates relate to the year 1929. On account of the fall of prices since 1929, the real burden of debts has considerably increased. For example, a debt of 135 crores (Punjab) in 1929 is equal to more than 270 crores at the present time.

Between 1921 and 1929 the rural debt of the Punjab increased by 50 crores. Debt per cultivated acre in 1929 amounted to 45 rupees, and per head of those supported by agriculture, to 104 rupees.

The causes of debt are well known. They have been divided into two classes by Mr. Darling. The peasant proprietor is obliged to borrow because (*a*) of the small size of his holding and its fragmentation, (*b*) losses of cattle from drought and disease, (*c*) his 'ingrained improvidence, the effects of which are greatly aggravated by insecurity of crops', and (*d*) his extravagant expenditure upon marriage and other ceremonies. The peasant proprietor *can* borrow because the money-lender is always ready to oblige him, and because of the expansion of credit due to high prices in the past and rise in the value of the land. The Agricultural Commission thus summed up the situation: "Causes which he (cultivator) seldom understands and cannot influence have endowed him with credit which he did not formerly possess, and he has found it difficult to resist the temptation to relieve present necessities by mortgaging his future income and even his capital" (p. 432).

The problem has changed during the past four years. The fall of prices has led to a contraction of the borrower's credit and at the same time reduced his capacity to repay debts.

The solution suggested by the Central Banking Enquiry Committee was debt conciliation on a voluntary basis. The details of the Committee's scheme are given below:

(1) Special officers should be appointed in each Province to persuade the lender and the borrower to agree to a redemption of standing debt on the basis of a cash payment or equated payments spread over a number of years.

(2) The existing co-operative credit societies should be utilized as the agency for the payment to the lender of the amounts payable under the terms of the settlement.

(3) The outstanding part of the settled debt will be treated as a deposit by the lender with the co-operative society. This will be paid to him in the settled annual instalments.

(4) Where part of the settled debt is to be paid in cash, Government should advance to the co-operative society the necessary funds which will be repaid by the society in annual instalments.

(5) In cases where a society is subjected to loss on account of the failure of the borrower to pay his instalments, the Government should come to the assistance of the society.

It is probable that many money-lenders would agree to substantial reductions of capital debt if the payment of the settled debt were guaranteed in the manner suggested above. But the payment of the debt in such cases would be spread over a number of years, say ten or more. The Punjab Provincial Banking Enquiry Committee pointed out that for such debts co-operative societies would require mortgage security. "But there are objections to village societies dealing in this form of security, and in the Punjab these objections have always been regarded as so weighty that mortgages are rarely taken" (p. 23).

The Central Banking Enquiry Committee, however, thought that there could not be any objection in principle to an ordinary co-operative society undertaking the work, as "the repayment of the settled amount of the debt will be made from long-term deposits either from the lender or the Government" (p. 66).

Voluntary debt conciliation, and the payment of the settled debt by instalments through co-operative societies would be a satisfactory arrangement; where the lender does not agree to a voluntary settlement of the debt, the Central

Banking Enquiry Committee suggested compulsory settlement by means of legislative enactment.

There is no objection in principle to the compulsory settlement of debts. Our brief review of Government measures of farm relief in different countries shows that in some cases the capital debt has been reduced as much as 50 per cent (Bulgaria and Rumania), while in Denmark, if the prices of bacon and butter do not rise, the reduction in capital debt would amount to more than 50 per cent. There is of course less objection to the remission of part or even whole of accumulated interest, to the lowering of the rate of interest, or to the prolongation of the period of payment of the settled debt. We have seen that in several countries short-term loans have been converted into long-term loans, and also that State banks have facilitated the payment of settled debts through the issue of bonds, carrying the guarantee of the State, which the creditors are obliged to take.

In view of relief granted to farmers elsewhere the proposal to grant such relief to farmers in India cannot be condemned as a communal measure. If voluntary debt conciliation fails, the State would be justified in suitably reducing both the accumulated interest and the capital debt.

It would be desirable to make a distinction between large and small proprietors. The strongest case exists for the reduction of debts owed by peasant proprietors, owing and cultivating 10 or 12 acres or less. The case for the reduction of debts owed by cultivating tenants is equally strong. No ground exists for debt reduction in the case of non-cultivating landlords, particularly when the debts were not incurred for agricultural purposes.

Relief from indebtedness is only one aspect of the problem of farm relief. The landholder, as we have seen, deserves relief from the heavy burden of taxation. And the worker deserves relief from the heavy exactions of the non-working landlord.

The land revenue should be abolished and agricultural incomes subjected to the income-tax. The water-rates should be reduced so as to be about equal to the cost of service (including interest on capital). The yield of the income-tax, as applied to agriculture, would be the Government's share in the real profits of cultivation, or the return to Government for its beneficent rural activities (including irrigation).

The reform of the system of rural taxation presupposes large changes in the administrative machinery of the Government. Land-taxation cannot be adequately reduced without a heavy reduction in the cost of administration, or without a simpler administrative machinery and cheaper officials.

Finally, there is urgent need for a comprehensive review of the relations between landlords and tenants, and a readjustment of these relations.

APPENDIX A

RELIEF OF INDEBTEDNESS IN THE PUNJAB

A Government bill for the relief of indebtedness in the Punjab has been introduced in the Punjab Council. Ground was prepared for legislative action by the work of the Indebtedness Committee, composed of members of the Punjab Legislative Council appointed in March 1932.

In the 'Statement of Objects and Reasons' it is explained that in formulating the legislative measures embodied in the Bill, "the Punjab Government have endeavoured to hold the balance fairly between the debtor and the creditor and to give the former such relief as is possible without making any change in the law which might have the effect of destroying or seriously impairing the whole system of rural credit."

The 'agriculturists' to whom relief is to be given shall include cultivating and non-cultivating owners, and tenants.

First, it is proposed to give the benefit of simplified insolvency procedure, provided in the Insolvency Act of 1920, to debtors whose debts exceed Rs. 250 and whose total property does not exceed Rs. 1000 (old limit Rs. 500 in both cases). The raising of the limit to Rs. 1000 is expected to extend the benefit of simplified insolvency procedure to nearly 80 per cent of the entire agricultural population.

The Committee on Indebtedness recommended the appointment of special Petty Insolvency Judges to administer justice in summary proceedings. The Committee expected that cases involving villagers will be settled as far as possible in the villages, not in the District Courts.

Second, a clear definition of 'excessive' interest has been framed. On loans advanced on the security of immovable property, or pledge of movable property, the court shall deem interest excessive if it exceeds 12 per cent compound interest with annual rests, or 15 per cent simple interest; on other loans 18 per cent compound interest with annual rests, or 24 per cent simple interest.

Third, it is proposed to set up Debt Conciliation Boards, on the lines recommended by the Central Banking Enquiry Committee.

A Debt Conciliation Board shall consist of a chairman and two or more members to be appointed by the local Government, for a term not exceeding 3 years.

An application for debt settlement may be made to such Board by a debtor or any of his creditors. When a debtor has applied for settlement, the Board shall call upon every creditor of the debtor to submit a statement of debts owed by the debtor. Every debt of which a statement is not submitted to the Board *shall be deemed for all purposes and all occasions to have been duly discharged.*

The creditor will be bound to furnish all necessary information to the Board, supported by documents, regarding his claim. The debtor will be called upon to explain his case, and finally the Board shall "use its best endeavours to induce them to arrive at an amicable settlement".

If the debtor and creditors to whom not less than 60 per cent of the total amount of the debtor's debts are due come to an amicable settlement, the Board shall forthwith reduce the settlement to writing. The agreement will then be registered and take effect as if it were a decree of a civil court.

If no amicable settlement is arrived at, the Board shall dismiss the application.

If a creditor refuses to accept what the Board considers a fair offer on the part of the debtor, the Board may grant the debtor a certificate in respect of the debts owed by him to such creditor. The advantage of this certificate to the debtor will be that if the cerditor sued him for the recovery of the debt, the court shall not allow the plaintiff (creditor) any costs in such suit, nor interest on the debt after the date of registration at more than 6 per cent per annum simple interest.

In a similar Bill prepared in the Central Provinces the debts payable under an agreement approved and registered by the Conciliation Board are recoverable as arrears of land revenue by the Collector, but if the Collector is unable to collect them, the agreement ceases to subsist and the creditor may sue in a civil court. "Thus the whole proceeding process becomes barren", is the comment of the Punjab Committee of Indebtedness. The proposed simplification of insolvency procedure, which is a part of the Punjab Bill, will prevent the work of our Conciliation Board from becoming barren. The agreement, as we have seen, after being approved and registered by the Conciliation Board, will have the character of a decree of a civil court. If the debtor refuses to pay according to the terms of the settlement, he will be dealt with by special Petty Insolvency Judges.

The amounts payable under an agreement must be paid before any debts incurred after the date of the registration of the agreement. Similarly, where the Board has granted a certificate to a debtor and an unsecured creditor sues for the recovery of a debt in respect of which a certificate has been granted, nothing will be legally payable until all amounts payable under an agreement have been paid.

It has been provided that no appeal or application for revision shall lie against any order passed by the Board, but the Board may review its own orders. Parties before the Board may be represented by agents, but not by legal practitioner.

The ancient principle of *Damdupat* has been applied to agricultural debts. In any suit brought against an agriculturist for the recovery of a loan taken after the commencement of the Indebtedness Act, no court shall pass a decree for a larger sum than twice the amount of the sum taken as principal. Loans made by a bank to an agriculturist will not be subject to this provision.

Finally it has been provided that an agriculturist debtor may, at any time, deposit in court a sum of money in full or part payment of his debt for payment to his creditor. From the date of deposit interest shall cease to run on the sum so deposited.

The Conciliation Boards will first be set up in one or two carefully selected areas. The system will be extended to other areas if it is found to work successfully.

There is no question that the proposed measure will give much-needed relief to the debtor. It is an interesting experiment, and the experiment is worth trying. Its success will largely depend on the composition of the Conciliation Boards and the spirit in which they work. It is possible that the fears of misuse of the provisions of the bill by the debtor to avoid making due payments to the creditor are groundless.

In the Bhavnagar State the State lent money at 4 per cent to the cultivators to enable them to pay off the amounts of debts settled by Conciliation Boards. This is impracticable in the Punjab. The creditors would readily accept cash payments of 8 or 6 annas in the rupee, or even less, but where is this money to come from? Taking the rural debt of the Province to be 135 crores, at 4 annas in the rupee, over 33 crores, equal to three times the annual revenue of the Punjab Government, would be required to pay off the debt.

Appendix B

THE LAND REVENUE AS A CAUSE OF DEBT

There is an interesting reference to this subject in the report of the Punjab Committee on Indebtedness (1934):

"It has been asserted before us that the land revenue is one of the main causes of indebtedness in the Punjab. While this assertion will not bear the test of figures, which show that the payment of land revenue is relatively a small item in the zamindar's budget, the fact remains that in bad years the zamindar finds all demands upon him hard to satisfy" (para 45).

The Committee (Chairman Mr. H. Calvert) did not admit that the land revenue was a cause of indebtedness, but since the Committee recognised that in bad years the zamindar found all demands upon him hard to satisfy, we may infer that the Committee would have probably conceded that in bad years the zamindar may sometimes incur debt to pay the land revenue.

What are the facts?

Normally the land revenue is a cause of indebtedness for it forms a considerable proportion of the cost of production of crops. In bad years it becomes a main cause of indebtedness. This is shown by the analysis of loans which is given every year in the official report on the working of co-operative societies, Punjab.

The analysis of loans for the year ending 31st July 1930, based on the records of 1,799 societies showed that approximately 12·66 per cent of the loans were taken for the payment of land revenue. Commenting on this in para. 27 of the Report the Registrar Mr. M. L. Darling, said: "Much the most significant of these figures is that for land revenue. Nearly 13 per cent of the amount borrowed is on this account as against a five years' average of less than 2 per cent."

In its review of the Report the Ministry of Agriculture thus commented on these figures: "The sudden rise from 1·95 to 12·66 per cent in the proportion of loans taken for the payment of land revenue as compared with the total amount borrowed from credit societies, shows how hard the zamindar has been hit by the fall in prices" (para 8 of the review).

The proportion of loans taken for land revenue was never 2 per cent or less. This is shown by the statement given below:

Loans by Co-operative Credit Societies in the Punjab
Proportion per cent of total

	Debt	Cattle	Revenue	Trade	Ceremonies
5 years ending 1923-24	22·0	20·5	13·0	6·5	8·0
1924-25	27·50	20·75	11·25	9·5	7·75
1925-26	26·0	20·5	3·75	8·5	7·0
1926-27	28·25	19·25	9·25	9·25	7·5
1927-28	26·9	18·2	9·3	10·2	9·8
1928-29	21·7	16·5	13·6	13·2	7·3
1929-30	23·48	17·43	12·66	10·83	7·58

(See analysis of loans in each year's report)

The average proportion of loans taken for land revenue in the five years ending 1928-29 was not 1·95 but 9·43 per cent. The average of 1·95 per cent is impossible as in no year was the proportion about 2 per cent. It will be seen that, excepting the year 1925-26, in each year the loans for land revenue have formed a considerable proportion of the total. The figures for 1931-32 and 1932-33 are given below:

Analysis of Loans made by Co-operative Credit Societies in the Punjab

Object of loan	Loans. Number 1932-33	Loans Amount 1932-33 1000 Rs.	Approximate Percentage	
			1932-33	1931-32
1. Repayment of debt	3,978	4,49	21·46	22·33
2. Cattle	5,297	3,49	17·06	17·27
3. Land Revenue	4,817	2,93	14·33	16·46
4. Trade	1,823	2,01	9·81	9·68
5. Building	1,129	1,44	7·05	5·91
6. Land Purchase	853	1,54	7·50	6·88
7. Ceremonies	1,367	1,36	6·63	7·31
8. Seed	1,306	53	2·61	1·72
Total	25,158	20,44		

(Source: Report on the Working of Co-operative Societies in the Punjab, 1932-33)

In 1931-32 the proportion rose to about 16½ per cent, but it fell to 14 ⅛ per cent in 1932-33. Loans for the payment of land revenue are third in order of importance; the land revenue, according to the official analysis of loans is one of the important causes of indebtedness. We may even call it a main cause of indebtedness at the present time.

The percentage of loans for the payment of the land revenue shows great variations in different districts:

1932-33

	Percentage of loans for land revenue to total loans taken from co-operative credit societies
Sialkot	1·48
Kangra	2·20
Jullundar ..	2·85
Dera Ghazi Khan ..	7·40
Gujrat	21·26
Shahpur	21·26
Gujranwala ..	23·40
Lyallpur	33·60
Multan	38·06
Montgomery ..	39·30

(Source: Punjab Co-operative Report, 1932-33, p. 30)

In some districts the land revenue is not only a main but the most important cause of indebtedness.

Incidentally we may note that a smaller percentage of loans is taken for ceremonies than for land revenue. It is gratifying to find that the proportion of loans for this purpose has fallen in recent years. This, as the Registrar says in his Report for 1932-33, implies that the agriculturist is re-adjusting the standards of expenditure which he accepted unthinkingly in the past. And the Registrar exclaims: "May this be the precious jewel in the head of the ugly and venomous toad, depression!" We join in the prayer.

Similarly in the United Provinces the percentage of loans taken from co-operative credit societies for marriages and ceremonies was only 4·33 per cent of the total in 1930-31 and it fell to 3·4 per cent in 1931-32. But 36·4 per cent of the loans in 1931-32 were for the payment of rent.

A novel suggestion has been made to ensure that Government income from the land revenue does not fall in bad years. Suppose a fund is started to which both the landholder and the Government contribute, the landholder paying his contribution in good years along with the land revenue. When bad times come, the Government at once remits the land revenue and balances its budget by drawing on the fund (Report of the Punjab Indebtedness Committee, p. 15). How very simple! It is surprising that no one ever thought of this solution before. The same safeguard may be proposed for an important source of Central revenues, the income-tax. Let a businessman, who is assessed to the income-tax at 1 anna per rupee when he earns an income taxable at that rate, pay an additional contribution of one anna per rupee to a special fund. If, next year, his income fell below the exemption limit he would of course pay nothing, but the Government would still have got something out of him to balance its budget. Is this over-taxation or not? Would such a proposal made in regard to the taxation of non-agricultural income be taken seriously by any one? And is the Indian agriculturist so prosperous in good years that he can bear to be over-taxed? Is the burden imposed by the land revenue on the landholder much lighter than that imposed by the income-tax on the non-agriculturist? The proposal in effect means that the Government should really never remit any land revenue at all.

In bad years the normal thing for a Government to do is to cut its expenditure so as to adjust it to the reduced income of the people. There is no way of escape from the difficulties created by the top-heaviness of the administration through increased taxation disguised as 'contributions', voluntary or otherwise.

Appendix C

GOVERNMENT VIEW OF WATER-RATES

The Government view of water-rates is expounded in a note pre-fixed to the report of the Abiana Committee. (This Committee, composed of official and non-official members of the Punjab Council, was appointed in July 1933). The non-official members of the Committee recommended "that a separate budget should be prepared and presented to the Council and the commitments of the department of Irrigation to contribute to the general finances of the Province should be restricted in their extent and regulated on some intelligible basis, as is done in the case of the railway budget in the Central Government". The Government, of course, cannot entertain such a proposal. The proposal, we are told in the Government review of the Report, "is based on a fundamental misconception, that the irrigation works of the Province were created and are maintained for the benefit of a particular class. This is not so". The irrigation works of the Province were created for the benefit of the whole population, and their construction was financed partly out of surpluses from the revenues of the Province and partly out of borrowed money advanced on the security of the general revenues, as well as from the sale of lands irrigated by the Canals. Further: "The water in the Punjab rivers and the Crown lands irrigated by them are the property of the State while the users of canal water are not the whole body of the citizens of the Province but a fortunate section comprising only about 34 per cent of the total population. If, therefore, a section of the people benefit directly by the use of that water, the rest of the population is equally entitled to benefit indirectly. The analogy of the Railways of India, which are used equally by the whole population, is not an exact one. The suggestion that after deducting a certain fixed return for the benefit of the State generally the remaining profits from a particular form of taxation should be expended for the benefit of the particular section of the population which pays the tax is not only indefensible in theory, but would in practice be unworkable. It could be used with equal justice by motorists, by users of excisable liquor or by those who provide the income from stamp duties of various kinds.... The *reductio ad absurdum* of the proposal of the non-official members would be that each citizen could only receive that share of the benefits provided by State, which was represented by his actual contribution to the general revenues" (para 7).

These observations are of extraordinary interest, particulary as they come from the head of the Punjab Government.

Firstly, the whole argument is based on the assumption that the water-rates are a tax, not a price charged for water. A tax, as we know, is not a *quid pro quo* for a specific service rendered by Government to an individual who pays the tax. It is a general contribution to the revenues of Government to enable the Government to carry on its administrative and other functions. We agree. It is also true that the agriculturist is exempt from the income-tax. The land revenue and the water-rates may be regarded as a substitute for the income-tax in the case of the cultivator.

But if the water-rates are a tax on income, the tax should be made to conform to the well-known principles of taxation. The burden of the tax should be adjusted to the tax-payer. But while the water rates are a tax, they are levied in the form of price. Every one who takes canal water pays the water-rates, just as every one who makes use of the railway, or the services of the postal or the telegraph department, pays the charge fixed for the service. In essence the supply of canal water to the cultivator is a service. To say that railways are used equally by the whole population while canal water is used by 34 per cent of the population means nothing. Actually the railways are not used equally by the whole population. Even if the analogy of the

Railways of India is not an exact one, take the telegraph service. Does a telegraph office exist in every village? In this service used equally by every one? The proportion of those who directly benefit most largely by it is less than 34 per cent of the population. Yet the charge for telegrams is based on cost of service. Even if this analogy is not an exact one, consider the charge for the use of electrical energy provided by the Mandi project. In theory the service may be used equally by the whole population, but in actual practice it will be used, for industrial purposes, by a very small section of the population. The development of the Mandi-Project may transform the industrial life of the Province, just as progress of Canal irrigation has transformed the agricultural life of the Punjab. Let us assume that in the beginning the charge for the use of this energy has been fixed low in order to make it attractive. Will there be any justification, when the energy is more largely used for industrial purposes, for raising the rates so that they cease to bear any relation to cost of service and assume the shape of a heavy tax on income? A charge for water, exceeding cost of service, is made even when cultivation ceases to be remunerative. Will any industrialist care to use electrical energy when the cost exceeds his net income, no allowance being made in the calculation of net income for the wages of his own labour and profits of enterprise?

The cultivator cannot refuse to take canal water. The Government has a monopoly of service, and possesses the means of realising its dues. That explains how water-rates are paid when the cultivator earns no net income in the true sense at all.

The non-official members demanded a reduction in the water-rates of 80 lakhs a year. The actual reduction sanctioned is 35 lakhs. In determining the amount of the reduction account has been taken not so much of the capacity of the cultivator to pay as of the capacity of the finances of the Province to bear the strain of reduction. If a situation arises in which it will become necessary to grant further temporary relief not only to the users of canal water but to all payers of land revenue, the crisis, it is promised, will be met "promptly and generously by throwing in the last reserves of Government. But until he must, the Governor-in-Council will not mortgage the future of the Province" (para 41).

The meaning of this is that the cultivator must continue to bear the whole burden of the top-heavy administration until nothing more can be got out of him.

PROFIT FROM CANALS

It is pointed out in the Government review of the Abiana Report that during the past 40 years the profit from canals, or the surplus which the sale of canal water to the cultivator provides, "has been the motive power of all progress in the Province" (para 6). During the 12 years ending 1922-23 the total revenues of the Province amounted to 116 crores, of which 46½ crores, or 40 per cent, were contributed by the Irrigation department, or rather the cultivator who used the canal water. It is argued that both the Government and the people in the past regarded the canals, "in the absence of alternative sources of revenue, as the most important source of financing the requirements of the Province irrespective of all theoretical considerations" (para 8). Admitting this, it may be asked whether the attitude of both the Government and the people toward Canals should not change when a heavy fall of prices has created a new situation?

Taking the view which the Government does of the function of Irrigation revenue, it is natural for the Government to say that a discussion of profits from irrigation is irrelevant to the present problem (para 8). But it is not irrelevant from the point of view of the cultivator.

Statement showing average annual return per cent on the total capital spent on the canal system of the Punjab as a whole:

Year	Total capital outlay in lakhs	Profit in Lakhs	Percentage of profit
1928-29	32,11	2,91	9·08
1929-30	32,88	3,06	9·31
1930-31	33,32	2,74	8·22
1931-32	33,71	2,91	8·64
1932-33	34,83	2,81	8·31
Average of 5 years ..	33,17	2,89	8·70

(Source: Abiana Report, p. 25 of Statements)

It is seen that the percentage of profit from canals has fallen inappreciably in spite of the severest agricultural depression of the past 75 years.

The water-rate per acre has varied as below:

	Rs. per acre
1900-01	3·0
1901-02 to 1906-07	3·3
1907-08 to 1909-10	3·6
1910-11 to 1915-16	3·7
1916-17 to 1923-24	3·95
1924-25 to 1925-26	4·77
1926-27 to 1928-29	4·5
1929-30	4·33
1930-31 and 1931-32	..

Had not special remissions of water-rates been given, the average rate would have been 4·38, i.e., much the same as in 1929-30. The actual rates were 3·88 in 1930-31 and 3·86 in 1931-32.

Between 1900-01 and 1917-18, the area assessed to water-rates rose from about 4 million acres to 6·2 million acres and the amount of the assessment from 119·0 lakhs to 242·6 lakhs. During this period Government took, as water-rates, from 1|7th to 1|10th of the value of the produce raised with canal water.

From 1918-19 to 1921-22, owing to the high price of agricultural produce, the Government's share in the form of water-rates dropped to about 1|16th. It rose after the increase in water-rates in 1924-25, and still further when prices fell. After allowing for remissions, it amounted to 15·2 per cent in 1930-31 and 13·3 per cent in 1931-32.

Statement showing Percentage Ratio of Occupier's Rate to Value of Crops on the Principal Canals in British Punjab

	Area assessed during the year in Million acres	Amount of assessment in Lakh Rs.	Rate per acre Rs.	Value of crops per acre Lakh Rs.	Percentage ratio of occupier's rate to value of crops
1900-01	3·9	119·0	3·02	15,61·4 / 5·9 = 26·4	11·4
1913-14	5·9	220·8	3·75	26,45·3 / 8·0 = 33·2	11·3
1917-18	6·2	242·2	3·90	33,370·0 / 8·2 = 40·5	9·6
1921-22	8·5	326·4	3·85	67,20·7 / 10·6 = 63·6	6·1
1924-25	7·9	378·4	4.77	57,71·1 / 10·1 = 56·9	8·4
1928-29	9·73	435·9	4·48	55,06.4 / 11·9 = 46·4	9·7
1929-30	9·99	433·0	4·33	49,27·0 / 12·0 = 41·0	10·6
1930-31	9·97	387·4	3·88	29,45·1 / 11·9 = 24·8	15·2
1931-32	9·30	359·3	3·86	32,73·8 / 11·2 = 29·1	13·3

(Source: Abiana Report, Statements)

The value of crops per acre in 1930-31 was actually less than that in 1900-01; the rate per acre was Rs.3·88 in 1930-31 as compared with Rs.3·02 thirty years before.

The percentage ratio of occupier's rate to value of crops is interesting for comparative purposes. For example, it rose to 15·2 per cent in 1930-31 as compared with 6·1 per cent in 1921-22. But the ratio tells us nothing about the burden that it imposes on the user of water. To discover that it is necessary to consider the proportion of the occupier's rate to the net income of the user of the water:

Proportion of water-rates to net income according to the Farm Accounts in the Punjab. 1930-31

Note.—**Net income in the Farm Accounts has been calculated without making any allowance for wages of labour of the cultivator and his family or profits of enterprise.**

Farm. Area and District	Net income per acre	Water rates	Proportion of water rates to net income per cent
	Rs. a. p.	Rs. a. p.	
27¼ acres, Lyallpur, Batai.	9 11 0	4 12 4	49.6
802.5 acres, Risalewala Govt. Farm. Batai.	23 4 5	4 11 10	20.3
25 acres, Montgomery. Batai.	14 4 6	5 2 10	36.2
55.5 acres, Sargodah. Siri.	6 2 6	2 12 4	45.0

Let us consider the meaning of these figures. In the year 1930-31 the cultivator of the farm of 27¼ acres in the Lyallpur district (we assume that the whole land had belonged to him) found that after meeting the cost of cultivation, apart from the water-rates, he was left with Rs. 9-11-0 per acre. If there were no water-rates to pay, that would have been his reward and that of his family for their labour on the land (four able-bodied members of the family worked on the holding). The reward was not liberal; about 3 annas per day per adult worker for a year's work on the farm. Of this income the State claimed about half (49·6 per cent), as the price for the use of water. Is this a fair price?

Fortunately for the Government the great majority of those who pay the water-rates are unable to read Government reports. Otherwise they may want to know why the canals earn a profit of over 8 per cent when they earn less than their subsistence.

The demand for the reduction of water-rates to the level of cost of service (including interest on capital) is reasonable. The State, as has been suggested above, may supplement its irrigation income by a graduated tax on agricultural income, with an exemption limit. For the rest, it must reduce its expenditure. The State must live within its means. There is a strange unwillingness in official circles to recognise facts. Present prices are more 'normal' than the prices of ten years ago. The prices of 1924-25 were wholly artificial. The income of those days was inflated income. Those days are definitely gone. Standards of State expenditure set up then cannot be maintained. There is a useless multiplication of Departments in the Provinces (to which we propose to make further additions when the new constitution is inaugurated). The need for simplifying administrative machinery and reducing the level of official salaries is apparent. Nothing of course, will be done, but we should have at least the fairness to admit that the inability of Government to reduce the cost of administration does not make the taxation of the subsistence of poor men, women and children in the villages morally justifiable or economically sound.

Appendix D

POPULATION AND FOOD SUPPLY

Is the outturn of food in India in excess of the needs of the population? The question is suggested by the heavy fall in the price of food-grains. If there is over-production of wheat, rice and other food-grains, it may be desirable to restrict production, in order to adjust supply to demand.

The Prices Enquiry Committee of 1910 examined the question of food supply in relation to the growth of numbers between 1890-91 and 1911-12. The Committee drew attention to the substitution of non-food-crops for food-crops in certain parts of India, as the result of which there was 'a diminution in the food supply of the country and a consequent rise of prices' (para 173). The general conclusion of the Committee was that during this period the requirements for food-grains for internal consumption increased in a larger proportion than the total production of food-grains (para 146). This conclusion was criticised by the Government of India in a note pre-fixed to the Report of the Committee. The Government referred to the untrustworthy nature of the estimates of area and yield of crops and their incompleteness, and maintained that the area under food-crops had increased in almost exact correspondence with the growth of population which, in view of the improvement in the means of transportation and the extension of irrigation, implied 'the production on the average of a relatively larger and more efficient food supply' (*Prices Report,* p. viii).

The rise of prices after 1905 was not due to comparative shortage of food but causes of a more general nature connected with the Indian monetary system.

What is the situation at present?

The following statement shows the area under rice and

wheat and the total area under food grains in British India in 1911-12 and the following years:

Area under Food-grains in million acres

	All food grains	Rice	Wheat
1911-12 ..	195·1	76·6	25·0
1912-13 ..	201·4	78·8	23·9
1913-14 ..	191·6	76·9	22·7
1914-15 ..	204·5	77·7	25·5
1915-16 ..	203·7	78·7	25·5
1916-17 ..	208·8	81·0	25·0
1917-18 ..	207·4	80·7	26·4
1918-19 ..	177·8	77·6	19·1
1919-20 ..	199·7	78·7	23·5
1920-21 ..	186·9	78·1	20·4
1921-22 ..	204·8	79·7	22·4
1922-23 ..	205·0	80·6	24·4
1923-24 ..	197·0	77·2	24·3
1924-25 ..	200·3	79·3	24·8
1925-26 ..	196·1	80·2	24·0
1926-27 ..	197·2	78·5	24·2
1927-28 ..	196·7	76·6	24·6
1928-29 ..	200·3	81·1	24·9
1929-30 ..	200·1	79·4	24·7
1930-31 ..	202·7	80·6	24·8
1931-32 ..	..	80·3	25·1
1932-33 ..	..	78·6	24·8

(Source: Statistics of British India for 1930-31 and Area and Yield of Principal Crops for 1932-33)

The averages for the five years ending 1915-16 are: rice 77·7 million acres, wheat 24·2 million acres and all food grains 199·3 million acres. The figures for recent years do not show any large increase over these averages.

The population of British India increased from 243·8 millions in 1911 to 271·5 millions in 1931 or by 11 per cent. It is evident that population has been increasing more rapidly than the area under food-grains in British India.

But we must not conclude in haste that there must be an actual shortage of food at the present time.

The production of food in British India in 1932-33 may be thus estimated:

	Area Million acres	Food Million tons	
Rice ..	78·6	29·8	
Wheat ..	24·8	7·6	
Barley ..	6·3	2·4	
Jowar ..	21·4	4·7	
Bajra ..	13·6	2·2	
Maize ..	6·3	2·1	
Gram ..	13·9	3·4	
Ragi for 1930-31 ..	4·0	1·3	at 8·6 mds. per acre[1]
Other food grains and pulses, 1930-31 ..	30·0	17·7	at 16 mds. per acre[1]
Total ..		71·2	

(Source: See Reports mentioned above)

The monsoon of 1932 was fairly normal and gave, on the whole, well-distributed rains all over the country. The yields in 1932-33 may be regarded as 'normal'.

The statement given below shows estimated consumption:

Outturn of food	..	71·2 million tons
Population	..	271·5 millions

[1] Estimate of yield per maund according to the *prices Report*, 1914.

		Million tons
Food	..	54·3 assuming that one ton of food will feed 5 persons for a year.
Seed	..	5·0 at 7 per cent of outturn.
Cattle food	..	3·6 at 5 per cent of outturn.
Wastage	..	3·6 at 5 per cent of outturn.
Total consumption		66·5 million tons.
Estimated surplus	..	4·7 million tons.

These figures are conjectural, but it is probably true that the surplus of food-grains at the present time is less than 9·53 million tons, estimated by the Famine Commission of 1898.

Allowance must also be made for an export of about 2 million tons of food at present.

It would seem that it is incorrect to speak of over-abundance of food in India. The restriction of food cultivation by the substitution of non-food crops for food crops may dangerously reduce such small surplus of food as exists, and inflict hardship on the consumer in a year of unseasonable rainfall.

Cultivation of food should be made remunerative by making it possible for the cultivator to reduce his costs, not by restricting supply.

The extension of canal irrigation in Sindh will make the reserve of food larger than it is at present and is therefore not unwelcome.

CHAPTER II

FOREIGN TRADE

In the case of a large country like India, internal trade, from the point of view of the home producer, is of greater importance than foreign trade. The internal demand is large, and it must grow with the growth of numbers. A rise in the standard of living of the masses would stimulate this demand enormously.

Of the rice crop before the War (1909 to 1913-14) 91 per cent was consumed in the country, and only 9 per cent exported. In the case of wheat, the percentage of exports to production was higher—14 per cent. At the present time there are practically no wheat exports. The exports of rice in 1933-34 represented 5% of the crop of 1932-33. The quantity of food exported at the present time is probably not more than 2 or 3 per cent of the total production.

This proportion is considerable in the case of raw cotton and raw jute—(about a half) and certain other articles (linseed and groundnuts). In the case of tea the proportion of exports to production is 90 per cent.

On the whole the foreign demand for our food-stuffs and raw materials is small as compared with the internal demand. But from the point of view of the balance of payments the foreign demand is of the greatest importance. A heavy and permanent reduction in it would produce serious consequences.

India is a debtor country. She must export goods in order to pay interest on Sterling loans, and funds invested in India by foreigners.

We are also a heavy importer of services—services of foreign administrators, soldiers, shippers, bankers, insurance agents and others.

Finally, there are imports of goods which are indispensable to us. There are many classes of consumers' goods which, in our present stage of industrial development, we must import (electrical goods and apparatus, railway material, motor cars, motor cycles and bycycles, rubber manufactures, dyestuffs etc.) While some progress has been made in the manufacture of consumers' goods, we do not make producers' goods at all. All classes of tools and implements and all machines used in factory production are imported.

We are not self-sufficient to-day, as we were under the Moghul Kings. Life in those days was simpler. The common man wanted no imported luxuries—they were meant for the rich. India then was what Werner Sombart would call *Ausfuhrland*. She exported goods because the world wanted her products. We are today an *Einfuhrland*—or we export goods to pay for goods and services which we must import.

The decline in exports in recent years suggests that Indian growers of food-stuffs and raw materials would have to rely on Indian demand more largely than before for the consumption of their products. And indeed, if the world will not buy our wheat, we shall consume it ourselves, as we are doing now—the unsatisfied demand for wheat in India, apart from exports, is considerable. Conceivably a great expansion of the cotton mill and hand-loom industry may render exports of cotton unnecessary. The development of the leather industries might absorb the hides and skins, raw, tanned and dressed at present exported. And so on. In this sense we can become self-sufficient,—more largely consuming our own products and relying on exports on a reduced scale to pay for such imported goods as we do not produce.

But how is the problem of foreign debts and imports of services to be solved? So long as India has heavy foreign obligations to meet, she must have an excess of exports of goods over imports at least equal in amount to these obligations.

Under existing conditions any serious diminution in the exports of primary products, either because of a fall in the foreign demand, or because of increase in home consumption, must turn the balance of payments against India and lead to the export of gold.

In 15 months from the end of September 1931 to the end of September 1932 our payments abroad were as follows:

Sterling debt, net reduction	£ 11 millions
Repayment of money invested in Indian Treasury Bills by foreign banks	£ 11¼ millions
Total debt payments	£22¼ millions
Current requirements of trade (sea-freights, interest and dividends on investments in India held abroad, family remittances, money spent by travellers from India etc.)	£ 14 millions
Government of India's current requirements	£ 34½ millions
Total current requirements	£ 48½ millions
Total of foreign payments	£ 70¾ millions

This is equal to a little more than 94 crores of rupees.

But for gold exports we should not have been able to meet these charges, for the excess of exports over imports of merchandise from the end of September 1931 to the end of December 1932 amounted to only £ 15 millions.

Apart from repayment of sterling loans, the current requirements of trade and the Government of India amount to about £ 43 millions, or a little more, in a year. If our favourable balance of trade is less than this amount, we must either export gold, or add to sterling debt.

It is this aspect of the question which invests the figures of our foreign trade in recent years with an extraordinary interest. And it is on account of our heavy annual obligations that increase of home consumption is not a satisfactory remedy for the decline of exports. If some exports decline, we must develop others, for the only alternative is bankruptcy. We cannot repudiate our obligations and it is impossible for any country to pay debts abroad year after year by exporting gold.

The following table shows our balance of trade and import or export of gold from 1924-25 to 1933-34 (1st April to end of March):

TABLE I

India's Foreign Trade. In lakhs of rupees

	Exports	Re-exports	Imports	Balance of trade	Gold, net import (—); net export (+)
1924-25	384,66	13,51	243,16	+155,01	— 73,93
1925-26	374,86	10,49	224,11	+161,24	— 34,85
1926-27	301,43	8,01	229,98	+ 79,46	— 19,40
1927-28	319,11	9,54	246,78	+ 81,87	— 18,10
1928-29	330,13	7,83	251,49	+ 86,47	— 21,20
1929-30	310,80	7,13	238,95	+ 78,98	— 14,22
1930-31	220,49	5,14	163,58	+ 62,05	— 12,75
1931-32	155,89	4,66	125,72	+ 34,83	+ 57,98
1932-33	132,43	3,22	132,27	+ 3,38	+ 65,52
1933-34	146,31	3,42	115,20	+ 34,71	+ 57,05

As compared with 1924-25, the value of exports of Indian merchandise fell 66 per cent in 1932-33 and 62 per cent in 1933-34. Exports sank to their lowest level in 1932-33, when including re-exports, they exceeded imports only by 3 1/3 crores of rupees. In 1933-34 exports increased, while imports continued to decline, so that the surplus of exports over imports rose to about 34¾ crores. It may be noted that this amount is not sufficient to cover the "Home charges" (more than 40 crores of rupees).

While both exports and imports have fallen, the decline in exports has been relatively heavier. As compared with 1924-25, exports, as we have seen, fell 66 per cent in 1932-33, but imports by only 46 per cent. The percentage decrease of exports in 1933-34, as compared with 1924-25, was greater than that of imports (62 per cent exports and 53 per cent imports), in spite of the continued fall in imports.

The net import of gold came to an end with the suspension of the gold standard.

The principal exports from India are small in number. Their value and quantity are shown separately in Tables II and III.

TABLE II

Exports of Indian Merchandise. In crore rupees

Year	Raw Jute	Gunny bags	Gunny cloth	Cotton raw	Seeds	Tea	Grain, pulse and flour	Hides and skins, raw	Total of all exports	Total	Percentage of col. 10 to col. 11
1	2	3	4	5	6	7	8	9	10	11	12
1924-25	29·1	23·2	28·3	91·2	33·2	33·4	65·1	6·8	310·3	384·7	80·7
1925-26	38·0	26·7	31·8	95·0	29·6	27·1	48·0	7·2	303·4	374·9	80·9
1926-27	26·8	24·4	28·5	58·6	19·1	29·0	39·3	7·2	202·9	301·4	77·3
1927-28	30·7	23·3	30·0	47·7	26·7	32·5	42·9	8·8	242·6	319·1	76·0
1928-29	32·4	24·9	31·6	66·3	29·6	26·6	33·7	9·6	254·7	330·1	77·2
1929-30	27·2	21·9	29·7	65·1	26·5	26·0	34·8	8·0	239·2	310·8	77·0
1930-31	12·9	14·6	16·8	46·3	17·9	23·6	29·9	5·5	167·5	220·5	76·0
1931-32	11·2	10·9	10·5	23·5	14·6	19·4	20·4	3·7	114·2	155·9	73·3
1932-33	9·7	11·2	10·2	20·4	11·3	15·2	16·1	2·8	96·9	132·4	73·2
1933-34	10·9	9·7	11·4	26·6	13·7	19·9	11·8	4·3	108·3	146·3	74·0

Index Numbers

		Raw Jute	Gunny bags	Gunny cloth	Raw cotton	Seeds	Tea	Grain, pulse and flour	Hides and skins, raw	Average	Total of all exports
1924-25		100	100	100	100	100	100	100	100	100	100
1925-26		131	115	112	104	89	81	74	106	102	97
1926-27		92	105	101	64	58	87	60	106	84	78
1927-28		105	100	106	52	80	97	66	129	92	83
1928-29		111	107	112	73	89	80	52	144	96	86
1929-30		94	94	106	71	80	78	53	118	87	81
1930-31		44	63	59	51	54	71	46	81	59	57
1931-32		38	47	37	26	44	58	31	54	41	41
1932-33		33	48	36	22	34	46	25	41	36	34
1933-34		37	42	40	29	41	60	18	63	41	38

TABLE III

Exports from India. Quantity

	Raw jute 1000 tons	Gunny bags Millions	Gunny cloth Million yds.	Raw cotton 1000 tons	Seeds 1000 tons	Tea Million lbs.	Grain, pulse and flour 1000 tons	Hides and skins, raw 1000 tons	Average
1924-25	696	425	1,456	594	1,328	340	4,260	47·7	
1925-26	647	425	1,461	745	1,250	326	3,063	50·8	
1926-27	708	449	1,503	569	838	349	2,429	50·6	
1927-28	892	463	1,553	480	1,210	362	2,784	64·4	
1928-29	898	498	1,568	663	1,328	360	2,300	66·1	
1929-30	807	522	1,651	727	1,195	377	2,510	53·1	
1930-31	620	434	1,271	701	1,195	356	2,614	45·3	
1931-32	587	389	1,021	423	988	342	2,614	33·6	
1932-33	563	415	1,012	368	733	379	2,056	27·3	
1933-34	748	401	1,053	489	1,124	318	1,807	41·6	
Index Numbers									
1924-25	100	100	100	100	100	100	100	100	100
1925-26	93	100	100	126	94	96	72	197	98
1926-27	102	106	103	96	63	103	57	106	92
1927-28	128	109	107	81	91	106	65	135	103
1928-29	129	117	108	112	100	106	54	139	108
1929-30	116	123	113	122	90	111	59	111	106
1930-31	89	102	87	118	78	105	61	95	92
1931-32	84	92	70	71	74	101	61	70	78
1932-33	81	98	70	62	55	112	48	57	73
1933-34	108	94	72	82	82	94	44	87	83

It will be seen that the heaviest decrease has occurred in the case of grain, pulse and flour, whose exports fell from 65 crores in 1924-25 to 25 crores in 1932-33 and further to 11·8 crores in 1933-34—a fall of 82 per cent in the value of exports. Next to grain, pulse and flour, raw cotton is the greatest sufferer. The fall in the value of exports of raw cotton amounted to 71 per cent in 1933-34 and 78 per cent in 1932-33.

On an average the quantity of these 8 principal exports decreased 27 per cent in 1932-33. The fall in value on an average amounted to 64 per cent in the same year. Roughly, for quantities 73 per cent of those of 1924-25 we got prices 64 per cent below those of 1924-25. The fall of prices thus amounted to 51 per cent, which means that if there had been no decrease in the quantities of these exports, the value of exports would have decreased not by 64 but 51 per cent.

In the case of tea in 1932-33 and raw jute in 1933-34 there was an increase in the quantity of exports, but the value fell heavily. In the case of grain, pulse and flour, the value contracted by 82 per cent and the decrease in quantity of exports amounted to 56 per cent. Allowing for the reduced quantity of exports, the fall in prices of the food-grains exported amounted to 36·4 per cent on an average as compared with 1924-25.

It is evident that exports have suffered both on account of reduced demand and the fall of prices. But Table III makes it clear that generally speaking the reduction in the value of exports has been comparatively small. It is the fall of prices which in most cases is the real cause of hardship.

The principal exports in the tables given above accounted for about 81 per cent of the total value of exports of Indian merchandise in 1924-25 and 1925-26. But their proportion to the total steadily grew less till 1932-33, in which year their value represented a little more than 73 per cent of the total. It is obvious that the decrease in the proportion of these exports was accompanied by increase in the proportion of some other exports. This is shown by Table IV.

TABLE IV

Manufactured exports from India in crore rupees

	Manufactured exports from India In crore rupees			Index numbers	
	Manufactured exports excluding jute manufactures	All exports (Indian merchandise)	Per cent of col. 2 to col. 3	Manufactured exports excluding jute manufactures	All exports
1	2	3	4	5	6
1924—25 ..	32·4	384·7	8·4	100	100
1925—26 ..	30·8	374·4	8·2	95	97
1926—27 ..	32·1	301·4	10·6	99	78
1927—28 ..	34·0	319·1	10·6	105	83
1928—29 ..	32·7	330·1	9·9	101	86
1929—30 ..	32·2	310·8	10·4	99	81
1930—31 ..	25·4	220·5	11·1	78	57
1931—32 ..	20·7	155·9	13·3	64	41
1932—33 ..	16·8	132·4	12·6	52	34
1933—34 ..	18·5	146·3	12·6	57	38

The proportion of manufactured exports (excluding jute) rose from 8·2 per cent in 1925-26 to 13·3 per cent in 1931-32. At the present time a little more than one-eighth of total exports are articles partly or wholly manufactured. The rise in the proportion does not mean greater exports, whether in value, or volume. The value of manufactured exports in 1931-32 had fallen by 36 per cent; in the same year the fall in the value of the principal exports mentioned in Table III amounted to 59 per cent. The comparatively smaller fall in the proportion of manufactured exports to the total is due to the smaller extent of the fall in the price of manufactured articles.

MANUFACTURED EXPORTS

Apart from gunny cloth and gunny bags, our manufactured export are of little importance. The most important

6

article, after jute manufactures in class III (articles wholly or mainly manufactured) is tanned or dressed hides and skins—(value of exports in 1933-34, 565 lakhs). The value of other principal exports is shown below:

Manufactured exports in 1933-34

	Value in Lakh Rs.
Chemicals, drugs and medicines	1,14
Dyes and Colours	81
Metals, iron and steel and manufactures thereof ..	1,07
Metals, other than iron and steel and manufactures	2,36
Cotton yarns and manufactures	2,73

The chief chemical exported was saltpetre (15 lakhs). Among dyeing and tanning substances the more important are cutch and gambier (about 4 lakhs), indigo (about 1 lakh) and myrobalans (about 56 lakhs). The exports of pig iron in 1933-34 amounted to 85 lakhs, steel bars 20 lakhs, old iron or steel for re-manufacture 23 lakhs, and piglead 1½ crore.

The exports of cotton piece-goods, in view of the growth of the Indian mill industry, are of greater interest and deserve fuller treatment.

The Government of India sent a Trade Mission to certain countries in the Near East and in Africa in 1928 to make a survey of their potentialities as markets for Indian cotton goods, and to make recommendations for the encouragement of the export of cotton manufactures from India. The Trade Mission, consisting of three members, spent five months in these countries and submitted a report which has been published.

The Trade Mission estimated the total demand of the Levant, South Africa, Persia and Iraq, Aden and the Sudan, and East Africa at 1,110 million yards, and India's share at 110 million yards or 10 per cent, varying between 42 per cent in the case of Persia to less than 1 per cent in the case of Turkey and Egypt. The consuming groups in the order of their importance are as follows:

1 Persia and Iraq, 70-75 million yards per annum
2 East Africa, 16-17 million yards and, 55,000 blankets
3 South Africa and Portuguese East Africa, 12 million yards
4 Aden and the Sudan, 9 million yards
5 The Levant 4 million yards

According to the Trade Mission the markets offering the greatest potentialities for development are the Levant and South Africa.

Since the Trade Mission's investigations the foreign markets for our cotton goods have much contracted.

This is shown by Table V:

TABLE V

Exports of Cotton Piece-goods. In million yards

	1924—25	1931—32	1933—34
Iraq	48·9	12·8	4·7
Aden and Dependencies	4·8	2·5	1·6
Arabia	6·5	6·2	4·4
Bahrein Islands	6·4	4·5	3·1
Persia	38·1	20·2	8·9
Ceylon	16·0	17·1	13·4
Straits Settlements	21·3	9·2	5·1
Siam	2·1	·7	·9
Egypt	1·9	·4	..
Union of S. Africa	1·2	·3	·2
Anglo-Egyptian Sudan	3·5	1·7	2·1
Mauritius and Dependencies ..	1·6	·6	·5
Portuguese E. Africa	9·4	6·1	2·8
Tanganyka Territory	6·8	10·7	2·8
Kenya, Zanzibar and Pemba ..	10·7	6·5	2·9
Other E. African Ports	2·1	1·1	·9
Other countries	4·3	4·1	2·1
Total ..	181·5	104·6	56·5
Value in lakh rupees	6,16	3,24	1,66

It will be seen that total exports fell from 181·5 million yards in 1924-25 to 104·6 million yards in 1931-32 and 56·5 million yards in 1933-34. The value of the exports has shrunk from over 6 crores to 1 2/3 crores. Exports to the countries included in the investigations of the Trade Mission (excepting the Levant for which separate figures were not available) in 1924-25 and 1933-34 were as follows according to Indian trade returns:

	1924-25 million yards	1933-34 million yards
Persia and Iraq	87·0	13·6
East Africa	19·	6·6
South Africa and Portuguese East Africa	10·6	10·6
Aden and Sudan	9·5	3·7
Total (Indian Trade Returns) ..	126·7	26·7
Trade Mission's estimate.. ..	107-113	--

In 1933-34 exports to these countries had been reduced to less than one-fourth of the figure for 1924-25.

Such is the present position. It is to be seen whether these and other countries will buy more of our cotton goods when prosperity returns.

The Trade Mission recommended the establishment in Bombay of a well-controlled organization for export-marketing, with branch offices abroad (at Baghdad, Alexandria, Aden, Port Sudan etc.). The Trade Mission pointed out that the only countries in which Indian cotton goods found a market were those where there was a considerable Indian mercantile community, or where, owing to proximity, the styles of piece-goods in demand were similar to those consumed in India. No effort had been made to study the nature of the foreign demand, or to co-ordinate the selling arrangements. The Trade Mission also recommended the appointment of three Trade Commissioners who were to be stationed at Alexandria, Mombassa and Durban. A Trade Commissioner for South Africa has been appointed.

Indian mill production now exceeds 3000 million yards annually. In 1933-34 the proportion of exports to mill production was less than 2 per cent.

The following table shows the imports of piece-goods:

TABLE VI

Imports of Cotton Piece-goods. In million yds.

	United Kingdom	Japan	Total (including other countries)	Indian mill production
1909—10 to 1913—14, average	2563·8	3·1	2631·7	1105·5
1914—15 to 1918—19, ,,	1702·1	97·6	1841·0	1444·0
1919—20 to 1923—24, ,,	1199·0	113·4	1351·9	1675·9
1931—32	383·5	339·8	775·6	2989·9
1932—33 . ..	597·1	579·7	1225·3	3169·9
1933—34	425·9	349·1	795·7	..

Attention may be drawn to the steady growth of Japanese imports up to 1932-33. In 1933-34 total imports of piece-goods fell 35 per cent as compared with the preceding year, British imports 29 per cent and Japanese imports 38 per cent. It is evident that the preferential tariff has played some part in stemming the rising tides of Japanese imports.

THE OTTAWA AGREEMENT

The statement given below shows the share of the United Kingdom, British Empire and foreign countries in India's exports and imports.

Direction of Trade

Imports from	United Kingdom Lakhs	British Empire Lakhs	Foreign countries Lakhs	Total Lakhs
1928-29	113·2	137·1	116·2	253·3
1929-30	103·1	125·9	114·9	240·8
1930-31	61·3	76·0	88·8	164·8
1931-32	44·8	56·6	69·7	126·3
1932-33	48·8	59·4	73·2	132·6
1933-34	47·6	57·7	57·4	115·4
Exports to				
1928-29	69·0	115·0	215·1	330·1
1929-30	67·3	111·0	199·8	319·8
1930-31	51·8	86·1	104·4	220·5
1931-32	43·5	68·7	87·2	155·9
1932-33	37·0	59·8	72·6	132·4
1933-34	46·6	67·6	78·7	146·3
Percentages				
Imports from				
1928-29	44·7	54·1	45·9	100
1929-30	42·8	52·3	47·7	100
1930-31	37·2	46·1	53·9	100
1931-32	35·5	44·8	55·2	100
1932-33	36·8	44·8	55·2	100
1933-34	41·2	50·0	50·0	100
Exports to				
1928-29	20·9	34·8	65·2	100
1929-30	21·7	35·7	64·3	100
1930-31	23·5	39·0	61·0	100
1931-32	27·9	44·1	55·9	100
1932-33	27·9	45·2	54·8	100
1933-34	31·9	46·2	53·8	100

It will be seen that imports increased in 1932-33 as compared with 1931-32—foreign imports by 3½ crores, and those from the British Empire by something less than 3 crores. Imports declined in 1933-34, which is probably explained by the growth of Indian production in some cases, and the reduced purchasing power of our masses in most others. But it is noteworthy that while imports from foreign countries in 1933-34 fell by no less than 15½ crores as compared with the preceding year, the decrease in imports from the British Empire was only about 2 crores, and in those from the United Kingdom about 1¼ crores. It is probable that but for Imperial Preference, the effects of our reduced demand would have been felt by British and foreign manufacturers in less unequal proportions. Imports from the British Empire are now equal to foreign imports.

Some examples are given below to show the effect in 1933-34 as compared with 1932-33 of the preferential tariff in encouraging imports from the United Kingdom and other parts of the Empire at the expense of foreign imports.

Woollen piece-goods. Britain's share increased from 52 lakhs to 57 lakhs, while those of her principal rivals fell heavily, (Germany, from 34 lakhs to 17 lakhs, France, from 42 lakhs to 23 lakhs).

Hardware (excluding cutlery and electro-plated ware) Britain's share increased from 91 lakhs to 97½ lakhs, while that of Germany fell from 108 lakhs to 86 lakhs.

Electric wires and cables. Britain's share increased from 16 lakhs to 21 lakhs, while those of Germany and Netherlands fell. Imports from Belgium advanced from 1¾ lakhs to 2¼ lakhs.

Telegraph and Telephone wires and cables. A striking increase in Britain's share from Rs. 44,000 to over 2 lakhs, while imports from other countries declined from Rs. 45,000 to Rs. 2,000.

Electric lighting accessories (including *switches*). Britain's share increased from 2 2/3 lakhs to 3½ lakhs, while that of Germany fell from 3 2/3 lakhs to 2¼ lakhs.

Total Electrical instruments, apparatus and appliances and parts thereof (including telegraph and telephone apparatus, not being machinery). Britain's share increased from 121½ lakhs to 130½ lakhs, while those of Germany and the United States fell substantially. Imports from Belgium, Italy and Netherlands also advanced, slightly in the case of Netherlands and Italy, and appreciably in the case of Belgium.

Lubricating oils. Britain's share in lubricating oils (except batching oils) increased from about 21 lakhs to 25½ lakhs, while that of the United States fell from 74 lakhs, to 72½ lakhs, and that of Belgium from 9 lakhs to ½ lakh.

Pneumatic motor covers (tyres). Imports from the United Kingdom increased from 45 lakhs to 71 lakhs, and those from Canada from 4¾ lakhs to 6¾ lakhs. The share of all other countries decreased, notably that of the United States, from 40½ lakhs to 16 1/3 lakhs.

Pneumatic motor cycle covers. Britain's share increased while of all other countries decreased.

Pneumatic cycle covers. Britain's share increased while those of Germany and France fell.

Cycles. Britain's share increased from 52 lakhs to 62 2/3 lakhs, while those of Germany, Japan and other countries fell.

Motor Cars (including taxi-cabs). Britain's share increased from 80 lakhs to 106 lakhs and Canada's from 6 lakhs to 25½ lakhs. Imports from Germany, France and Italy fell, but those from the United States increased from 18½ lakhs to 36 1/3 lakhs.

In his *Survey of the Import Trade of India* during the first nine months of 1933-34 His Majesty's Senior Trade Commissioner in India renders thanks to the Ottawa duties for the increase in Britain's share in many classes of imports. He finds it "most encouraging to note that, largely on account of the 10 per cent preferential duty", Britain's share in the imports of hardware increased, despite a reduction in total imports (p. 11). "Thanks to the preferential duty" (p. 12), again, Britain's share in the imports of electrical instruments, apparatus etc., increased while those of Germany, U. S. A., and Japan decreased. He finds it "most satisfactory to record that the share of the United Kingdom (in lubricating oils, excluding batching oils in which the United Kingdom is not interested), mainly due to the preferential margin of 2 annas per gallon and also to improved marketing organization" (p. 18) rose substantially, both in regard to quantity and value of imports. Satisfaction is also expressed at the increase in Britain's share in other imports.

In the coming years, British imports may be expected to expand further. The advantage of preference in the case of manufactured goods is real. There are many rivals, and competition is keen. Any preference is therefore of value.

While the favourable effect of the Ottawa Duties on imports from the United Kingdom and other parts of the Empire is undeniable, it is difficult to say how far our exports as a whole have benefited from preferential duties.

The share of the United Kingdom in our exports in 1933-34 as compared with 1932-33:

Raw Jute. Total exports increased and, with the exception of Australia and three or four foreign countries, exports to all countries show an advance. The increase in Britain's share amounted to 31 lakhs, and in Germany's share 44 lakhs. Exports to Germany slightly exceeded those to the United Kingdom. Britain's share in exports of raw jute in 1933-34 was a little over 23 per cent.

Gunny bags. Total exports fell. Exports to the United Kingdom decreased from 107 lakhs to 98 lakhs. There was an increase in exports to New Zealand, Argentine, Chile and Egypt, but these are small buyers. Ten per cent of the exports went to the United Kingdom in 1933-34.

Gunny cloth. Total exports increased, but those to the United Kingdom fell from 63 lakhs to 57 lakhs. The principal buyer is the United States of America whose purchases increased from 510 lakhs to 660 lakhs (58 per cent of total). The share of the United Kingdom is 5 per cent.

Raw cotton. Total exports increased and also exports to all countries with the exception of Japan. Britain's share increased from 161 lakhs to 337 lakhs (12·7 per cent of total). The exports to Britain exceeded those to China (322 lakhs), but were one-third of those to Japan (1053 lakhs). Japan's share is about 40 per cent of total exports.

Tea. Total exports increased. Britain's share increased from 14¾ crores to 17½ crores. Britain's share in the total is about 89 per cent.

Seeds

Castor. With the exception of Italy, exports to all countries decreased, those to Britain declining from 33 lakhs to about 19 lakhs.

Groundnuts. With the exception of Italy and Germany, exports to all countries decreased. The principal buyer is France whose purchases declined from 366 lakhs to 187 lakhs. The total value of exports in 1933-34 was 663 lakhs. Britain's share decreased from 58 lakhs to 31 lakhs.

Cotton. Exports to the United Kingdom increased from Rs. 85,000 to Rs. 1,89,000 and to other countries from Rs. 82,000 to Rs. 136,000.

Linseed. Total exports (due to the failure of the Argentine crop) increased from 91 lakhs to 458 lakhs, and those to United Kingdom from 16½ lakhs to no less than 181 lakhs. There was also an increase in exports to Netherlands, France, Spain, Italy, Greece, Japan and Australia.

Rape. There was a decline in total exports from 154 lakhs to 81½ lakhs, chiefly due to the fall in the Italian demand from 91 lakhs to 11 lakhs. Exports to the United Kingdom increased from 14 lakhs to 18 lakhs.

Sesamum. Total exports increased from 19½ lakhs to 22 lakhs. The United Kingdom does not buy this seed.

Lac

Button. Total exports increased very slightly, and those to the United Kingdom from 4·6 lakhs to 4·7 lakhs. She is the principal buyer.

Shell. Total exports increased from 83 lakhs to 194 lakhs, the increase in exports to the United Kingdom being notable—from 25 lakhs to 123 lakhs. The United Kingdom is the principal buyer.

Stick. The value of exports is small, 1½ lakhs in 1933-34, of which Belgium bought the largest quantity—1 lakh.

Hides and Skins

Hides and skins, tanned or dressed. The principal buyer is the United Kingdom. Total exports increased from 466 lakhs to 564 lakhs, and those to the United Kingdom from 436 lakhs to 530 lakhs.

Hides and Skins, raw

Buffalo. Total exports about doubled. Exports to Germany increased from 1·3 lakhs to 2·6 lakhs, and those to Greece from 2 to about 4 lakhs. Exports to the United Kingdom increased from Rs. 36,000 to Rs. 47,000 (less than 4 per cent of the total).

Cow hides. Total exports increased from 54 lakhs to 87 lakhs, and also exports to almost all countries. The principal customers are Germany (31 lakhs) and Italy (16 lakhs). Exports to the United Kingdom increased from 4 lakhs to 9 lakhs.

Calf skins. Exports to all countries increased. Britain's purchases are inconsiderable, Rs. 3,660 in 1933-34 out of a total of 2,41,000.

Goat skins. Total exports increased from 179 lakhs to 277 lakhs. The principal customer is the United States whose purchases increased from 87 lakhs to 152 lakhs. Exports to the United Kingdom increased from 50 lakhs to 77 lakhs.

Sheep skins. Total exports increased from 5·3 lakhs to 11·3 lakhs. The principal customer is Italy whose purchases increased from 3 lakhs to about 5½ lakhs. Exports to the United Kingdom increased from Rs. 68,000 to Rs. 1,95,000.

Other skins. Total exports increased from 29 lakhs to 35 lakhs. Exports to France, the largest single purchaser, decreased from 12 lakhs to about 11 lakhs; those to United Kingdom increased from 3 lakhs to 5 lakhs, to Germany from

4·9 lakhs to about 6·9 lakhs, and to Italy from 4·7 lakhs to 6·8 lakhs.

FOOD GRAINS AUD PULSES

Rice not in the husk. Total exports decreased from 1418 lakhs to 1052 lakhs owing to decrease in the demand of the principal buyers—Ceylon, Germany, Straits Settlements and China. Exports to the United Kingdom increased from 54 lakhs to 64 lakhs. The proportion of exports to the United Kingdom to total exports is 6 per cent.

Wheat. Exports decreased from about 4 lakhs to 3 lakhs. The United Kingdom purchased wheat worth 11 rupees in 1932-33 and 17 rupees in 1933-34.

Wheat flour. Exports decreased from about 28 lakhs to 16 lakhs. The United Kingdom bought 6 tons of wheat-flour in 1932-33 and 10 tons in 1933-34.

Barley. Exports decreased from 10½ lakhs to Rs. 11,000. The demand of the United Kingdom fell from 8 lakhs to Rs. 645.

Jwar and Bajra. Exports fell from 13 lakhs to about 5 lakhs. The demand of the United Kingdom fell from 5½ lakhs to nothing.

Beans. Exports decreased from 16 lakhs to 12 lakhs. The demand of the United Kingdom fell from 4½ lakhs to 2 lakhs.

Gram. Exports decreased from 29 lakhs to 26 lakhs. There was a very slight increase in exports to the United Kingdom, from 14·9 lakhs to 15·2 lakhs.

Other sorts. Exports decreased from 43 lakhs to 39 lakhs, and those to the United Kingdom from 9·1 lakhs to 8·6 lakhs.

Others

Oil-cakes. Total exports decreased from 197 lakhs to 165 lakhs, while those to the United Kingdom increased from 72 lakhs to 80 lakhs.

Vegetable Oils. Total exports increased from 54 lakhs to 57 lakhs; those to the United Kingdom decreased from 23 lakhs to 17 lakhs.

Unmanufactured Tobacco. Total exports increased from 73 lakhs to 90 lakhs, and those to the United Kingdom from 36 lakhs to 47 lakhs.

Carpets and rugs, woollen. Total exports increased from 64 lakhs to 73 lakhs, and those to the United Kingdom from 45 lakhs to about 56½ lakhs.

The principal increases in exports to the United Kingdom in 1933-34 as compared with 1932-33 were cotton (176 lakhs), tea (275 lakhs), linseed (164 lakhs), shellac (98 lakhs) and hides tanned or dressed (94 lakhs). It is difficult to say whether the increase in these exports is to be wholly ascribed to preferences, or partly to other causes, such as the revival of trade. In some cases exports would have probably increased even if there had been no preferences.

The increase in the exports of linseed is very satisfactory, if it is not followed by a setback. India's share in the total imports of linseed into the United Kingdom fell from 48 per cent in 1914 to 32 per cent in 1930 and 3 per cent in 1932.

France was an important purchaser of our groundnuts. Before the war 58 per cent of her total imports were supplied by us. The proportion fell to 49 per cent in 1929 and 40 per cent in 1931. In 1932 there was a revival, the percentage rising to 44. In 1933-34 as compared with 1932-33 exports of Indian groundnuts to France decreased by 180 lakhs. Is this an indirect result of Imperial Preference?

Our advantage in regard to tea is limited by the fact that Ceylon is a competitor, and Ceylon enjoys the same preference as we do. In 1932 imports of tea into the United Kingdom amounted to 567 million lbs., of which India's share was 312 million lbs. (56 per cent) and Ceylon's 172 million lbs. (30 per cent).

It may also be noted that the increase in the value of exports in 1933-34 was wholly due to the rise in price. The quantity of tea bought by the United Kingdom fell from 330·7 million lbs. in 1932-33 to 276·5 million lbs. in 1933-34. It is improbable that preference will cause the British consumer to drink more Indian tea. But if we did not enjoy the preference, the share of Ceylon might increase at our expense.

Cotton is an important article of export, particularly from the point of view of the Punjab. The Indian Delegation to Ottawa raised the question of a duty on foreign cotton in the United Kingdom but it was made plain to the Indian Delegation that the British Delegation "could not entertain this suggestion, and that the interests of their own industry placed it out of court" (Report p. 21). The Indian Delegation recognised the importance of cheap raw material to the British cotton industry. It is not possible for the United Kingdom to ruin her industry by raising the cost of cotton to the British manufacturer. But attempts are being made to persuade the British spinner to buy more Indian cotton and, as we have seen, exports of raw cotton to the United Kingdom are increasing.

An unsatisfactory feature of the situation is the decline of exports to Japan. The decline was comparatively small in 1933-34 (about 11,000 tons), and it was more than counterbalanced by increase in exports to Italy of 20,000 tons, and to China of 26,000 tons. But a continued and heavy fall in exports to Japan, which was not accompanied by a corresponding increase in exports to the United Kingdom, would inflict serious injury on the Indian cultivator.

Preference would be of the greatest value to us if, while the British demand for our principal exports increased, the demand of foreign countries did not fall. Preference is of doubtful value to us because (1) no hope can be entertained of any considerable expansion of our principal exports to the United Kingdom, and because (2) with the limitation of imports from foreign countries into India, their demand for Indian exports must shrink.

It is too early yet to strike a balance of advantages and disadvantages of the Ottawa Agreement. The adjustments in foreign countries to our Trade Agreement will take several years. For example, Japan will endeavour to lessen her dependence on Indian raw cotton and to develop other markets for her cotton goods. The future of our exports of cotton to Japan will depend on the extent to which Japan is able to use the newly acquired territory in China for cotton growing, and the use of American cotton instead of Indian in Japanese mills. In regard to American cotton, there was a remarkable increase in its consumption in Japan in 1932:

Imports of raw cotton into Japan in million lbs.

From	11 months of 1932	1931	1930
British India	342	614	597
U.S. A.	1,122	582	469
Egypt	37	33	22
China	60	85	81
All other	4	2	10
Total	1,565	1,316	1,179

The increase in the consumption of American cotton was partly due to the spinning of finer counts "but it was mainly caused by the fact that American parity prices were cheaper than Indian"[1].

Normally Japan uses more Indian than American cotton. In 1931, 6 lbs. of Indian cotton were imported to every 5 of American. But in 1932 the proportion was 3 lbs. of Indian cotton to over 10 of American. "Nothing is more remarkable", says Mr. G. B. Sansom, "than the facility with which Japan seems to switch from the one to the other". "It might be thought", he continues, "that the change could not be effected without temporary loss of efficiency and differences in

[1] "Economic conditions in Japan to Dec. 1932". G. B. Sansom, Commerical Councillor to H. M. Embassy, Tokyo, 1933 (54-541).

quality. But no such effects are apparent. This talent of the Japanese spinner has been commented on more than once but it can scarcely have ever been put to such a test as in the last few years"[2].

This talent of the Japanese spinner is a source of danger to our exports. Indian exports of cotton, it seems, are not indispensable to Japan.

Japan was expected to go back to the 1931 proportion —6 lbs. of Indian cotton to every 5 of American, in 1933. It is not yet known whether she has done so.

It is evident that in this respect India is vulnerable. At present it is impossible to think that the United Kingdom will replace Japan as a consumer of Indian cotton, and even if she does, there is no net gain to India from the Ottawa Agreement.

Another article of export in which the Punjab is interested is wheat. Bengal is interested in rice. Is there any hope of greater exports of food-grains to the United Kingdom?

The answer is in the negative—the figures for 1933-34 are not encouraging. Our wheat prices are above export parity and, as exporters, we have formidable competitors in Australia and Canada. The extension of canal irrigation in Sind will increase the 'surplus' for export. But no export can take place unless the price falls to about 1 rupee per maund—a ruinous price from the point of view of the cultivator.

Our principal purchasers of rice are foreign countries. If there is 'over-production', or danger of 'over-production' of rice, we shall get little help from the United Kingdom in getting rid of the surplus. Generally speaking the possibilities of expansion of the British market for Indian food-grains are extremely limited.

What is the advantage of the preference on jute? The quantity and value of exports of gunny cloth and gunny bags to the United Kingdom fell in 1933-34. Exports of raw

[2] *Ibid*, p. 49.

jute as we have seen, increased, but not as an effect of preference. At present there is nothing else that the United Kingdom can buy in place of jute.

Exports of cotton, jute and jute manufactures, tea and food grains accounted for 90 crores out of total exports of Indian merchandise amounting to 146 crores in 1933-34 (62 per cent). As we have seen, in the case of tea, there is no hope of gain from the Ottawa Agreement, but only hope of avoiding losses which might have resulted from the non-acceptance of the Agreement. In the other cases the hope of net gain to India is so small as to be negligible.

The prosperity of the great mass of cultivators in the Punjab and other large parts of India depends on greater exports and higher prices of wheat and cotton, and of cultivators in Bengal on greater exports and higher prices of jute and rice. Rice is also the staple export of Burma. These are our principal crops. It may be possible to show that under Imperial Preference the United Kingdom will buy more pig iron, pig lead, paraffin wax, leather and hides, or even particular seeds. These are no substitutes for our principal crops. Generally speaking, the growth of exports to the United Kingdom under Imperial Preference will leave the great mass of our agriculturists unaffected.

On account of the very nature of our exports, the advantage to us from preferential tariffs will be comparatively small.

Retaliation

The chief ground on which Lord Curzon's Government opposed Imperial Preference in 1903 was the danger of retaliation. Sir Edward Law argued in his minute that, excepting a few cases, unless Imperial Preference secured 'very great advantages' for India's exports to the United Kingdom and the Colonies, it was more in the interests of India to leave matters as they were. This was not a verdict in favour of Imperial Preference. Lord Curzon's Government still thought that Sir Edward Law had underrated "both the power of retaliation which foreign countries possess and also their readiness to use it". "We cannot feel confident", they wrote to the Secretary of State for India, "that the conditions and requirements of foreign countries have yet been ascertained with the precision and fulness necessary to make them a sufficiently broad and stable basis on which to rest a fiscal policy of very problematic value to India, whilst the consequences of failure might result in irreparable disaster".

We have embarked on that policy at a time when the conditions and requirements of foreign countries are less stable, and when our position as an exporter is weaker than before. The tendency of scientific research and economic progress in recent years has been to render foreign countries less dependent on us for the supply of primary products. We are more vulnerable now than 30 years ago, and the power of foreign countries to retaliate has increased.

The danger foreseen by Lord Curzon's Government is slowly materialising. It cannot be said that the present tariff relations of the United Kingdom with Japan, France and other countries are of the friendliest nature. A sort of tariff war is already in progress, which will ultimately react on India.

From the point of view of India no time worse than the present could have been chosen for new tariff experiments. Lord Curzon's Government in their note on the subject referred to India's sterling obligations, which then amounted to £16 millions per annum, for the payment of which it was necessary, in the interests of national solvency, to preserve a favourable balance of trade of equal amount. "It is therefore a vital object with us", they wrote "to stimulate our exports by every means in our power, to seek new markets and develop old ones, and to remove all obstacles which stand in the way of growing external demand" (para 16). We have adopted Imperial Preference at a time when the Home Charges exceed our favourable balance of trade, and we are exporting gold to keep solvent. This is no method of stimulating exports, of seeking new markets and developing old ones.

Lord Curzon's Government feared that under Imperial Preference India might be forced to shape her policy not in accordance with her own needs but in accordance with the interests and demands of other constituents of the Empire. Imperial Preference is not very old yet. The struggle for the Indian market in its new form has just commenced. It is certain that foreign countries, whose position is being assailed by Imperial Preference, will not give up the Indian market without a struggle. If foreign countries, aided by improved marketing organization, or cheaper labour, or more efficient methods of production, are able to offer more effective competition, and the 10 per cent preference is found insufficient by British manufacturers, an interesting situation may arise. The path of protection, whether national or Imperial, is an inclined plane—once one has started downward, it is easier to continue in the same direction. Imperial Preference has come to stay, and there will be more rather than less of it in the future.

The Consumer

Imperial Preference ignores the consumer completely. Sometime ago the interests of the Indian consumer were held to be paramount. Under protection we sacrificed the consumer at the altar of nationalism. Imperial Preference imposes sacrifices on the consumer, not in the interests of national but Empire industries. It may be admitted that the interests of the Indian manufacturer have been duly safeguarded. But where there is no competition between imported goods and products of Indian industries, it is the right of the consumer to buy in the cheapest market. He may be deprived of this right, but only if it can be shown that as a compensation for the injury inflicted on him, very great advantages would be secured to the country as a whole. When these advantages are more unreal than real, Imperial Preference means taxing the Indian consumer for the good of Empire producers.

Imperial Preference and Reciprocal Preferences

It is argued in the Report of the Indian Delegation to Ottawa that the British Import Duties Act, which changed the British fiscal policy from free trade to protection, created an entirely new situation. "It was no longer a question of what India stood to gain but of what she stood to lose". If we had stood aloof, our goods would have been subjected to the British 10 per cent duty, and thus admitted into the United Kingdom on less favourable terms than those of the Dominions and Colonies. Some of our exports would undoubtedly have been adversely affected by British protection. But it should not be forgotten that whilst the United Kingdom is the largest single purchaser of our products, foreign countries, against whom we have adopted a policy of discrimination, buy more from us than the whole of the British Empire. If Imperial Preference leads to retaliation by foreign countries, and if our exports to them shrink, our injury will far exceed that which the British 10 per cent duty would have inflicted on us.

The fact that we granted preferences to the United Kingdom to avoid the application of the British Import Duties Act to our exports, does not alter the character of the Ottawa Trade Agreement. It is in essence the Imperial Preference of 30 years ago. That also meant reciprocal preferences. One-sided preferences were never contemplated, nor would have India ever agreed to a one-sided arrangement. The only difference is that we are now permitted to protect our manufacturing industries against British competition.

We might have safeguarded our position against the British 10 per cent duty by lowering the rate of exchange to 16d. sterling. This aspect of the question has never been considered.

CHAPTER III

GOLD EXPORTS

India imported gold and silver on a large scale under the Moghul Kings. This was due to the character of our balance of trade in those days.

The balance of trade is still in our favour. But our favourable balance of trade is now a sign of our debtor position. The Home charges amount to £30 millions annually; this is expenditure charged to the revenues of India. Apart from the Home charges, there is an annual drain from India of profits of important industries, which are a monopoly of, or controlled by foreign capital, as tea, coffee, rubber, petroleum, jute, coal and others of less importance. In addition, invisible imports in the shape of services of foreign shippers, bankers and commission agents have to be paid for. While the balance of trade is generally in our favour, the balance of payments is against us, and we pay our debts abroad by exporting goods greater in value than goods imported.

The situation was different in the past. The demand for our manufactures was keen in the markets of the world while our demand for the manufactures of other countries was so small as to be negligible. Indian produce was exported in Indian ships manned by Indian sailors, and the natives of the country largely earned the profits from exchange and the provision of credit needed for trade. Not only the balance of trade but the balance of payments was heavily in our favour. In other words, India was a creditor country, and the world paid her tribute in silver and gold.

Van Twist in his *Generale Beschrivinghe van Indien* (1638) tells us that although there were no gold or silver mines in India, large quantities of both were imported from foreign countries, and that it was forbidden to export them. "India is rich in silver," wrote Hawkins, "for all nations bring coyne and carry away commodities for the same; and this coyne is burried in India and goeth not out."[1] Terry estimates that an Indian ship returning from the Red Sea was usually worth two hundred thousand pounds sterling, most of it in gold and silver. "Besides," he adds, "for what quantity of monies comes out of Europe by other means into India, I cannot answere; this I am sure of that many silver streames runne thither as all rivers to the sea, and there stay, it being lawful for any nation to bring in silver and fetch commodities, but a crime not less than capitall to carry and great summe thence"[2]. Mandelslo also noted that it was "prohibited, upon pain of death, that any should transport either Gold, Silver, or coined Brass out of the Country"[3].

India imported gold heavily also from 1900-01 to 1930-31 as is shown by the table below:

Gold, lakhs of Rs.

	Imports	Exports	Net imports
1900-01 to 1904-05	75,33	44,14	31,19
1905-06 to 1909-10	87,45	28,73	58,72
1910-11 to 1914-15	149,59	22,87	126,72
1915-16 to 1919-20	98,22	31,16	67,06
1920-21 to 1924-25	182,24	38,69	143,55
1925-26 to 1930-31	121,53	1,01	120,52

It is seen that imports of gold exceeded exports by about 548 crores of rupees. The import of gold came to a sudden end when England abandoned the gold standard, and we linked the rupee to sterling. Since 21st September 1931, gold

[1] Foster Early Travels in India, p. 112
[2] Foster, p. 302
[3] Travels into the Indies, p. 68

exports amount to over 183 crores of rupees (May 1934), and gold continues to flow out.

This movement of gold from India was entirely unexpected. The Gold Delegation of the Financial Committee of the League of Nations thus speculated about the Indian demand for gold in the depression.

"No doubt the present economic depression may result in some temporary weakening of the Indian demand; on the other hand, it is quite possible that the recent decline in the price of silver will lead to increased purchases of gold. We understand that attempts are being made to extend banking and investment habits in India, but we do not think it would be safe to anticipate any material reduction in the Indian demand for many years to come" (interim Report, p. 14).

Since 21st September 1931, no remarkable change in the banking and investment habits has occurred in India. But we have not only suspended our purchases of gold, but are selling gold to the world on an unprecedented scale.

Price of Gold

We are tempted to sell gold by the rise in its price. Why has the price of gold risen?

The lowest London New York Cross rate (dollars to pound sterling) in September 1931 was 3·60 (parity 4·866 dollars to the pound). This signified a rise of about 35 per cent in the price of dollars in terms of the pound sterling.

The Mint price of gold in England per fine ounce was £4-4-9¾. The highest price of gold in London in September 1931 was £ 5-14-9. The rise in the London price of gold was about equal to the depreciation of the pound sterling in terms of the gold dollar.

The price of gold rose in India as we had linked the rupee to sterling.

The highest price of country bar gold at Bombay rose from Rs. 21-5-6 in August 1931 to 25-4-0 in September, and steadily to Rs. 30-12-0 in December. Thereafter, between January 1932 and September 1932 it fluctuated between Rs. 28-4-0 and Rs. 29-12-0. In November 1932, as the dollar rose in terms of the pound sterling, and with it the London price of gold, the rupee price rose to Rs. 31-15-6. In March 1933 the highest price was Rs. 29-4-6. A sudden rise above Rs. 34 took place when the United States devalued the dollar. The explanation is as follows:

The new gold dollar of the United States contains 13·71 grains of pure gold. As compared with the old gold dollar, which contained 23·22 grains of pure gold, this represents a reduction of about 41 per cent in the fine gold contents of the dollar. The sovereign contains 113·00 grains of pure gold. The old parity between the dollar and the sovereign was 4·866=1 £; the new parity is 8·24=1 £.

But, to take an example, on May 4, 1934, the dollar was quoted in London at about 5·12 to the £ sterling. This is equal to a rise of about 61 per cent in the price of the dollar.

(On May 4, 1934, the closing rate for the French franc was 77·28 for the pound sterling. The parity being 124·21 francs to 1 £ (gold), the rate of 77·28 francs to the £ sterling represents a rise of about 61 per cent in the price of francs in terms of the £ sterling).

The price of gold per fine ounce in London on May 5, 1934 was £ 6-16-2 which represents a rise of 60·6 per cent above the old Mint price of gold.

The London price of gold rises and falls, with the rise and fall in the price of the dollar. If the dollar rose to its old parity, (or the cross-rate fell from 5·12 to 4·86 dollars to the £ sterling), the London price of gold would rise to £ 7-3-8 (69·5 per cent above the old Mint price of gold).

Before England and India abandoned the gold standard on September 21, 1931, the £ was equal to 4·86 dollars, the rupee was equal to 18d. gold and the price of gold per tola was Rs. 21-3-10 (making no allowance for cost of transportation).

If now the cross-rate were stabilised at 4·86 dollars, as we have seen, the London price of gold would rise by 69·5 per cent. Other things being equal, the Indian price would rise to the same extent, or to Rs. 36 per tola.

Actually, if India continues to sell gold, the Indian price would be below Rs.36.

The connection between the price of gold and exports of gold is shown by the fact that a rise in price leads to greater exports. For example, the London price rose in December 1931; exports of gold from India in that month amounted to about 17½ crores of rupees. Again in December 1932 exports rose to about 10 crores on account of the rise in the London price. In February 1934 exports exceeded 10 crores, as compared with about 5 crores only in February 1933. It was the devaluation of the dollar that raised the price of gold in February 1934.[4]

COMMODITY PRICES

By selling gold amounting to over 183 crores of rupees, the people of India increased their purchasing power to the same extent. What was the effect of this increase in their purchasing power on the level of commodity prices?

The Calcutta index number of prices rose from 91 in September 1931 to 98 in December of the same year. Prices then fell. The index number for December 1932 was 88, for December 1933, 89, and for April 1934 also 89.

The rise of prices in the last quarter of 1931 was accompanied by an expansion of the currency.

From 1st January 1931 to 31st August 1931, there was a return of notes to the Government amounting to 18,49 lakhs, and of rupee coin amounting to 18,99 lakhs, or a total contraction of the circulation by 37,48 lakhs. From September 1, 1931 to February 29, 1932 there was an absorption of currency: notes 34,69 lakhs and rupee coin 15,72

[4] After a temporary suspension for two weeks India resumed gold exports when the price of gold rose above 141 shillings at the end of August 1934.

lakhs. This may be attributed to the stimulus given to trade by the abandonment of the gold standard.

The stimulus was temporary and the demand for currency ceased. In the year 1932-33 there was a return of the currency: notes 12,55 lakhs, and rupee coin 4,56 lakhs—or a contraction of the circulation by 17,11 lakhs, in spite of gold exports in 1932-33 amounting to about 65½ crores of rupees.

In 1933-34 gold exports attained a total of 57 crores. The index number of prices, however, shows no tendency to rise. It is obvious that the sale of gold has served only to replace some of the purchasing power lost by the agricultural section of the population on account of the fall of prices. Under normal conditions the aquisition of new purchasing power amounting to 183 crores would have sent up prices with a rush.

Advantages Claimed for Gold Exports

Gold exports have formed the subject of much controversy in India. Non-official opinion regards gold exports with disfavour. The policy of the Government in permitting an unrestricted flow of gold from India has been severely criticised both in the press and in the Assembly.

The official view, on the other hand, to which expression has been given both by the Viceroy and the Finance Member of the Indian Government, is that gold exports are of direct economic advantage to the country.

The interest of British M.P.'s in our gold exports and the dumb millions of India is shown by a question asked early in March 1932 in the House of Commons by Mr. Peter McDonald M. P., suggesting the desirability of Government action with the object of making the rise in the price of gold widely known throughout India. Sir Samuel Hoare assured Mr. Peter McDonald that the fact that gold was realisable at advantageous prices was already widely published in the country.

What is the benefit that gold exports have conferred on the masses of India or the country in general?

Gold exports have enabled the United Kingdom to pay part of her debts to France and the United States. This aspect of gold exports does not interest official India, and we shall say no more about it. The advantages which are emphasized in official utterances and in official reports (*e.g.*, Report of the Controller of the Currency) are the following:

(1) Gold exports have led to an improvement in the credit of the Government.

This has several aspects, of which not the least important is the maintenance of the 16d. sterling exchange.

At a time when exports of commodities were declining, the maintenance of exchange without exports would have proved difficult, if not altogether impossible. From April 1, to the end of September 1931 the highest rate for telegraphic transfers on London was a little less than 18d. In September the highest rate was 17¾d. which is equal to gold export point. But as soon as gold exports began, exchange improved. By the end of October 1931 it had risen to 18 1|33d. Tenders invited for £500,000 at the end of October were allotted at 18 $^{3}|_{32}$d. The weekly offer of sterling was gradually raised to £1 million. Exchange weakened in the latter half of November, but, says the Controller of Currency in his report for 1931-32, "there was no week in which Government was not able to obtain the full amount offered for tender and effect purchases of intermediates at 1|32d. above the tender rate" (pp. 12-13).

In 1932-33 Government purchased about £36 millions at an average rate of 18·15d. Exchange fell early in June on account of the scarcity of export bills. The improvement of exchange from the middle of June was partly the result of an increase in gold exports due to rise in the price of gold.

Exchange stability improves Government credit. Government credit also improves when Government is able to meet its maturing obligations. The export of gold conferred a double benefit on the Government of India in enabling it to maintain exchange and to meet its obligations. The Controller of Currency says in his report for 1931-32.

"One result [of gold exports] was that the Government of India was able to purchase large amounts of remittance which not only materially improved its credit abroad by enabling it to pay off the 15 millions sterling debt maturing in January, but also enabled it to reduce its floating debt in India by the creation of the fresh currency required to pay for the gold" (para 11).

It is stated in the same officer's report for 1932-33 that the improvement in the financial position of the Government in this year was "mainly due to the continuance of the export of gold on a large scale" (para 6). The Government made purchases of sterling in excess of its requirements, which enabled it to "reinforce the position of the Home Treasury". Further the "immense improvement" in the credit of the Government enabled the Government to borrow funds for short periods at very low rates, and to fund a substantial proportion of its short term loans into long-term loans at very favourable rates. The treasury bills outstanding on the 31st of March 1933 amounted to Rs. 26 crores against Rs. 47½ crores on April 1, 1932, or there was a reduction of 21½ crores in the amount of these obligations. The average treasury bill yield in March 1933 was 1·36 per cent as compared with 5·13 in April 1932—a very substantial reduction. The rate of interest on medium and long-term loans was reduced gradually from 5½ per cent to 4 per cent.

Sir George Schuster drew attention to the improvement of Government credit resulting from the paying off of treasury bills and sterling debts in his budget speech for 1932-33. In the 15 months from the end of September 1931 to the end of September 1932 gold exports were valued at £80 millions. Of this gold Government acquired £70 millions and £10 millions was used to repay foreign funds temporarily invested in India. Out of the £70 millions of gold which the Government had acquired by open purchases in the market as currency authority, it used £34½ millions to meet its own current requirements and £ 35½ millions to repay sterling loans and strengthen its reserves. "Therefore", Sir George concluded, "out of the total £ 80 millions of gold proceeds only £ 34½ millions were used to meet current requirements, and the balance of £ 45½ millions went to reduce India's external obligations and strengthen her public reserves".

(2) Gold exports strengthened India's public reserves. It may be thought that the reserves were strengthened by the addition of gold. No. We had no use for gold in the reserves. At the close of the year 1932-33 the gold holdings of the Government amounted to 44,36 lakhs, an increase of 2 lakhs as compared with the position at the close of the proceeding financial year. The market value of the gold reserves increased from 58 crores to 63 crores. "In other words", says the Controller of Currency in his report for 1932-33, "there was practically no increase in the quantity of gold in the reserve during the year but the value at the market rate increased by nearly 5 crores over that of the last year" (para 32). To the suggestion that the Government, instead of permitting gold to flow abroad, might have bought, at any rate, some of it for addition to the reserves, Sir George Schuster's reply was: "We already have our proper proportion of gold in our currency reserves" (para 26 of the budget speech for 1933-34). What we wanted in the reserves was not gold but sterling securities. We sold the gold to the United Kingdom, and added sterling securities to the reserves.

(3) Gold exports have meant the conversion of one form of reserve into another.

What is the nature of the gold sold by the general public? Is it 'distress' gold, sold by necessitous persons, or is gold sold by well-to-do individuals as a "business proposition"?

We have seen that there is a connection between the London price of gold and gold exports. A large rise in the London price causes exports to increase. It is evident that the desire for gain has induced many persons to part with their gold.

Still it is beyond question that a large amount of the gold has been sold by the agricultural population to meet daily necessities and to pay Government dues.

The comparative inelasticity of Government dues and the heavy losses suffered by cultivators on account of the fall of prices have been discussed in a preceding chapter.

An Associated Press telegram, which was published in the *Tribune* of Lahore of 27th February, 1932, thus explained the flight of gold from Siraj Ganj (Bengal): "Hard pressed by acute financial stringency the middle class people, agriculturists and even some landlords have been selling the ornaments of their wives and other family women".

According to a statement made by Sir L. Hudson in the Legislative Assembly on March 2, 1933, a very large percentage of the sale of gold represented "the forced sale of capital resources to provide for ordinary, every day necessities of daily life".

Some of the gold proceeds have been converted into interest-bearing Government obligations. In this sense the sale of gold represents the conversion of hoards, a useless form of reserve, into Government paper, a useful form of reserve. But it is not 'distress' gold that has been converted into Government paper.

In a sense, even the sale of 'distress' gold means the conversion of one form of reserve into another. Food and clothing represent reserves of concentrated energy. The payment of Government dues is a source of moral satisfaction. The cultivator who has sold his gold reserves to meet Government dues and current requirements may be said to have converted barren reserves into valuable reserves of moral and physical health and strength.

(4) Gold exports have encouraged the flow of international trade.

It is pointed out in the report of the Controller of Currency for 1932-33 (para 6) that gold exports brought increased revenue from certain import duties, "as it is clear that a proportion of the profits on gold sales must have been utilized for increased purposes of imported articles". There is a more explicit reference to this advantage of gold exports in Sir George Schuster's Budget speech for 1933-34. Imports of goods in 1932-33 were valued at about 132½ crores of rupees. To this 45 crores of customs duties must be added, for the consumer of imports must pay the price of the imported goods *plus* the duty. The total cost of imports was thus Rs.177½ crores. Exports of Indian merchandise in the same year amounted to Rs.132 crores. Thus gold proceeds equal to Rs. 45½ crores were used to pay for imports. (Thereby we avoided reducing our consumption to the desperately low level which would otherwise have been necessary). And to the same extent we encouraged the flow of international trade. Sir George Schuster referred to artificial restrictions on imports by way of high duties and exchange restrictions, which he described as "the worst feature of the present world situation". And he added: "This is checking the flow of international trade, so that its channels are gradually becoming completely dry." We ourselves have sinned in this respect. And, but for the export of gold, imports of goods into India would shrink still more. "India in fact", said Sir George Schuster, "has been able to release into the world a commodity for which alone there is an undiminished market and the possession of which, if it is used as a basis for currency, does not diminish but rather increases the purchasing power of the countries which absorb it" (para 19 of the budget speech for 1933-34). Our gold exports thus acquire an international significance. They have not only helped India to buy more foreign goods, but benefited the whole world. If an economic policy designed to benefit others merits a reward in heaven, India, by exporting gold, has been accumulating huge reserves of credit in the other world, which may be described as a process of conversion of material into spiritual reserves.

If the purchasing power of other countries increases,

they may buy more of our goods. Gold exports may therefore be regarded as a disguised stimulus to exports of goods. By exporting gold, India, as Sir George Schuster said, is increasing "the purchasing power of her own potential customers". We might have attempted to develop exports by increasing our own power of potential competition. But this is a difficult process.

Incidentally we may note that in spite of heavy gold exports in 1932-33, exports of Indian Merchandise continued to decline month after month; for the whole year the excess of exports (including re-exports) was only 3½ crores, as compared with about 35 crores in the preceding year. The revival of exports in 1933-34 cannot be attributed to increase in the purchasing power of world due to our gold exports; it is due to the slowing down of growth of stocks of primary commodities.

(5) The export of gold means that the people of India are using their reserves as they are meant to be used.

The Viceroy in the course of an address to the Legislative Assembly on January 25, 1932 said:

'A time has indeed come when India's huge investments in gold—which have for many years been barren and unproductive—are proving profitable to the private holders and to the State alike. Those who would press a contrary view profess to argue that India is weakening her position by this process. But if the holding of gold in a country is to be regarded as an investment and a source of strength, of what use is it if it is never to be drawn upon? What is the use of a reserve against bad times, if when the bad times come it is not to be used?"

"Reserves are being drawn upon in hard times", said Sir George Schuster, "and as His Excellency asked, 'of what use is a reserve if it can never be drawn upon?'" If gold "is *never* to be used, it might just as well be at the bottom of the sea".

This implies the admission that the gold that has been

sold is 'distress' gold, or that people are selling it to tide over 'terribly difficult times.'

If that is so, the sale of gold means a process of living on capital—a dangerous process in the case of a country as in the case of an individual. When terribly difficult times come the first duty of the Government is to reduce tax burdens and to increase the purchasing power of the people so that they are not forced to live on capital. The realization of capital is a process of impoverishment, not enrichment of a country.

Taking the view of gold exports that they did, our highest authorities have encouraged the Indian holder to part with his gold. "In fact it is clear", said the Viceroy, "there is not only no cause for anxiety in what is now happening, but that it is conferring a great benefit on both public and private interest." In his budget speech for 1932-33 the Finance Member, with all the weight of his great authority, advised the people to sell gold. Gold was over-valued. England, and with her more than half the world, had abandoned the gold standard. America was still on gold, but she was straining every effort to bring about a rise in the gold prices of commodities. That meant that the value of gold would fall. If America succeeded in her attempt to lower the gold prices of commodities, she might save her currency system. If she failed, she would have to go off gold. "It is impossible to escape the conclusion", concluded the Finance Member, "that the world is faced now with two alternatives, either to find some means (by better international arrangements and the better use of the available monetary stocks of gold) for reducing the real value of gold as expressed in commodities, *or* to abandon gold altogether as the basis of currency. If those are the two alternatives then surely one is forced inevitably to the conclusion, that in either case—whichever of the two alternatives actually happens, it would, taking a long view, pay to part with gold now. Why therefore should the people of India be deprived of the right to exercise their own judgment in this matter and sell their gold?" (para 73).

Which of the two alternatives happened? About a year later the United States devalued her dollar, the direct effect of which was not to lower but to raise the price of gold. The highest price of gold in March 1933—it was early in March 1933 that the Finance Member advised the people of India to part with their gold—was £6-1-11½. Early in February 1934 the London price of gold was 140 shillings. The highest price of country bar gold in Bombay in March 1933 was Rs. 29-15-6; on February 2, 1934, it was more than Rs. 35, and at the present time it is about Rs. 34.[5] Further, if the dollar appreciates to 4·86 to the £, as we have seen, the Indian price may rise to about Rs. 36. Those who, following the advice of our greatest financial authority, parted with their gold in March 1933, would have certainly lost nothing by holding on to gold for a year more.

Sir George Schuster's last budget speech, for 1934-35, contained no reference to gold exports or the price of gold. It would have been interesting to learn from him if we may 'part with gold now', or wait until the price of gold rises to Rs. 36|-.

Future Price of Gold

Many Indian holders sold their gold thinking that the price of gold was not likely to rise further. Our financial authorities publicly encouraged them to do so. If the price of gold falls, as they have been told it will, they may buy gold back at a profit.

It is not impossible, but wholly improbable.[6]

Let us re-consider Sir George Schuster's two alternatives.

We have seen that the currency changes in the United States have not lowered but raised the price of gold. Would the price of gold fall if France abandoned the gold standard?

[5] More than Rs. 35 in the first week of Sept. 1934.
[6] Written in May 1934.

The answer is 'no'. The price of gold would then be determined by the value of the pound sterling in terms of Dutch currency.

It deserves to be clearly stated that the rise in the price of gold is due to the depreciation of sterling (to which the rupee is linked) in terms of gold. In fact, it is incorrect to speak of a rise in the price of gold. It is not gold that has risen, it is paper that has fallen.

If, then, France abandoned the gold standard, the value of French paper money in terms of Dutch currency will fall. That is all. If the purchasing power of the pound sterling in terms of Dutch florins did not alter (£ =7·53 florins on May 4, 1934), the London price of gold would remain as high as it was before (£ 6-15-10 on May 4, 1934). There is no reason why the pound sterling should buy more Dutch florins because France chooses to abandon the gold standard.

What would happen if, after France, Holland, Switzerland, Belgium and other countries, whose currency is still linked to gold, went off gold? The whole world goes off the gold standard. Will the price of gold fall then?

It may be argued that the monetary demand for gold then would heavily decrease. The price of gold must fall.

It will fall if France, Holland, U S. A. and other countries immediately start getting rid of gold. Suppose they said: "We are off gold. Gold has therefore become a thoroughly useless commodity. Let us sell our gold reserves to England and replace the gold by interest-bearing sterling securities". In that case the price of gold must fall. But it will be long before U. S. A., or European countries are persuaded to believe that the replacement of barren gold in the reserves by interest-bearing sterling securities is sound finance.

The scramble for gold will continue. Even when every country is off gold, each will endeavour to add to its gold holdings, in the hope that a larger gold reserve may facilitate the eventual return to gold.

If we return to gold, the price of gold will entirely depend on the rate at which the rupee is re-stabilised in relation to gold.

Stabilisation of different currencies at present rates has been often suggested. If this suggestion is accepted, and the £ is stabilised at the rate of about 77 francs, or 7·53 Dutch florins, the price of gold will remain what it is today—about 136 shillings. The price of gold will fall if England chose a higher rate of stabilisation. 124·21 francs to the pound will bring down the price of gold to the old level. Is it probable that England, having learnt by bitter experience what a high value of the pound means for her exports, will repeat her mistake of 1925?

Even if England chose a rate of stabilisation higher than the present, it is not possible for India to do so.

Before we went off the gold standard, Rs. 13-5-4 were equal to 20·43 marks, or a rupee was equal to about 1½ mark. Similarly Rs. 13-5-4 were equal to 124·21 French francs, or a rupee was equal to about 9 $^1|_8$ francs. On May 4, the rupee was quoted in Berlin at 0·96 mark (a rupee equal to something less than a mark), and in Paris at 5·82 francs. Even at these rates we find it difficult to develop our exports to Germany and France. A higher value of the rupee would kill exports.

While it is wholly improbable that we should deliberately raise the gold value of the rupee above its present level, it is not at all improbable that the gold value of the rupee may fall. Gold exports, as we have seen, explain the strength of the present exchange. When gold exports decline or cease, unless exports of merchandise miraculously reach the level of 1928-29, the sterling exchange will fall.

In the general interest of the country it would be desirable to lower the exchange value of the rupee. If exchange is stabilised at a lower rate, the price of gold in rupees will rise. The result would be the same if adverse trade conditions brought down exchange.

It deserves to be emphasized that for countries which do not produce gold, the price of gold depends on the exchange value of their money in terms of currencies which are linked to gold. The price of gold in London is 136 shillings; in Australia it must be 25 per cent higher, since 125 Australian pounds are equal to 100 British pounds. Suppose Australian currency is stabilised in relation to the British pound at par. The price of gold in Australia will then fall. If Australian currency was stabilised at the present rate, the price of gold in Australian money will remain what it is now.

Let us consider finally whether the price of gold would fall if there was a better distribution of the world's monetary stocks of gold. With the increase of gold reserves steps may be taken in many countries to expand the currency, and commodity prices may begin to rise. Let us suppose that the United Kingdom is one of these countries: her gold reserves expand, and on that basis more credit money is created. The resulting rise of prices may effect the exchange value of the pound.

It is extremely improbable that prices would rise to the same extent in all countries. Even when the world's commodity prices are going up, the rise may be greater in some countries than in others. Any considerable rise of prices in one country, say the United Kingdom, above the level of prices in other countries would restrict British exports, and adversely affect Britain's balance of trade. If, as a consequence, it became difficult to maintain the exchange value of the pound and exchange fell, the price of gold, in British money, would go up. Similarly if, on account of inflation, or 'reflation', the prices of our primary products began to rise, it would become more, not less difficult for us to compete in foreign markets, and the decline of exports, unless it was counterbalanced by a reduction in our external obligations of an equal amount, will lower the exchange value of the rupee, and thus raise the price of gold.

If we assume that prices rise to about the same extent everywhere, so that exchange stability is maintained everywhere, the price of gold in each country would depend on the rate of stabilisation in terms of gold.

We may summarise the whole arguments as follows:

1. The abandonment of the gold standard by France or Holland will raise the price of gold in France or Holland, and will have no effect on the price of gold elsewhere—the price of gold in India would, as before, depend on the exchange value of the rupee in terms of currencies that were still linked to gold.

2. The price of gold will fall if the universal abandonment of the gold standard led countries with large stocks of monetary and non-monetary gold to dispose of their stocks. If gold was being sold as a useless commodity and no one was willing to buy it, its price must fall.

3. But this is wholly improbable. The universal abandonment of the gold standard would not diminish the gold hunger of the world.

4. If there is a return to the gold standard with currencies stabilised at present rates, the price of gold in India and England will remain what it is now.

5. Stabilisation of the rupee at the present rate (rupee = 5·82 francs) would mean a devaluation of the rupee in terms of gold amounting to a little more than 37 per cent.

6. If a higher or lower gold rate than the present was chosen, the price of gold would alter. If we chose stabilisation at 18d. gold, the price of gold would be Rs. 21-3-10 per tola; at 2 shillings gold it will be still lower.

7. If we followed the example of Australia and New Zealand and depreciated the rupee, say 25 per cent below the sterling level, and this lower sterling value of the rupee was the rate chosen for stabilisation, the price of gold in rupees will rise.

8. A better distribution of world's monetary stocks of gold may lead to a rise in commodity prices. If the rise of prices does not affect the stability of exchange rates, the price of gold will neither fall nor rise in any country. A rise of prices in a given country above the level of world

prices may lower the exchange value of the money of that country, and thus raise the price of gold in that country.

DEMAND AND SUPPLY

If we consider the production of gold in relation to demand, a fall in the price of gold again seems improbable. According to Sir Joseph Kitchin, the total value of the world's output of gold between 1893 and 1929 was about 4,412 million pounds (at 84|11½ per fine ounce). Of this, gold worth about 1,406 million pounds was produced between 1851 and 1900, and of the value of about £ 2,356 millions in 1901-1929. The output in 1929 was valued at £ 83·5 millions (Transval £ 44·3 millions, U. S. A. 9·1 millions, India £1·5 millions).

Gold is used in the arts all over the world, and till recently our absorption of gold was heavy. Mr. Kitchin estimates that of the world output amounting to £ 772 millions in 1920-29, about 21 per cent (£ 162 millions) was used in industrial arts and 25% (£195 millions) was absorbed by India, leaving 54% of the output (£ 415 millions) for use as money.

In estimating the future non-monetary demand for gold the Gold Delegation assumed that it would increase between 1930 and 1940 at the rate of 1 per cent per annum.

As regards the supply of gold the Gold Delegation, on the basis of both official and non-official estimates of production, came to the conclusions that the supply, after increasing for three or four years would begin to decline. Mr. Kitchin's estimates are shown below:

World's gold output. In million £.

1929	83·5	1935	82·8
1930	83·1	1936	81·5
1931	82·6	1937	80·5
1932	84·3	1938	78·9
1933	83·6	1939	76·0
1934	82·8	1940	76·0

The rise in the price of gold has stimulated gold production. For example, the output of South Africa in 1932 reached the record figure of 11·6 million ounces, worth £49 millions at par. Production fell to 11·0 million ounces in 1933, valued at £47 millions. The estimated value of South African production for 1932 was £43·8 millions and for 1933 £42·5 millions.

India, as we have seen, has ceased to be a buyer, and has become a seller. The increase in gold production and the cessation of Indian demand are factors which modify the relation of supply to demand as worked out in the report of the Gold Delegation. Still it is beyond question that unless new discoveries are made, gold production will decline.

Mr. Kitchin wrote in 1930:

"There is reason to believe that 1915, with its total of £96,400,000—apart from some outstanding new discovery—will prove to have been the zenith of the world's gold output and that, though the production, after falling to £ 68,000,000 in 1921, has recovered to £83,500,000 at the present time (55 per cent. of this recovery being due to the New Rand and the balance to Canada and Russia), the prospects are that there will be no further recovery, but rather a decline, increasing with time, after about 1934" (Report of the Gold Delegation, 1930, p. 58).

The advance of metallurgy is not expected to lead to greater gold production:

"It has already been indicated", says Mr. Kitchin, that little is to be hoped from improved metallurgy, while the limits and possibilities of existing gold fields are, perhaps, fairly known. Subject to the qualification as to the possibility of some outstanding new discovery, there seems to be no prospect that the world's production will advance beyond the present level" (*Ibid*, p. 60).

Mr. Kitchin anticipated that gold production would decrease after 1934—"at first very slowly and then at a greater rate" (p. 61).

It is difficult to estimate the monetary and the non-monetary demand with accuracy in this rapidly changing world. But unless the whole attitude of the world toward gold changes, in view of the anticipated decline in gold production, a rise in the price of gold seems more likely than a fall.

Why Gold Exports should be Prohibited

1. If it is certain that the price of gold will fall in the near future, it would be desirable as Mr. Peter McDonald M. P. suggested to Sir Samuel Hoare in the House of Commons, to make the fact of the rise in price widely known in India. The rise in price may be announced by beat of drum in every village and in every town, and the people exhorted, as Sir George Schuster exhorted them in 1933, to part with their gold now. It would be profitable to sell gold at about Rs. 34, and to buy it back later, say at Rs. 21 or even less. But it has been argued above that the price of gold is not only not likely to fall, but will probably rise. The sale of gold then is not a profitable transaction. The export of gold means loss to India, for India may have to buy gold later at a price higher than the present selling price.

2. Even if Empire Trade Agreements did not limit the expansion of our exports to foreign countries; even if exports were not restricted by the rise of national economies, tariffs, quotas and prohibitions—in view of the revolution of agricultural methods and practices in the West, and the difficulty of modernising Indian agriculture, Indian exports in the coming years would expand slowly if at all. India, even if she wants to buy gold, will possess very limited means to pay for it.

3. Unless the present relation between the prices of primary products and manufactured goods is reversed, the process of buying gold in the future will be costly for India. We exported wheat worth 17 crores in 1924-25. In the first place no one wants our wheat now. In the second place, on account of the lower price of wheat, much greater quantities

of wheat will have to be given to acquire a given amount of gold. The terms of foreign trade have moved against us, thus increasing the cost of gold in terms of food-stuffs and raw materials.

4. Gold is not like tea, jute or cotton. We do not raise crops of gold. The more of gold goes out, less of it remains in the country. And considerations advanced in the preceding paragraphs suggest that the gold which leaves us now will never come back. It leaves us for good.

5. Gold is not like other commodities. It is the sinews of war. It is the basis of credit. Even if gold in our hoards is barren it would be better to keep it than to lose it. It may be utilised later as reserves for a widely extended system of banking.

6. The individual holder for various reasons, is forced to realise his capital, but that does not mean that gold must be exported. The Government may buy it and preserve it in the general interests of the country.

7. The export of gold has enabled the Government to maintain its credit and the rate of exchange at a heavy cost to the country. Certain Empire countries, Australia and New Zealand, depreciated their currencies below the sterling level without losing prestige.

The force of these arguments may be admitted, but it may still be argued that on account of the fall in our exports of merchandise, the export of gold was inevitable. But then, in the first place, there is no occasion for rejoicing because we are exporting gold; nor is the export of gold to be looked upon as a profitable business. In the second place, it is imperatively necessary to cut down the expenditure of the Indian Government in England, so as to reduce the heavy burden of our annual sterling obligations. And in the third place, expenditure in India should be cut down ruthlessly, so that those who have been brought to the verge of ruin by the fall of prices are not forced to realise their assets in order to pay Government dues. These measures of economy should be supplemented by a constructive programme of economic development, and particularly agricultural reform and reorganisation, with the object of reducing the imports of goods and services and increasing the cultivators' power of international competition.

The reader may be reminded that the amount of gold exported is no longer negligible, and gold has not ceased to flow out. Referring in January 1932 to 40 crores of gold exported since September 1931, the Viceroy said that the volume was "of no appreciable importance compared with what has been imported in recent years alone", and His Excellency spoke of "vast stores which must have been accumulated before 1900". Within 2½ years we have lost gold which we took more than 12 years to accumulate (1900-01 to 1912-13). If we do not put our house in order, in a few years more we may lose all the gold imported since 1900-01, and then start consuming the capital accumulated before 1900. It is easy to consume one's patrimony, or inherited wealth; it is difficult to add to it.

CHAPTER IV

INDIAN FINANCE

The economic depression is responsible for decrease in revenue and increase in taxation.

The main sources of Central revenues are the Customs and the income-tax. The heavy fall in the value of imports meant loss of revenue from import duties. The Finance Member in his budget speech for 1934-35 gave an example to show the effect of the depression on the income-tax. The annual profit of companies and registered firms in India fell from an average of over 53 crores in the eight years ending March 31, 1930 to under 29 crores in 1932-33. The fall in Customs and income-tax receipts diminished the tax-revenue of the Government. Non-tax revenue also contracted. In 1923-24 non-tax revenue amounted to Rs. 30½ crores, in 1929-30 Rs. 19½ crores, and for 1934-35 it is estimated at only Rs. 5¼ crores.

In certain cases the fall in Customs revenue is due to the development of home industries. For example, customs duties on cotton piece-goods yielded 6,04 lakhs in 1928-29, but their estimated yield in the budget for 1934-35 is only 4¼ crores. Imported sugar yielded 10½ crores in 1930-31. In 1933-34 it was expected to bring in 6,10 lakhs, but the actual receipts were 5,00 lakhs. The income budgeted under this head for 1934-35 is 2,05 lakhs. The fluctuations of income under the principal heads are shown below:

Lakhs

	1930—31	1931—32	1932—33 Revised	1933—34 Revised	1934—35 Budget
Customs ..	46,81	46,44	52,29	46,87	44,62
Taxes on Income	16,00	17,45	17,70	17,13	17,25
Salt ..	6,83	5,58	10,38	8,55	8,73
Opium ..	2,53	2,07	95	1,59	95
Other heads ..	2,03	2,09	1,91	1,86	1,82
Total principal heads ..	74,21	76,77	83,22	76,00	73,37

BUDGETS 1929-30 TO 1934-35

Heavy additions have been made since 1930-31 to the burden of both direct and indirect taxation.

Sir George Schuster took charge of our finances in 1929 and left us in 1934. His first budget was that for the year 1929-30. Estimates of revenue and expenditure for that year showed a deficit of 120 lakhs as compared with a surplus of 30 lakhs realised in 1928-29. The Finance Member decided to draw upon the Revenue Reserve Fund for the balance of 90 lakhs. He did not think it justifiable to impose new taxation until he was convinced that there was permanent need for it. His review of general conditions in 1928-29 showed that while they were bad in patches, there was no ground for "serious pessimism". Besides, he was new to the country and wanted time to study more fully the expenditure side of the budget as well as economic conditions throughout the country.

In his next budget speech Sir George Schuster referred to the New York Stock Exchange crisis: "The collapse seems likely to result in a period of business stagnation in America, which has already produced a serious fall in the prices of all commodities. While the effect of these events on monetary conditions in India has been apparent throughout the year under review [1929-30] the effect of the fall in prices on trade is only now beginning to be felt".

The depression, which was just beginning, produced deteriorations of revenue under Customs, Miscellaneous payments, Railways, Posts and Telegraphs and other heads. The total net deterioration was 66 lakhs, which, combined with the anticipated deficit of 90 lakhs, raised the total deficit to 156 lakhs. The deficit was exactly balanced by a payment to India of 156 lakhs in connection with the German Liquidation Account under the Treaty of Versailles.

But the gap between income and expenditure had not been really filled. There were some abnormally high receipts under particular heads (*e.g.*, interest on the Gold Standard

Reserve), and windfalls under other heads (one of 30 lakhs as the net result of certain judgments in the Privy Council).

The financial position was not satisfactory in spite of the balanced budget for 1929-30. The estimates for 1930-31 showed a gap of 5,52 lakhs, and new taxation was necessary to fill the gap.

The changes in taxation were the following:

1. The export duty on rice was reduced, which was estimated to cost the Government 30 lakhs.

2. In addition to the 15 per cent revenue duty a 5 per cent protective duty with a minimum of 3½ annas per lb. on plain grey goods was imposed on cotton piece-goods imported from countries outside the United Kingdom.

3. The excise duty on kerosine was increased from 1 anna to 1 anna 6 pies, while the import duty was reduced from 2½ annas to 2 annas 3 pies.

4. The duty on sugar was increased, so as to yield an additional 1,80 lakhs.

5. The income-tax on *personal* incomes of Rs. 15,000 and upward was raised by 1 pie in the rupee and a corresponding increase was made in the super-tax in all grades. The Finance Member did not consider it desirable to impose fresh burdens on industry or commercial enterprise.

6. The old import duty on silver of 4 annas per ounce was re-introduced.

In justifying the need for fresh taxation the Finance Member said that, if things went well, the new taxes would create a margin which would enable the Central Government "to give a fair measure of assistance to the Provincial Governments in the next chapter of their history".

The budget for 1930-31, as finally passed, provided for a surplus of 86 lakhs. The revised estimates in March 1931 showed a deficit of 13,56 lakhs. "Times are bad", said the Finance Member as a preface to his business statement. A further heavy fall in the tax revenue was anticipated in 1931-

32 and new taxation had to be imposed. Was this to be of a temporary or permanent nature? The Finance Member thought that of the new taxes, some at least would be permanently needed, or at least could not be abolished unless substitutes were found—for behind the temporary needs of the Central Government there lay a permanent need for more resources for the Provinces.

The most important of the Customs sur-charges was that of 5 per cent on the general revenue schedule of 15 per cent. The 5 per cent sur-charge was placed on imported cotton goods also. The duties on special articles as alcoholic drinks and sugar were considerably enhanced. The additional yield of the Customs was estimated at 9·82 crores.

Changes were also made in the income-tax and the super tax, but the taxable minimum income for the income tax, Rs. 2000, was not lowered.

The duty on silver was increased from 4 annas to 6 annas per ounce. The re-introduction of the duty of 4 annas in the budget for 1930-31 had not checked the consumption of silver.

The net result of these changes was to give the Finance Member a surplus. Still the Finance Member added a word of caution: "Expenditure and revenue returns will have to be carefully watched, and if conditions show signs of deterioration, it may be necessary to take interim measures to counteract that. It is vitally important to the financial stability of the country that we should not find ourselves at the end of another year with a large realised deficit."

The budget, as, finally passed, provided for a small surplus of 1 lakh.

There was a supplementary budget at the end of September 1931. The returns of the 5 months, from 1st April to the end of August, showed a heavy fall in revenue. Taking into account the anticipated surplus of 1 lakh, the net deficit at the close of 1931-32, was estimated at 19,55 lakhs. The increase in taxation took the form of a sur-charge of 25 per cent on the rates in force, lowering of the exemption limit of the income tax to Rs. 1,000, curtailment of the list of goods imported free of duty, the imposition of special rates of duty on some imports (*e.g.*, boots and shoes and artificial silk piece goods) and an enhancement of postal rates.

The justification of the proposals for new taxation was that India had abandoned the gold standard, and financial stability was essential if public confidence in the currency was to be maintained: "for once a country's currency is cut adrift from the moorings of a stable standard such as Gold, it is particularly necessary to avoid getting into any sort of inflationary position resulting from a failure to balance current expenditure with current revenue." In the concluding portion of his speech the Finance Member again referred to the connection between budgetary deficits, note printing and collapse of confidence in a country's currency and said: "We want to erect a solid barrier against the possibility of India getting on to that slippery slope. That is the essential justification for our proposals."

The new proposals were meant not only for the remaining months of 1931-32 but also for the whole year 1932-33. The two years ending March 31, 1933 were to be considered together. It was anticipated that the year 1931-32 would close with a deficit of 10·17 crores, but that in the following year a surplus of 5·23 crores would be realised. When the position was examined in March 1932, it was found that deterioration in revenue had increased the deficit in 1931-32 to 13·66 crores; the surplus in 1932-33 was also not expected to exceed 2·15 crores.

A year later, the actual figures for 1931-32 showed an improvement of about 2 crores, while the surplus realised in 1932-33 was 2,17 lakhs; so that on the combined result of the two years there was a deficit of 9,58 lakhs. On the other hand, provision had been made in these two years for reduction or avoidance of debt amounting to 13,73 lakhs. On the combined result of the two years then there was a surplus of receipts over expenditure other than reduction of debt amounting to 4,15 lakhs.

The changes in taxation in the budget for 1933-34 were of minor importance, relating to import duties on uppers of boots and shoes, artificial silk goods and mixtures. The budget provided for a revenue of 124,35 lakhs and an expenditure (exclusive of reduction of debt) of 117,22 lakhs, leaving a surplus of 7,13 lakhs. The revised estimates showed a considerable fall in revenue under Customs, the Income-tax and a slight fall in a number of other heads. Against a total fall in revenue of a little over 4 crores, expenditure decreased by 2,20 lakhs, so that the surplus realised (without making any allowance for reduction of debt) was 4·29 lakhs. Of this the Government decided to utilise 3 crores for debt reduction. The remaining sum, 129 lakhs has been set apart for earthquake relief.

As compared with 1933-34 (revised figures), the revenue position was expected to get worse in 1934-35 by 2,80 lakhs (chiefly due to the falling off in sugar import duties), and as regards expenditure an increase of 2 lakhs was anticipated. An estimated expenditure of 79,61 lakhs (net) against an estimated revenue of 78,08 lakhs left a deficit of 153 lakhs to be provided for.

This has been met by excise duties on sugar and matches, readjustment of tobacco duties, and reduction in the import duty on silver from 7½ to 5 annas.

The Sugar Excise

The sugar excise has been much criticised. The old duty was Rs. 7-4-0 per cent plus a sur-charge of Rs. 1-13-0. Rs. 7-4-0 was the basic protective duty for sugar recommended by the Tariff Board. The Tariff Board also recommended that Government should have the power of increasing the measure of protection by 8 annas per cwt. when Java sugar was being imported at a price less than Rs. 4 per maund into Calcutta. Assuming that the conditions justifying this extra margin of protection were likely to cotinue in existence for the present, the Government fixed the level of the excise at

Re. 1-5-0 per cwt., leaving a protective margin of Rs. 7-12-0 per cent.

Indian producers of factory sugar take an entirely pessimistic view of the sugar excise. It is feared that it will lead to the disappearance of the smaller factories, and make heavy inroads into the legitimate profits of bigger concerns.

In so far as the effect of the excise is to reduce the output of factory sugar, the cane-grower will not escape injury.

On the other hand, there is not much evidence to show that the cane-grower has substantially benefited by the growth of factory production. The sugar-refining industry absorbs only a very small proportion of the sugar-cane grown in India. In 1932-33 out of a total of about 48½ million tons of cane produced in India only 4½ million tons was required by factories producing refined sugar. Of the balance, about 5½ millions tons was taken by khandsari factories, leaving 38½ million tons for other purposes. The capitalist interests are not sympathetic towards the cane-grower. It deserves to be recorded that when in 1933, it was proposed, in the interests of the cultivator, to fix the price of cane for factory purposes, among those who opposed the proposal was the Honourable Minister for Local Self Government and Industries, Punjab!

The Government of India now propose to ensure that the agricultural producer gets his full measure of benefit out of the policy of protection. No one will grudge the cultivator a few extra pice per maund that he may thus be able to secure.

In defending the sugar excise the Finance Member also referred to "a real danger of over-production on a scale which may lead to very serious reactions both on the manufacturing industry and on the cane-growers who rely on it".

The sugar industry has indeed been expanding rapidly. The number of factories increased from 68 in 1932-33 to 130 in 1933-34, and the output increased from 351,000 tons to 647,000 tons (estimate). But there is still considerable scope for the expansion of the industry, for estimated consumption exceeds the output of sugar factories. In the year 1933-34, 231,454 tons of Java sugar were imported; the imports exceeded 800,000 tons in 1929-30. The market which Indian factories can hope to capture is equal to imports at the present time, that is over 231,000 tons. But the decline in imports is not solely due to the growth of the Indian industry. It is partly due to the fall in our purchasing power. The market will therefore expand as economic conditions improve. Further, next to the United Provinces, Bihar and Orissa have the largest number of factories (35 in 1933-34 with an estimated output of about 229,000 tons as against 67 factories with an estimated output of 326,000 tons in the United Provinces), and considerable damage has been done to sugar-factories in Bihar and Orissa by the earthquake. The Finance Member admitted that the earthquake had "affected an important sugar-growing area", but he did not consider the loss of producing capacity in Bihar and Orissa a sufficient reason for altering his whole plan.

Viewing the situation as a whole there does not seem to be much justification for the application of the brake in the shape of the excise at this stage. The needs of Government finance have led to the imposition of the excise, not so much the fear of over-production.

An excise on matches was recommended by the Federal Finance Committee. In the words of the Finance Member, India, under the new constitution, "will need to take advantage of all possible sources of indirect taxation. An excise duty on matches is and has always been recognised as an obvious expedient". And he thought it desirable to have this duty in operation in advance of the new constitution.

The excise duty on matches having been accepted, half the export duty on jute next year amounting to 1,89 lakhs after allowing for the cost of collection, will be handed over to the jute-growing provinces. Bengal is to get 167 lakhs, Bihar and Orissa 12½ lakhs and Assam 9½ lakhs. Bengal badly needed this help. She has been accumulating deficits since 1930 at the rate of 2 crores annually.

The duty on raw tobacco has been slightly increased and that on imported cigarettes reduced. This will lead to a revival of imports of cigarettes, and produce more revenue for the Government.

The other changes in the budget for 1934-35 are the abolition of the export duty on hides, and a reduction in postal and Telegraph rates. Allowing for the loss of 5 lakhs on the abolition of the export duty on raw hides, the changes in taxation are expected to yield 169 lakhs, which will cover the anticipated deficit of 153 lakhs, and leave a small surplus.

Expenditure

The situation created by the depression has been met, as we have seen, by making considerable additions to taxation. At the same time attempt has been made to reduce expenditure. The following statement shows gross and net expenditure of the Government of India since 1930-31.

		Expenditure in lakhs	
		Gross	Net[1]
1930-31	Actual	1,30,03	93,20
1931-32	"	1,26,50	88,78
1932-33	"	1,18,00	80,59
1933-34	Budget	1,17,22	79,21
1933-34	Revised	1,15,02	76,59
1934-35	Budget	1,15,10	76,61

Since 1930-31 gross expenditure has fallen by 15 crores, and net expenditure by 16½ crores.

Military expenditure in the budget for 1934-35 is 44·38 crores, or about 58 per cent of the total estimated net expenditure of the Government of India in that year. It amounted to 55 crores in 1928-29. For four years, beginning from 1928-29, the Government of India had agreed to provide Rs. 55 crores annually for Defence (net). Out of this stabilised 4 years' budget, the Army authorities had to find 10 crores, which they needed for their re-equipment programme.

[1] Net expenditure found by taking net figures for Interest and Defence.

They got the stipulated amount for two years only. Still the greater part of the re-equipment programme has been accomplished.

The reduction of Military expenditure by 10¾ crores since 1928-29 has been made possible by the fall in prices (1 crore), revision of pay of British soldiers (1 crore), the recent contribution of 2 crores by the British Government towards Indian Defence expenditure (this is to be an annual payment), and to the emergency pay cut (½ crore). In addition, 6 crores have been saved by the postponement of the re-equipment and building programme, by reduction of stocks of stores, and by "real and permanent retrenchments and economies".

The Military authorities, however, decline to accept 44·38 crores as a new permanent level of Defence expenditure. They regard it as an emergency budget "which barely covers the obligatory charges of maintenance".

In the emergency budget of September 1931 a 10 per cent cut had been applied to salaries of Government servants (including railway employees) drawing 40 rupees a month or more. The cut was of a temporary nature, and it was not intended that it should remain operative beyond March 31, 1933. In the budget for 1933-34 half of the cut was restored. This partial restoration of the cut was "an essential part of the budgetary plan". After allowing for the gain to the Government on account of the withdrawal of the exemption of income-tax sur-charges and the tax on incomes below Rs. 2,000 from Government officials (including Railway officials and officials serving under the Provincial Governments), the net cost of the restoration to the Central Government was 55 lakhs.

The cost was comparatively small, but in making out a case for the restoration, the Finance Member laid down principles which will not command general approval. "I wish particularly to emphasize", he said, "that this must not be regarded as optional expenditure to be weighed in the balance against other possible demands on the public funds.

Government is not really meeting its full obligations as long as it is not paying the fixed rates of pay of its officials—rates, moreover, which, in certain cases, are guaranteed by the Government of India Act. Government is therefore bound to regard the task before it as one of producing a balanced budget after including full pay to its servants". It is forgotten that the 'full pay' of Government servants is fixed on a scale which bears no comparison to the income of the masses of the population. Further, when national income falls, as it has fallen in India, there may be and is full justification for permanent, and drastic cuts in salaries. And when economic conditions and finances improve the person first entitled to relief is not the over-paid official but the over-taxed tax-payer. The 50 per cent restoration of the cut in the Central budget was immediately followed by a similar restoration of the cut in Provincial budgets, even when, as in the Punjab, the main burden of Provincial taxation rested on the cultivator whose real net income had fallen to practically nothing.

Indian Railways

Reference has been made above to the heavy decrease in the Government of India's non-tax revenue. Of the sources of non-tax revenue railways were the most important. In the period of 5 years ending 1928-29 the average annual contribution of the railways to the general revenues was about 6 crores. In this period the net revenue of the railways exceeded the interest charges each year by 9¾ crores on an average. In the year 1929-30, net revenue was still greater than interest-charges, but only by 4,04 lakhs, and therefore the contribution to the general revenues of 6,12 lakhs was paid by drawing on railway reserves for the difference. Beginning with 1930-31 interest charges each year have exceeded the net railway revenue. The railways paid a contribution of 5,74 lakhs to the general revenues in 1930-31; nothing after that.

The Railway deficit amounted to 5 crores in 1930-31, 9¼ crores in 1931-32 and 10¼ crores in 1932-33. Thereafter the deficit fell, which may be attributed to improvement in the economic situation. It is expected to amount to 7¾ crores in 1933-34 and about 5¼ crores in 1934-35. The deficits have been met by loans from the Railway Depreciation Fund.

It is claimed that the deficits do not reveal any inherent defects in the railway organisation. In his speech introducing the railway budget for 1934-35 the Commerce Member explained that even in the worst year of the depression (1932-33 for the railways) the net revenue from commercial lines alone amounted to 23¼ crores and the railways put by to the depreciation reserve a sum of 7¼ crores more than what was actually required to withdraw for current expenditure on renewals and replacements. The full interest charges payable in that year were 32½ crores, which sum exceeded the earnings from commercial lines (including the 7¼ crores mentioned) by only one crore. The Commerce Member added that similarly in 1933-34 and 1934-35 net revenue would be over 32 crores if payments to the depreciation reserve were confined to what was needed to meet only urgent and necessary requirements.

The financial position of the railways, therefore, is not so bad as the bare figures of annual deficits during the past 5 years indicate.

The more rapid increase in operating expenses as compared with gross earnings between 1913-14 and 1929-30 is shown by the following statement:

RAILWAY STATISTICS

	Gross earnings lakhs,	Working Expenses lakhs	Percentage of working expenses to gross earnings
1913-14	63,59 (100)	32,93 (100)	51·79
1917-18	77,36 (122)	35,37 (108)	45·79
1921-22	92,89 (146)	70,80 (215)	76·22
1925-26	113,39 (178)	71,09 (216)	62·69
1929-30	116,08 (183)	75,49 (229)	65·02

(Source: Stat. Abs. for British India)

While gross earnings increased 83 per cent in 1929-30 (1913-14=100) working expenses rose 129 per cent. The percentage of working expenses to gross earning naturally rose.

After the recent reduction in railway expenditure no further saving can be effected from major retrenchments, and the hope of further economies lies in the results of the detailed job analyses now being conducted by a special temporary organisation set up on various railways.

Income-Tax in India and England

Having studied the financial adjustments in India occasioned by the depression, we are now in a position to consider the general burden of taxation at present.

The burden of taxation, both direct and indirect, is not light. It is heavy.

The general ad valorem rate of the Customs tariff has risen by gradual stages from 5 per cent before the war to 25 per cent, and there are heavier duties on special articles.

More important than Customs duties are the rates of the income-tax and the super-tax. The following table shows the percentage of the income taken in the form of income-tax and super-tax in India in 1924 and 1932-33. Figures for England have been added for the sake of comparison.

Proportion of income taken in Income-tax and Sur-tax

	India		England (a)		England (b)	
	1924	1932-33	1924	1932-33	1924	1932-33
£ 100 = Rs. 1,333	..	..	..	..	..	..
£ 130 = Rs. 1,733	..	2·1	..	..	..	2·9
£ 200 = Rs. 2,666	2·6	3·9	..	..	..	6·3
£ 300 = Rs. 4,000	2·6	3·9	..	·8	6·8	9·4
£ 400 = Rs. 5,333	3·1	5·9	..	1·3	..	..
£ 500 = Rs. 6,666	3·1	5·9	3·3	3·0	12·5	15·6
£ 1,000 = Rs. 13,333	4·7	7·8	10·8	10·8	18·8	20·3
£ 2,000 = Rs. 26,666	7·8	12·4	17·0	16·7	22·7	22·7
£ 5,000 = Rs. 66,666	11·5	20·4	28·0	28·4	30·8	30·8
£ 10,000 = Rs. 1,33,333	14·6	25·9	38·0	38·5	39·0	39·7
£ 50,000 = Rs. 6,66,666	32·9	46·2	50·0	56·6	50·0	56·8

(*a*) Tax for a married man with three children, with income all 'earned'.

(*b*) Tax for a bachelor with income all 'investment'.

Source: For 1924 see Report of Taxation Enquiry Committee, 1924-25, p. 199. The amount of tax payable in England, in 1932-33 is given in the *Economist* Budget Supplement, April 14, 1934.

The figures for India show a very considerable increase throughout the scale. In England the increase up to £ 10,000 is less marked. The bachelor up to £ 1,000 pays more; the position of married couples, generally speaking, is the same as before.

A comparison of the burden of the tax in India in 1932-33 with that of the British income-tax yields interesting results. Up to £ 500, the percentage of income taken in India is higher than that taken in England. After £ 500 the burden of the British tax relatively grows heavier.

In the budget for 1934-35 the standard rate of tax has been reduced from 5 shillings (the rate in force in 1932-33) to 4*s*. 6*d*. The effect of this reduction would be to lower the British percentages for 1932-33 given above.

The British Income-Tax

The method of graduation in the United Kingdom is different, and various allowances are also given. In India the whole of net income, when it exceeds Rs. 1,000 is taxable income. In England, total. income, assessable income and taxable income mean different things.

The assessable income is found by deducting one-fifth (not exceeding £ 300) from the total income earned by an individual, and adding to it the whole of the unearned or investment income.

The tax is charged, not on assessable but taxable income. This is found by deducting from the assessable income £100 for a single person and £150 for a married couple, and also the allowances in respect of children, dependent relatives, or house-keeper, but not assurance premiums.

The Standard rate of tax in 1932-33 was 5 shillings in the £ (6 shillings from 1918-19 to 1921-22, 4 shillings from 1925-26 to 1928-29, and 4s. 6d. in 1929-30 and 1930-31). Half the standard rate, or 2s. 6d. was charged, on the first £ 175 of the taxable income and the full rate of 5 shillings on the remaining taxable income, whether earned or unearned.

Income is exempt from taxation when in the case of a single person it does not exceed £ 125, if all earned, or £ 100 if all unearned; and in the case of married couples when total income does not exceed £187 10s., if all earned, or £ 150 if all unearned.

Allowances are given of £ 50 for one child and £ 40 for each additional child under the age of 16, or who, if over 16, is receiving full-time instruction at any university, college, school or other educational establishment. In 1930-31 the deduction allowable was £ 60 in respect of the first child and £ 50 in respect of each additional child. These allowances are deducted from the assessable income.

Further, an allowance of £ 25 is made from assessable income in respect of a widowed mother, or a relative incapacitated by old age or infirmity from maintaining himself and whose income does not exceed £ 50 a year.

An allowance of £ 50 from the assessable income is made in respect of a resident female relative (or stranger) of a widower or widow.

It is seen that for purposes of income-taxation, a distinction is made in England between earned and unearned income, and between married and unmarried persons. It is also recognised that those having more children and dependents have a smaller tax-bearing capacity than others less burdened in this respect.

The super-tax, now called sur-tax, is an additional graduated income-tax levied on all personal incomes exceeding £ 2,000 per annum. The combined income and sur-tax rates rise from 6 shillings (plus 10 per cent sur-charge imposed in

1931-32) on each pound between £ 2,001 and £ 2,500 to 12s. 6d. (plus 10 per cent sur-charge) on each pound on incomes of £ 50,001 and over.

The effect of allowances in reducing the burden of the income-tax may be shown by an example.

If Ram Lal in India has an income of £ 500 or Rs. 6,666 in a year, he will pay the income-tax at 9 pies in the rupee, plus 25 per cent sur-charge, or at 11·25 pies in all, equal to 5·9 per cent of his total income. We assume that Ram Lal supports a widowed mother and three children under 16 who live with him, or who if over 16, are receiving instruction in a college or other educational institution. Ram Lal will get no relief in respect of the children or his widowed mother, and he will pay the same tax whether his income is wholly earned, or wholly derived from investment.

Let us now take the case of Mr. Smith in England with a total income of £ 500. We assume that Mr. Smith's income is wholly earned, and that his family responsibilities are the same as those of Ram Lal in India. What is the amount of the income-tax that he will pay?

Mr. Smith

Earned Income	£ 500
Deduct earned income allowance one-fifth ..	£ 100
Assessable Income	£ 400
Deduct Personal allowance	£ 150
Deduct three children, £ 50+£ 40+£ 40 ..	£ 130
Deduct widowed mother	£ 25
Total Relief ..	£ 305
Taxable Income ..	£ 95

Tax on £ 95 at 2s. 6d. in the pound .. £ 11-17-6.

£ 11-17-6 out of a total income of £ 500 is equal to 2·4 per cent of the income.

If Mr. Smith's earned income is £ 2,000, to find his assessable income, we shall deduct not one-fifth (£ 400), but the maximum allowed, £ 300. His relief in respect of children and widowed mother, and personal allowance would remain the same, so that the taxable income would be £ 2,000 less £ 605, or £ 1,395. On the first £ 175 of this taxable income, the rate of tax will be 2s. 6d. (equal to £21-17-6) and on the remaining £ 1,220 at the full standard rate of 5 shillings (equal to £ 305). Mr. Smith will now pay a total tax of £ 326-17-6, which amounts to 16·34 per cent of his income.

The absence of allowances makes our income-tax very burdensome for persons of moderate means.

It appeared to the Indian Taxation Enquiry Committee of 1924-25 that "it would be best under Indian conditions to set off the higher exemption limit (then Rs.2,000) against the absence of allowances in respect of dependents, in other words, to maintain the *status quo* in both matters" (p. 196). But in the first place the exemption limit is lower now, and in the second place the exemption limit, whether it is Rs. 1,000 or 2,000 confers no benefit on those who pay the income-tax, for they have to pay the tax on the whole of their income. The exemption limit benefits only persons with an income of less than Rs. 1,000.

It cannot be pretended that the taxable capacity of a person above the exemption limit is equal to the whole of his income. As in the British income-tax assessable income should be determined after making a deduction in every case from the earned income. The deduction would be a kind of subsistence allowance.

Dr. Paranjpye, an Indian member of the Taxation Enquiry Committee, was in favour of an abatement of Rs. 200 for one wife and Rs. 150 for each minor son or unmarried daughter to a maximum of Rs. 950, provided it was claimed (p. 196). The case for a personal allowance for married couples and deductions for children and dependent relatives is a strong one. The cost of education in India, for Indian conditions, is fairly heavy, and the taxable capacity of different families with different numbers of children, unmarried daughters and dependent relatives is certainly not equal. Under existing conditions the Indian income-tax is a rough and ready method of direct taxation, with no attempt to adjust the burden to the capacity of the tax-payer.

It has been suggested in a preceding Chapter that the income-tax should be applied to agricultural incomes. When this is done, a distinction must be made between earned and unearned income. Unearned income from non-agricultural sources is growing with the development of industries and the expansion of towns. Still relatively to agricultural unearned income it is at present small.

We have seen that up to £ 500 the percentage of the total income taken in the form of the income-tax is higher in India than in England. This may be defended on the ground that the cost of living in India is lower. We may assume that the taxable capacity of a person with an income of Rs. 6,666 in India is greater than that of £ 500 in England. But the table given above shows that after £ 500, the percentage of income taken in England steadily rises relatively to the Indian percentage. It is not intelligible, how, as compared with England, taxable capacity in India can be greater for the taxation of particular incomes and lower for the taxation of higher incomes!

In spite of its defects, however, the Income-tax is a better tax than Provincial taxes in the shape of land revenue and water-rates. The burden imposed by the Income-tax and the Customs tariff is not only lighter in comparison, but rests largely on the middle and the upper-classes.

Taxable Capacity

The taxable capacity of a people is the maximum amount that they can contribute towards the expenses of the State. It is found by deducting from their total income from all sources the minimum amount required for consumption, for replacing old capital and for new additions to capital.

If allowance is not made for the replacement of capital as it wears out and for additions to the country's apparatus of production, industrial efficiency will suffer, which must react on the income-earning capacity of the people. Further, minimum consumption does not mean bare subsistence, or the amount required to keep a worker's body and soul together. Minimum consumption must be interpreted as consumption necessary for efficiency. Taxable capacity, or the taxable surplus, is a surplus of production over costs in this sense. J. A. Hobson says:

> "I may summarise this analysis of ability to bear in the following general terms. Those elements of income which are necessary payments to owners of productive agents, in order to sustain the productive efficiency of an agent and to evoke its application, rank as 'costs' of production, and have no ability to bear taxation. The standard wages required to keep a working-class family on such a level of efficiency and comfort as will maintain and evoke the regular application of its labour-power constitute labour 'costs'. Such salaries, fees and profits as are necessary under existing social and economic conditions to secure the supply of the requisite amounts of business and professional ability needed for the initiation, organization and management of productive enterprise, must similarly rank as 'costs' of ability or brain-labour. To these must be added, under any system of private enterprise, the minimum interest required to evoke the amount of saving and the application of new capital needed to furnish the plant, tools and materials for the productive processes".[2]

In his *Science of Public Finance*, Mr. Findlay Shirras attempted to determine India's taxable capacity and on the basis of his figures he reached certain conclusions regarding the burden of taxation in India, as compared with that in England, in the year 1922. The figures are interesting. Mr. Shirras found that effective taxation in the case of India in that year was 4 per cent of the gross income as compared with 24 per cent in that of the United Kingdom, and 30 per cent of taxable capacity as against 82 per cent in the United Kingdom. He indeed points out that the figures "must not

[2] *Taxation in the New State* by J. A. Hobson, pp. 41-42.

be interpreted too rigorously"; still the impression that they leave on the reader's mind is that India is, comparatively, a lightly taxed country. We are also often told by propagandist writers, who have never made any study of the subject, that India is the most lightly taxed country in the world.

Now it is almost impossible to make international comparisons of tax-burdens. This is chiefly because the things that we compare are not the same. The economic organizations of two countries like India and England are different: in an agricultural country the flow of production and income is less regular and constant (as it depends on the vagaries of the monsoon) than in a manufacturing country; the systems of taxation are also different: our land revenue, for example, is a peculiarly Indian product, and the Indian income-tax, both in regard to the basis of assessment and the method of assessment, differs from the British income-tax; the levels of income or prosperity in the two countries are not the same, and this vitally affects tax-bearing power; finally, the burden of taxation also depends on such factors as (*a*) the objects on which the income of the State is largely spent and (*b*) whether the proceeds of taxation are spent in the country in which the taxes are raised, or a considerable proportion is spent outside the country, as in the case of India. It will be seen that, apart from the difficulties involved in measuring taxable capacity, international comparisons of taxable capacity must take account of so many different and involved factors, that conclusions based on them, as in the case of India and Great Britain, are scarcely of any value.

In the case of India there is the further difficulty that reliable estimates of national income do not exist. Dr. Bowley and Dr. D. H. Robertson, have recently made suggestions regarding an economic census of India. They were so much impressed by the difficulties of the task, (caused by the lack of reliable and accurate data) that they did not recommend for India at present any estimate of national wealth as a whole. For rural income they have advocated an estimate of the quantity and value of all produce and all services by the method of intensive surveys in selected villages, and for urban areas, in the first instance, surveys of the larger towns. These surveys of selected rural and urban areas will make it possible to estimate national income within certain limits.

It is obvious that where accurate information about the volume and value of national production is not available, any estimate of national income must be a guess, more likely to be wrong than right. The conjectural nature of such estimates may be shown by an example. Mr. Shirras estimated the production of milk in British India in 1921-22 at 290,665,151 maunds; the value of the milk was estimated at 310,36 lakhs[3] equal to 15·6 per cent of the total value of all produce.

Now it may be doubted if the number of milch cows and buffaloes in the whole of British India is exactly known. Even if our information on this point is reliable, there is room for great uncertainty and difference of opinion as regards the production of milk in a given year. If lower figures were taken for the production of milk and its value, the amount of national income would fall, and taxable capacity would fall too.

While for reasons stated above, it is impossible to determine the proportion of taxation to taxable capacity in India at present, there is some indirect evidence to show that the proportion is high.

In the case of the Income-tax, we have seen that up to £500 (Rs. 6,666) a year, a higher percentage of income is taken in India in the form of the income-tax than in England. The greater number of income-tax payers are included in the classes from Rs. 1,000 to Rs. 5,000. But our masses are rural. They are not touched by the income-tax. For the

[3] *The Science of Public Finance*, p. 140.

landholder Government dues in the shape of the land revenue and the water rates (where there is canal irrigation) have the effect of a direct tax on income. We have already seen that the charges for water are frankly levied as a tax, that is they are so fixed as to exceed the cost of supplying the water.

Facts relating to agricultural income at the present time, given in a preceding chapter, lead to the certain and indisputable conclusion that over large parts of the country the taxation of the agriculturist encroaches on his subsistence. In other words, the agriculturist is being taxed beyond his taxable capacity.

Indirect evidence of this is furnished by (1) the high proportion of loans made by cooperative credit societies to their members for the payment of land revenue, and (2) the sale of gold by necessitous agriculturists. The facts, both in regard to the land revenue, and 'distress gold', are incontestable, and they have only one meaning—that in the case of large masses of the population, on account of the heavy fall in income, taxation today rests not on any 'surplus', but subsistence.

The situation demands prompt remedies. It is not necessary to wait for action until an economic census of India has revealed the exact amount of our national income. An economic census may help us to determine more exactly the degree of our poverty—income per head may be found to be not 6 pice per day, but, let us say, 3 annas. That would not profoundly alter the economic situation. An economic census of India would not make the burden of taxation lighter, nor *per capita* income higher. The census may be undertaken when we have time and money for it.

What is needed immediately is practical measures to augment national income and reduce the cost of administration.

FEDERAL FINANCE

We have studied the present financial situation. Important changes in the financial relations between the Central and Provincial Governments are contemplated when the reforms are inaugurated and a Federal Government established at the Centre.

The Percy Federal Finance Committee prepared a forecast of Federal and Provincial finances for 1935-36. The revenue forecast of the Committee for the Federal Government is based on rates of taxation imposed by the first Finance Act of 1931; in other words, the Committee did not take into account the special surcharges on customs, income-tax and salt imposed in the Supplementary budget of September 1931. Working on this basis the Committee estimated the revenue of the federal Government at 84,60 lakhs (net) and expenditure (net) at 80,10 lakhs, which gives a surplus of 4½ crores.

The Provincial forecasts for 1935-36 showed a deficit of 3,82 lakhs (to which Bengal's contribution is 2 crores). "Our estimates show", wrote the Percy Committee, "that on the basis of their present revenues, most of the Provinces will be in a difficult position at the outset of federation, even if they balance their budgets during the intervening period and carry over into the federation only the liabilities which they have already incurred, including those in respect of budget deficits up to 31st March 1932" (p. 7). The chief cause of the difficulty is inelasticity of provincial sources of revenue. The Punjab, for example, under existing conditions, is overtaxed. There is little hope of expansion of revenues, unless, somehow, prices return to former levels.

In view of the anticipated Provincial deficits, amounting to about 4 crores, and the present serious financial situation in the Provinces, the anticipated federal surplus of 4½ crores is inadequate. "The Government of India," wrote the Percy Committee, "may well have to consider how that surplus can be not only realised, but increased" (p. 8).

The Committee examined possible new sources of revenue, both federal and provincial. Its conclusion was that such provincial taxes as appeared to be within the sphere of practical politics in the immediate future "could not be relied on to yield any substantial early additions to provincial revenues" (p. 11). In the federal sphere the Committee took into account only one tax, the excise on matches, which was estimated to yield 3 crores in all, and of which 2·50 crores was the estimated yield in British India. The federal surplus thus rises to 7 or 7·50 crores.

The Peel Committee had recommended that taxes on income should be transferred to the provinces. If this transfer was made at the outset of federation, to meet the resultant deficit, the Federal Government, would be obliged to levy Provincial contributions, until the growth of its revenue enabled it to remit the contributions. The Peel Committee had recommended that the constitution should provide for the extinction of provincial contributions by annual stages over a definite period, such as 10 or 15 years. The Percy Committee found it impossible to specify an annual rate of reduction of contributions, or a definite period within which they should cease.

The net yield of the income-tax was taken at 17,20 lakhs of which 3,70 lakhs (the yield of super-tax on companies, tax on salaries of federal officers and personal income-tax and super-tax levied in Federal areas) was to be retained by the Federal Government. The balance available for distribution to the Provinces was thus 13,50. The Percy Committee suggested the following distribution of income-tax, and Provincial contributions:

(In lakhs of rupees)

	Distribution of income-tax	Contributions proposed	Final surplus
Madras ..	1,83	1,41	22
Bombay* ..	3,43	2,48	9
Bengal ..	4,05	2,05	Nil
United Provinces ..	1,23	95	53
Punjab ..	91	70	51
Bihar and Orissa ..	1,07	35	2
Central Provinces ..	59	37	5
Assam ..	29	Nil	36
N. W. F. P.** ..	10	..	..
Total	13,50	8,31	

Assam will still have a deficit, but the Percy Committee thought that Assam might be made self-supporting by a well-considered programme of development and land settlement financed by federal loans.

We started with a surplus of 7 or 7½ crores for our Federal Government; of this surplus 5 crores is to be set apart for the Provinces (13½ crores of income-tax distributed among them *less* 8½ crores of provincial contributions). Thus the Federal Government is left with a surplus of 2 or 2½ crores.

The financial prospects are not cheerful. The cost of setting up the Federal Government will absorb a great part of the anticipated surplus. The Percy Committee hoped that the cost of introducing the new reforms would be reduced to a minimum, both at the Centre and in the Provinces; "It would be deplorable", the Committee wrote, "if the first result of the reforms were a large addition to the over-head charges of Government" (p. 16). Our past experience in

*Includes Sind

**The share due to N.W.P. Province will presumably go in reduction of the sub-vention to that Province.

this respect is deplorable, and unless steps are taken to carefully watch and control the new reforms expenditure, old financial history will repeat itself.

A more real danger is that of contraction of Central revenues. The anticipated surplus of 7 or 7½ crores may not be realised. The Percy Committee estimated the net yield of customs at 50,30 lakhs, *without* the surcharge on customs. *With* the surcharges the anticipated yield of customs in the budget for 1933-34 was 51,25 lakhs. The yield, according to revised estimates, was Rs. 46,87 lakhs in 1933-34, and in 1934-35 the Customs tariff is not expected to bring in more than 44,62 lakhs. The Percy Committee put the railway contribution at 5 crores, but who can say when the railways would again be in a position to contribute anything to the general revenues? Today the Percy Committee's estimate of federal revenue seems a little too optimistic. The actual drop of about 6 crores in the Customs revenue alone is sufficient to upset all calculations. A rise in the cost of defence (net) from 44,38 lakhs (budget 1934-35) to 47 crores (Percy Committee) would increase the confusion.

Whatever the political value of the reforms, from the financial point of view they cause serious misgiving.

CHAPTER V

EXCHANGE AND PRICES

Mint Par

When two countries use gold as their standard of value, there is a definite relation between their standard gold coins, determined by the amount of pure gold that the coins contain. This relation is known as the Mint Par. Before the recent devaluation of the dollar, the sovereign was equal to 4·866 dollars. This was the Mint Par between England and the United States determined by the relation between the fine gold contents of the dollar and the sovereign.

Suppose our standard of value was a gold *mohur* containing 113·00 pure grains of gold. Then one gold *mohur* would be equal to one sovereign, for the sovereign also contains 113·00 grains of pure gold. If one *mohur* was equal to Rs.13-5-4, that would also be the value of the sovereign in terms of rupees.

Before the outbreak of the Great War the sovereign formed part of our circulation and was legal tender at Rs.15. The gold value of the rupee was thus 16d. This was the rate at which rupees were converted into British money. And exchange rose and fell, according to the supply of and the demand for foreign remittances within the specie points determined by the cost of transportation of gold.

Specie Points and Gold Imports and Exports

In 1927 the sovereign ceased to be legal tender, but the rupee was made convertible into gold bullion at the rate of 1s. 6d. per rupee. This was our new par. It cannot be called 'Mint Par', because the rupee is a silver coin; further, the sovereign had been demonetised also in England. But our 18d. par was a real good par so long as we obtained gold without difficulty in exchange for rupees at that rate.

The cost of transportation of gold between India and England being equal to ¼d. per rupee, the new specie points were 18¼d. and 17¾d.

Exchange in London is quoted in pence per rupee. If we get more than 18d. per rupee, exchange is favourable to us and unfavourable to England; less than 18d. means a rate favourable to England and unfavourable to India.

If bills on London (which are drawn in English money) are scarce in India, their price will rise. In other words, we shall get less pence per rupee, and the rate of exchange will fall.

If the supply of bills on London exceeds the demand, the bills will become cheaper, or we shall get more pence per rupee.

In London, on the other hand, bills on India would be said to be dear or cheap according as more or less pence, respectively, had to be paid for a rupee.

A rise of exchange on India in London means a rise in the price of Indian bills, reckoned in English money. A rise of exchange on London in India, on the other hand, means that English bills have become cheaper.

In Italy exchange on London is quoted in Lire per £. A rise of exchange on London would therefore indicate a scarcity of bills on London, and a fall in the value of Italian money in terms of English money. Exchange on London would be said to improve when the rate of exchange fell, *i.e.*, a smaller quantity of Italian money was given in exchange for a pound.

Having understood what a rise or fall of exchange means, let us consider the effect on the rate of exchange of an unfavourable balance of trade.

When imports into India exceed exports, the demand for bills on London would be greater than the supply. The price of these bills will rise, or the rate of exchange will fall.

But, in normal circumstances, it cannot fall below 17¾d. per rupee. Supposing the rate of exchange was less than this, Indian importers will buy gold and send it to their British creditors. They lose only ¼d. per rupee by sending gold. They will lose more if they bought bills, for, by assumption, bills on London are being sold at rates more unfavourable to importers than 17¾d. If bills were sold at 17¾d. it would be a matter of indifference to importers whether they sent gold or bills. Some gold would begin to flow out even at 17¾d. This rate is therefore known as the gold export point for India.

Similarly a British debtor in London would not buy a bill on India at a rate more unfavourable to him than 18¼d. If the price is just 18¼d. per rupee, he may send a bill or gold. Some gold will leave England even at 18¼d., and this rate is known as the gold import point for India.

Between 1927 and September 21, 1931, the rupee exchange was maintained within the gold points.

Gold Parity and Purchasing Power Parity

Does gold parity signify purchasing power parity?

It must have that meaning if gold prices, or the purchasing power of gold in terms of goods and services, is everywhere the same.

It is argued that if gold prices in India are higher than gold prices in England, imports of goods into India will tend to increase and exports to decrease. Gold will tend to flow out and our prices will fall. If the gold goes to England, prices there may presumably rise. A tendency towards equality of prices in this sense may be said to always exist, assuming that gold is free to flow in and out.

In such a case, always assuming that the movement of gold corrects the disequilibrium between international prices, gold prices every where will be equal. If now a sovereign is equal to 4·866 dollars, the purchasing power of a sovereign in terms of goods which enter into international trade will be equal to the purchasing power of 4·866 dollars in the United States in terms of the same goods.

But, as a matter of fact, the internal purchasing power of money is reckoned in terms of all kinds of goods and services, all of which do not enter into international trade. Secondly, the movement of gold from one country to another is never so rapid nor so adequate as to bring about the necessary adjustments in international price levels. Making allowance for cost of transportation, the price of gold is everywhere the same, but even under the gold standard the purchasing power of gold in terms of goods and services is different in different countries. As Dr. Joseph Gruntzel says: "The purchasing power of a gram of gold in the United States was always less than in England and in England less than in Germany, and that permanently" (*Geldwert und Wechselkurs*, p. 29).

If the purchasing power of gold in terms of goods and services is greater in India than in England, then even if exchange is steadily maintained at 18d. gold, the purchasing power of a rupee in terms of goods and services in India will be greater than that of 18d. gold in England. As a matter of fact those who have lived in India and England know that one rupee goes, further in buying goods and procuring services in India than 18d. in England.

Under the gold standard, then, a rate of exchange determined by the relation between the fine gold contents of two standard coins (they may or may not be in circulation) does not express any equality between the purchasing power of the two units of currency. The rate of exchange is not based on any comparison between the purchasing power of the respective coins; it is simply determined by the relation of the fine gold contents of the one coin to the fine gold contents of the other coin.

Gold parity is not purchasing power parity.

Purchasing Power Parity when the Gold Standard Breaks down

As we have seen, when the gold standard is functioning, the value of one currency in terms of another can be easily known (assuming that the two countries concerned are on the gold standard). Suppose both countries abandon the gold standard. How will the rate of exchange between them be fixed?

If inflation takes place in both the countries, say A and B, and the amount of inflation is greater in A than in B, the value of A's money in terms of B's money will fall. Thus, it is argued, a comparison of the degree of inflation in the two countries will give us the new rate of exchange.

For example, if both England and India abandon the gold standard and resort to inflation, and if prices quadruple in India and only double in England, the new rate of exchange will be half of the old (9d. instead of 18d.).

When the rate of exchange falls to 9d. the internal and the external purchasing power of money will be equal. So long as they are not equal, exports from one country and imports into the other will be stimulated, which will tend to restore equilibrium.

For example, if the rate of exchange is one shilling, a stimulus will be given to imports of goods into India, while our exports will be discouraged. The consequent increase in the demand for English money will raise its price, or lower the rate of exchange.

Under the assumed conditions a stimulus will be given to imports because the external purchasing power of money is greater than the internal purchasing power in the ratio of 10:9. English money being comparatively cheap, it will be profitable to buy English goods.

If, on the other hand, the rupee is under-valued, our imports will be penalised and exports subsidized. Equilibrium will be restored by an increase in the demand for rupees and a rise in the exchange value of the rupee in terms of English money.

Such is the world-famous and much-discussed theory of purchasing power parity put forward by Prof. Gustav Cassel many years ago, to explain rates of exchange between depreciated paper currencies in the post-War period of currency confusion.

Assumptions

The theory is true if we assume: (1) that the rate of exchange is not influenced by such factors as the speculative buying or selling of currencies, which has not much to do with commodity prices, nor with movement of funds from one country to another due to banking requirements or Government transactions, which are again unrelated to changes in commodity prices; (2) that the movement of all goods, which enter into the calculation of purchasing power parities, from one country to another is absolutely free, and not restricted by prohibitions or quotas; and (3) that we have a satisfactory method of calculating the index of purchasing power.

In real life these conditions are never realised.

Speculative buying or selling of a currency, owing to changes in political conditions or other causes, may raise or lower its price independently of changes in commodity prices. In India, Government remittances play the most important part in determining the rate of exchange. At a time when exchange is tending to fall, Government can bring about a rise by limiting their demand for remittance, or by actually appearing in the market as a seller of sterling. They can prevent exchange from rising by beginning to buy sterling heavily—the price of sterling will rise or exchange will tend to fall. A sudden increase in the demand of bankers for sterling will have the same effect. It cannot be argued that bankers' operations or Government exchange transactions are directly governed by changes in commodity prices.

Nor can we ignore restrictions on the movement of goods. In view of the difference between the internal and the external purchasing power of the yen, a stimulus may be given to Japanese exports. But the difference will remain uncorrected if quotas and prohibitions abroad limit imports from Japan.

Finally, index numbers of wholesale prices in different countries are useful only for comparing the general trend of prices in different countries. For exact calculations of purchasing power parities it will be necessary to construct them on a uniform basis. Further, if index numbers include commodities which do not give rise to exchange operations, purchasing power parities calculated with their aid will not coincide with actual rates of exchange, except by chance.

Incidentally it may be mentioned that in India we have three sets of index numbers, for Calcutta, Bombay, and Karachi. In January 1934, the Calcutta index stood at 90, Bombay 95 and Karachi 97. If the method of calculating the average were changed, a different figure in each case would be obtained. A change in weights will again alter the result. It would appear that our index numbers serve to roughly indicate changes in the purchasing power of money; they cannot be used for deducing exact exchange quotations.

The Rupee and the Australian Pound

The rise in the exchange value of the rupee during and after the war is explained by the rise in the price of silver and our favourable balances of trade. There was a sensational fall in exchange between February and December 1920, which was partly due to unfavourable trade conditions, and largely to the sensational fall in the price of silver. This explanation takes no account of purchasing power parities.

Do purchasing power parities furnish a satisfactory explanation of exchange fluctuations at the present time?

A peculiar feature of the existing situation is that while our exchange has fallen considerably in terms of gold, there is no inflation. The Calcutta index for April 1934 (89) was two points below the index for September 1931 (91).

The rupee is linked to sterling, but Australia has depreciated her currency 25 per cent below the sterling level. 18d. sterling (British) is equal to 22·5d. Australian.

Here are two countries India and Australia, both off gold. For about two years both exchanges have preserved a stable relation to sterling, India's rupee=18d. sterling, and Australia's £ 125=£ 100 sterling. Is the fact that the rupee is worth 25 per cent more in Australian currency than in sterling, deducible from index numbers of prices in India and Australia, *i.e.*, from the comparison of purchasing power of money in terms of goods in India and Australia?

There is as little evidence of any inflation in Australia as in India. Prices in Australia (annual average) fell from 131·3 in 1931 to 129·7 in 1932 and 129·5 in 1933. The movement of prices in the two countries has been in the same direction.

The lower value of Australian money should give a stimulus to exports from Australia. If obstacles to the development of Australian exports in the shape of high duties in countries whose currency is less depreciated did not exist, the increase in the demand for Australian goods abroad, would lead to a rise of prices in Australia, which would tend to reduce or altogether remove the difference between the internal purchasing power and the external purchasing power of Australian money.

But, at the present time, the movement of goods is not free. The effect of tariff barriers is to create national price levels in the case of even important food-stuffs and raw materials, which are in universal demand.

It has been pointed out above that if goods which are consumed locally are included in the calculation of purchasing power of money in different countries, purchasing power parities will not coincide with actual rates of exchange, except by chance. If now every country has its own national price of wheat, cotton, coal and other products, produced by national demand and supply plus tariffs, quotas and prohibitions, purchasing power parities cease to have any relation to rates of exchange.

To take an example, suppose the price of a given quantity of wheat is Rs. 13-5-4 in India and one £ in Australia, and that the rate of exchange between Australian and Indian money is 18d. per rupee. As wheat is the only commodity considered, the internal purchasing power of money in India must be equal to that of Australian money in Australia. If the price of wheat rose in India, while it remained unchanged in Australia, India would import wheat from Australia until the price of wheat in the two countries became equal.

If the price of wheat, owing to inflation, rose 50 per cent in India, and also 50 per cent in Australia, the internal purchasing power of money in India and Australia would be still equal, and the rate of exchange would be 18d. per rupee as before. The rate of exchange would be equal to purchasing power parity.

Let us next assume that Australia depreciates her currency so that a rupee is equal to 22·5d. If the price of wheat in Australia is £ 1 for the given quantity of wheat, it must fall in India, since the value of Australian money has fallen. At 22·5d. per rupee, the £ would be equal to Rs. 10-10-8. If the price is higher in India, it would be profitable to import wheat from Australia, and imports will continue until the Indian price fell to Rs. 10-10-8. When wheat actually begins to sell in India at Rs. 10-10-8, the purchasing power of money in India would be again equal to that in Australia. The exchange rate of 22·5d. would be equal to purchasing power parity.

But suppose we do not let Australian wheat come in, or subject imports to heavy duties. While the value of Australian money falls, we maintain our price at Rs. 13-5-4 as before.

It is evident that in such a case the rate of 22·5d. per rupee is not equal to purchasing power parity.

This is a simple example, but we may complicate it by reckoning purchasing power in terms of a number of commodities whose prices are controlled in the two countries and, further, goods and services for which the demand is purely local.

The connection between rates of exchange and purchasing power parities breaks down altogether. Another explanation of rates of exchange must be sought and this is in terms of depreciation of paper in relation to gold. The gold standard has broken down but gold is still the regulator of the exchanges.

Depreciation in terms of Gold

Our paper money is legally convertible into silver rupees. So long as no difficulty is felt in converting notes into silver rupees, 100 rupees in notes would be equal to 100 silver rupees.

Suppose the facilities offered for the conversion of notes into silver were much curtailed, so that in effect paper money became inconvertible. A discount on notes would immediately appear.

In the first quarter of 1918, notes practically became inconvertible and they depreciated, the discount on notes in different parts of the country varying from 5 to 20 per cent. The depreciation of notes in such circumstances is wholly due to inconvertibility; and the extent of depreciation depends on the credit of the issuing authority, and faith in the ultimate conversion of notes. If there is a serious loss of confidence, the discount on notes will be heavy.

Now suppose that all forms of token money are convertible by law into gold at a given rate. So long as this convertibility is maintained, the price of gold in terms of token money (paper or rupees) will remain unchanged. But as soon as token money ceases to be convertible by law into gold, it will depreciate—or the price of gold in terms of token money will rise.

The amount of depreciation would be shown by the rise in the price of gold and of currencies which are still linked to gold. This depreciation, it may be noted, is simply due to inconvertibility—it has directly nothing to do with commodity prices.

The dollar was quoted at 4·85 31|32 on September 17, and at 3·88 on September 24, 1931, which shows a loss of about 20 per cent in the gold value of the pound sterling. This loss of value measured the depreciation of the pound sterling in terms of gold, not in terms of commodities and services.

When a number of countries abandon the gold standard, the extent of depreciation in different countries is unequal. There are then different prices of gold in different countries at the same time. The price is highest where the depreciation is greatest.

Let us take two countries A and B which were on the gold standard, but have now abandoned it. In both A and B paper has depreciated in terms of gold, but let us assume that while in A 25 per cent more paper has to be given to buy an ounce of gold, in B the depreciation is twice as heavy. What will be the relation of the paper money of A to that of B?

If 125 paper pounds of Australia are equal to 100 sovereigns, while in New Zealand 150 paper pounds are required to buy 100 sovereigns, 100 paper pounds of Australia will buy 120 paper pounds of New Zealand.

Under paper standards, then, the rate of exchange will depend on the degree of depreciation of paper money of the two countries in terms of gold or currencies linked to gold. If, for example, the French franc has not depreciated in relation to gold, the cost of francs in Australian money will rise 25 per cent. The relation between the paper money of Australia and that of New Zealand may be determined by comparing the extent of the rise in the value of francs in the two countries.

This explanation ignores the levels of commodity prices and deduces rates of exchange from the degree of depreciation in terms of gold alone. Since gold has no fixed price under paper standards, causes which raise or depress the price of gold in terms of paper in any country would produce variations in its rate of exchange with other countries.

Gold still the Regulator

It would appear that even when the gold standard breaks down, the price of gold still regulates the rates of exchange. When the gold standard is functioning, the Mint Price of gold in different countries gives the rate of exchange between them. When the gold standard ceases to function, the price of gold in terms of paper varies from day to day and differently in different countries. The rates of exchange between gold standard and paper standard countries on the one hand, and between different paper standard countries on the other, must, therefore, also vary, the variations being determined by the rise or fall in the price of gold in each country.

When allowance has been made for the differences in the rates of exchange, the price of gold in different countries will be the same. For example, the price of gold may appear to be lower in terms of Australian money, if Australian money has depreciated less in terms of gold than, say, the money of New Zealand. But since the cost of Australian money in terms of the money of New Zealand will rise, the price of gold in the two countries, after allowing for the rise in the price of Australian money, will be the same.

If it is not the same, it will be profitable to sell gold where it fetches a higher price.

It should not be forgotten that even under paper standards gold is everywhere in demand. No country refuses to import gold. In the case of other goods, duties may be levied in the interests of national industry. In the case of gold, the question of 'protection' does not arise. Export of gold may be prohibited or subjected to control in certain cases, but the amount of gold which is free to move is considerable. And this gold will go where it commands the highest price.

The effect of currency instability in increasing the demand for gold is thus described in the *World Economic Survey for 1932-33:* "In a perfectly free economy, the lessened demand for gold might have been expected to lower its value and cause prices to rise. But on the contrary, the demand for gold did not lessen. The increasing gold production of the world, supplemented by large amounts released from hoards in India and China was readily absorbed at higher prices in terms of the managed currencies and in terms of commodities. The gold standard countries, and many countries which had abandoned that standard, continued to buy gold as their resources permitted, and, in addition, a large demand for private hoarding sprang up in Europe and North America as currency instability became more wide-spread" (p. 42).

So long as gold is being bought and sold, its price will tend to be equal over the whole market comprising its buyers and sellers. The abandonment of the gold standard has brought no change in this respect.

Purchasing power in terms of gold is a more definite conception than purchasing power in terms of goods and services in general. It will be admitted that the concept of the general level of prices, though useful for many purposes, is vague. In fact there is no such thing as a general level of prices. The idea of purchasing power of money, based on the movement of an average constructed in a particular manner, is a fiction. The purchasing power of money is different in different provinces of India and it varies in different parts of the same province.

The price of gold, on the other hand, has a perfectly definite meaning. And differences in the price of gold in different parts of the world do not exceed the cost of transportation.

Secondly, it is conceivable that when a country is off the gold standard, the price of gold may rise when those of other goods and services are stationary, or even falling. The price of gold is subject to peculiar influences of its own. If, then, the purchasing power of paper money in terms of gold falls (even when the purchasing power of paper money in terms of goods and services may be rising), the rate of exchange will at once show the effect of the rise in the price of gold—more paper money will have to be given for purchasing foreign currencies linked to gold.

It is difficult to see why a rise in the price of gold must coincide with a rise in the prices of commodities and services. The forces of demand and supply determine the prices of goods and services. Their action may lower the prices of goods and services reckoned in paper money, while the effect of the forces of demand and supply is to raise the price of gold in terms of the same paper.

The Balance of Payments

If we are forced off gold, while England is maintaining the gold standard, the price of gold or gold bills will be determined by our balance of payments and be influenced by all factors which affect the balance of payments.

The depreciation of our paper money will be heavy if exports of goods from India continue to decline while imports, both visible and invisible, are increasing. If we are successful in raising loans abroad to pay off our creditors, the rate of exchange will improve. The raising of foreign loans amounts to export of securities.

The movement of funds by bankers and speculative dealings in foreign currencies, as we have seen, affect the rate of exchange by influencing the balance of payments.

Apart from the balance of payments, a rise or fall in our credit would produce changes in the rate of exchange. Political disorder and a chaotic state of national finances would raise the premium on gold and the price of gold bills.

The Role of Prices

Under the gold standard and a fixed mint par commodity prices play a passive monetary role. They do not determine the rate of exchange, but adjust themselves to the rate of exchange.

Similarly if the exchange value of the rupee is artificially fixed at 18d. gold and is maintained at that rate, there will be a tendency towards the adjustment of gold prices in India to gold prices in other countries at that rate. The adjustment, however, is never perfect and is hindered by economic friction in various forms, and chiefly by obstacles to the movement of goods in the shape of tariff barriers, quotas and prohibitions, which produce inequality in the purchasing power of money in terms of goods and services in different countries. The point which deserves emphasis is that so long as exchange is fixed, commodity prices are determined by the rate of exchange; they do not determine it. The result is the same when a country abandons the gold standard, but maintains the value of its paper currency with the help of an Exchange Equalisation Fund at a chosen level below gold. In effect this amounts to *de facto* devaluation of the currency.

Goods are imported or exported at certain prices. Variations in prices cause variations in exports and imports and thus affect the balance of trade and the balance of payments. Prices, thus, indirectly influence the rate of exchange.

This indirect connection between prices and exchange is not an argument in support of the theory of purchasing power parity. Whether a country, over a given period, will have a favourable or an unfavourable balance of payments depends on many factors, of which commodity prices are only one.

Commodity prices themselves are governed by production and demand. Production expands or contracts according to changes in cost of production or methods of production; demand increases with the growth of numbers and rise in the standard of living. In this sense there is no change of any economic significance, whether in the field of production, exchange, distribution or consumption of wealth which cannot be shown to be indirectly related to exchange. In explaining the rise or fall of foreign exchanges, however, attention has necessarily to be directed to phenomena and causes which have a direct bearing on the exchanges.

THE SILVER EXCHANGES

The theory of purchasing power parity has been applied to exchange between gold-using and silver-using countries. In a popular text-book of economics we read:

"Putting the matter generally, therefore, we say that the world price of silver in terms of gold tends to measure the purchasing power parity between the two metals, and the rate of exchange between a gold standard country and a silver standard country maintaining free mintage of silver will tend to be determined by that purchasing power parity" (*Elements of Economics* by S. E. Thomas, 6th edition, p. 542).

The rate of exchange between a gold standard country and a silver standard country is determined by the value as bullion of the silver coins of the silver standard country in terms of gold, or the value as bullion of the gold coins of the gold standard country in terms of silver. Whenever the market value of silver in terms of gold changes, the rate of exchange between the two countries must change. And silver may rise or fall in terms of gold (or gold may appreciate or depreciate in terms of silver) owing to changes directly affecting silver or gold, which are unconnected with commodity prices.

Suppose the monetary demand for gold increases while its production is stationary, or increasing at a comparatively slow rate. If at the same time the monetary demand for silver decreases on account of its demonetization by several large countries, the price of silver in terms of gold will fall, and the rate of exchange between a gold standard country and a silver standard country will fall immediately, and in a measure more or less exactly corresponding to the fall in the gold price of silver. This is the explanation of the fall in our rate of exchange between 1873 and 1892.

Again, if the price of silver rose on account of a serious shortage in production, the price of silver in terms of gold would rise. Such a rise in the price of silver took place in 1917—1920. Our token rupee became a full value coin and in spite of attempts to control exchange, the gold value of the rupee rose.

The point which deserves emphasis is that the rate of exchange between a gold standard country and a silver standard country has nothing to do with the relation of commodity prices in the two countries. It just depends on the market-value of the one metal in terms of the other.

The adjustment of prices to the rate of exchange comes later. It does not produce the rate of exchange, it is produced by the rate of exchange. Price adjustment is an effect, not a cause. Further, as we have already seen, this adjustment takes place very slowly, and on account of various obstacles to the exchange of goods, imperfectly.

The rate of exchange between a silver standard country and a gold standard country, found by comparing the purchasing power, in terms of goods and services of a given amount of silver in the silver standard country with that of gold of corresponding value in the gold standard country, will not coincide, except by chance, with the actual rate determined by the market value as bullion of the silver coins in terms of gold.

II

The Ratio Controversy

In the light of the foregoing discussion it may be interesting to re-examine the official case for the 18d. gold rate as argued by Sir Basil Blackett in the Indian Legislative Assembly in introducing the Currency Bill providing for the fixation of the gold value of the rupee at that rate. The ratio controversy possesses more than academic interest. At the present time the gold value of the rupee is something less than one shilling. Sooner or later the question of stabilisation will be again discussed. The question is thus of practical interest; it also involves some considerations of theory which deserve our attention.

The Finance Member advanced 11 arguments in support of the 18d. gold rate, which are reproduced below:

(1) The Silver rupee has no natural value other than the value of the silver bullion which it contains. Any other value than this for the silver rupee must be artificial.

(2) No one ratio for the rupee can possibly be permanently more advantageous for India than another. The question is not and never can be whether one particular ratio, say, 1s. 6d., is permanently more advantageous for India than some other ratio, say 1s. 4d. or 2s.

(3) All arguments based on the belief that the fixation of one particular ratio is definitely and permanently advantageous or disadvantageous to this or that interest are entirely irrelevant.

(4) A rising rate of exchange tends temporarily to assist imports and discourage exports, but this tendency is often counteracted, in whole or in part, by movement in world prices, as happened in the case of India from 1922 to 1925.

(5) A falling rate of exchange has the opposite tendency. But this again is often counteracted by external causes affecting the levell of prices.

(6) A fluctuating rate of exchange restricts the volume of trade and commerce and subjects both the producer and the consumer to losses without necessarily profiting the middleman who is often unwillingly made a speculator when he would prefer to do safe business.

(7) A stable exchange is what everyone wants and is to everybody's interests.

(8) In considering the fixing of the ratio at the present time, the first question must be "Is the time ripe for fixing the ratio"? The Currency Commission are unanimous in saying that it is.

(9) The only other relevant question is: "At, what ratio can stability of exchange be most easily and quickly secured"? The Commission are unanimous on this point also.

(10) The Commission are unanimous in saying that if prices have adjusted themselves in a preponderant degree to the ratio of 1s. 6d., it is in the interests of India that the ratio should be fixed at 1s. 6d.

(11) If it is accepted that the time is ripe for stablishing the rupee, the only point open to argument is whether prices have adjusted themselves in a preponderant degree to the 1s. 6d. ratio. This is a question of fact to be examined as such.

We may accept points (1), (6) and (7) without discussion. The gold value conferred on the rupee was wholly artificial, and, other things being equal, a stable exchange is better than an unstable exchange.

Sir Basil Blackett's explanation of points (2) and (3) is so interesting as to deserve reproduction .

"Nothing is gained by the Indian exporter or any one else if he receives in payment for what he sells a larger number of rupees of less value instead of a smaller number of rupees of greater value, if the gold or commodity value of what he receives remains unaltered. This is exactly what happens, as the following analysis will show:

A sells produce with a world market or destined for export for 1,333 rupees with exchange at 1s. 6d. for which, if exchange were 1s. 4d., he would get Rs. 1,500. The contention is that he loses 167 rupees owing to exchange being at 1s. 6d.

But it is agreed by all that under a gold standard the only thing that matters is the gold value of the money which a man gets for what he sells and pays out for what he buys. It is important to remember that though for convenience we talk of stabilising at 1s. 6d. what we really mean to do is to fix the gold value of the rupee at 8·4751 grains per rupee. The habit of talking of the rupee in relation to its sterling value is responsible for more than one fallacy in the Currency League's propaganda. The theory of a gold standard is that all money transactions take place either in gold or in legal tender notes or coins with a fixed gold value, and all prices are gold prices. Now, with the rupee at 1s. 6d., the rupee has a value equal to 8½ grains of gold. With the rupee at 1s. 4d., the rupee has a value of 7½ grains of gold. I ignore the decimal points for convenience. Now our friend A at present with the rupee at 1s. 6d., receives 1,333 rupees, each worth 8½ grains of gold. With the rupee at 1s. 4d., he receives 1,500 rupees each worth 7½ grains of gold. A simple sum in multiplication will show that in each case he receives rupees worth exactly the same amount in gold, *viz.*, approximately 11,300 grains of gold. If A desires to spend the whole of his rupees in buying gold, he gets exactly the same amount of gold whatever the exchange rate, since all values under a gold standard are gold values, determined, that is, by the value of gold, the rupees he receives in either case give him exactly the same power of purchasing commodities whatever the commodity he desires to purchase. (An Honourable Member: "Question"). It is easy enough to question arguments but it is difficult to question facts."

The Honourable Member who interrupted the Finance Member was evidently not satisfied with the explanation. Nor would any student of economics. The 'fact' mentioned by the Finance Member cannot be questioned. The gold value of 1500 rupees, when exchange is 16d. gold, is equal to the gold value of 1,333 rupees when exchange is 18d. gold. In both cases the rupees received by the cultivator are worth approximately 11,300 grains of gold. If no further questions are asked, the cultivator is neither a gainer nor a loser by the fixation of exchange at the higher or the lower figure.

But when the cultivator receives 1500 rupees (instead of 1,333 rupees) in exchange for his produce sold at 16d. gold, does he say to himself "The extra 167 rupees mean nothing to me, for the gold value of Rs. 1,500 at 16d. is just equal to that of Rs. 1,333 at 18d."? Is the cultivator in the village interested in the gold value of the rupee?"

The extent to which the cultivator is a consumer of imported goods is so small as to be negligible. He consumes kerosine oil and, in some parts of the country, a little foreign salt. For the most part he dresses in Khaddar, the product of his village hand-loom. When he pays an instalment of debt to the mahajan or the co-operative credit society, again, he is concerned with the number of rupees, not their gold value.

The gold value of the rupee has little to do with the cost of production of crops. The main elements of cost, as we have seen, are Government dues and bullock labour. Bullocks are a home-grown commodity, whose price is reckoned in rupees. Government dues, similarly, are paid in rupees, which is also true of charges when paid in cash, for the winnowing or harvesting of crops. Finally the cultivator's implements are, in most cases, indigenous, not foreign.

It would appear that the cultivator is not concerned with the gold value of the rupee. What he wants is a sufficient number of rupees to meet his charges. If now he obtains in exchange for his produce Rs. 1,500 instead of Rs. 1,333, he is a clear gainer to the extent of Rs. 167. After paying Government dues and meeting other charges in connection with the raising of crops the cultivator would be left with more money in his pocket for his personal expenses.

The cultivator would certainly get the same amount of gold for his rupees, whatever the rate of exchange was, but it is emphatically not true that "all values under a gold standard are gold values". Under a gold standard all values are not determined by the value of gold—only such values are determined by the value of gold as have some connection with exports and imports. We have already seen that gold is different from other commodities. Owing to its great value in small bulk the cost of transportation of gold is small and under the influence of a world-wide demand, it moves quickly from one country to another. Other commodities move with more difficulty. But in the present case we are concerned with commodities which do not move at all. Our plough-bullocks do not enter into international trade—there is no competition between them and British plough-bullocks. Our village menials, carpenters, shoe-makers, and agricultural labourers do not enter into international trade either. It may be said that water-rates and the land revenue have a gold value in the sense that if the rate of exchange fell, the burden of the 'Home Charges' would increase, and heavier taxation would have to be imposed all round. But, conceivably, the situation may be met by economies in Government expenditure; conceivably more revenue may be got out of other sections of the population and the cultivator left alone.

The view that the level of exchange is a matter of indifference to the cultivator, since all values under a gold standard are gold values, is a deduction from the theory of purchasing power parity, but it is a deduction made blindly and in ignorance of the facts.

No one with any experience of Indian village life, or of the conditions under which the cultivator lives and works, would seriously maintain, as Sir Basil Blackett did, that more rupees, which a lower rate of exchange would give to the cultivator, would mean nothing to the cultivator since their gold value would be the same as that of a smaller sum at a higher gold rate.

We may now consider points 4 and 5 according to which the artificial exchange stimulus to exports or imports is counteracted by 'movements in world prices'. It would be simpler and more to the point to consider adjustments in India to a rising or falling exchange.

If exchange is rising, it becomes cheaper to pay for imported goods, and imports increase, which may injure home industries. But in the long run, home manufacturers will increase their power of competition by reducing costs of production and introducing improvements in organisation. The weaker businesses will be eliminated; but those which survive will offer effective competition to imports. In the long run, then, when exchange becomes stable, the stimulus to imports ceases to operate.

In the beginning a rising exchange may restrict exports, but if home producers of food-stuffs and raw materials reduce their costs of production, the handicap imposed upon them will be temporary.

A falling exchange would restrict imports by making them dearer. The home manufacturer is benefited thereby, for he can charge higher prices for his goods, or undersell his foreign rivals. But this advantage will disappear when his wages and other elements of cost rise. Similarly, the exporter makes a gain when exchange is falling, for he receives a greater number of rupees for the same amount of produce exported. But in the long run his costs of production will rise. So long as the costs of production do not rise, the exporter makes a gain, but at the expense of other factors of production. Giving evidence on this point before the Rowler Committee on Indian Currency (1898) Dr. Marshall[1] insisted that it was incorrect to say that a falling exchange gave a bounty to employers and that any stimulus to exports relatively to imports which was not accompanied by lending to foreign countries, or returning loans, must

[1] "Now if any one says that the export trade of a country is conterminous with the under-takers of business enterprise, who are generally employers, and that anything that benefits the employers is a bounty on the export industry, then the proposition may be conceded. But, as I hold that the creditors who finance an industry that produces for export have some share in the export trade, and that the employees who make the thing for export have a very large share—quite as large a share as the undertaker—holding that I do not admit the proposition. If the statement is that a depreciating currency gives a bounty to the employer who is producing for export, I admit it; only, I add, the bounty is just the same, and at the expense of just the same people, as that which he would get from a depreciating currency if he were producing for his home market, and not for export."

necessarily lead to an equal reduction of exports relatively to imports.

When these adjustments are complete, and prices are stabilised at the new gold value of the currency "there is" as Sir Basil Blackett said, "and can be neither loss nor gain to the producer or the exporter or any one else.".

When the gold value of our rupee rises, rupee prices will adjust themselves to world gold prices by falling, if the world gold prices are stable. If the gold value of the rupee is falling, the adjustment will take place through a rise of rupee prices, world gold prices remaining stable.

The Finance Member did not doubt that rupee prices had adusted themselves to the 18d. gold rate. If, under such conditions, there was a return to a lower rate, say 16d. adjustment would mean a rise of rupee prices by 12½ per cent, a rise in the cost of living by the same amount, and a reduction in real wages by 11 per cent. "Does the House want to reduce by 11 per cent the real wages of all wage earners, agricultural and industrial", asked Sir Basil Blackett, "of all clerks and shop-hands in private employ, of postal employees, railway employees, to reduce the value of every fixed income by 11 per cent?" The answer of the House was 'No'. The 18d. gold rate was duly placed on the Statute Book. Sir Basil Blackett himself looked forward to the future with hope and confidence[2].

[2] "And what does the admission, that prices have adjusted themselves in a preponderant degree, mean? It means that there is no more reason to-day for disturbing the 1s. 6d. ratio than there was for disturbing the 1s. 4d. ratio in, say, 1907. It means that we have come to the end of a long struggle to restore equilibrium to currency and exchange and prices after the war upheaval. It means that the supply of currency has been brought into harmony with the demand at the existing level of prices and internal prices into harmony with each other and with world prices. It means that businessmen and traders of all kinds can go ahead, once the last remains of uncertainty are removed by placing 1s. 6d. on the Statute Book with confidence and hope to expand their activities, to launch out into new and promising ventures, without any fear of seeing all their bright hopes upset by the vagaries of exchange, and with a prospect of reasonably stable prices also, knowing as they do that strong influences are at work to keep world prices steady at about the present level, they can look forward to normal conditions generally and expanding opportunities in every direction."

The influences which were expected to keep world prices steady ceased to work almost immediately and influences which were to lower prices began to make themselves felt. Businessmen and traders who were bidden by Sir Basil Blackett to look forward to normal conditions generally and expanding opportunities in every direction were soon to be overwhelmed by a crisis of extraordinary intensity and still more extraordinary persistence. It would seem that in spite of the *de facto* 18d. gold rate, Sir Charles Addis and Calcutta exchange bankers who supported him were right after all in thinking that it was open to question whether gold prices and conditions generally the world over had sufficiently settled down in 1927 to justify the stabilisation of rupee exchange[3].

The course of wholesale prices in India and certain other countries between 1922 and 1931 is shown by the table given below:

[3] In a pamphlet entitled "Indian Currency Reform", published in 1926 I pointed out that the fall which had occurred in rupee prices from January to September 1925 was in sympathy with the fall in English and European gold prices and summarised my conclusions on the question of the 18d. gold rate thus:

"It would thus seem that, on the basis of the information that is available, it is impossible to dogmatise, as the Currency Commission have done, about the adjustment of Indian prices to the rate of exchange; and if the proposal to stabilise the rate of exchange at 1s. 6d. gold rests mainly on this supposed adjustment, it obviously rests on a very weak foundation" (p. 63).

The general conclusion was stated thus:

"No sensible man in India would insist that the Government should immediately proceed to inflate the currency with the definite object of raising prices in the country above the level of world prices, so as to reduce the exchange value of the rupee to 1s. 4d. But it is the greatest mistake to think that because 1s. 6d. is the prevailing rate, little difficulty will be experienced in maintaining exchange at that rate in the future. Let us gain some more experience of the 1s. 6d. exchange before permanently fixing the exchange value of the rupee at this rate.

"What I have said in the preceding Chapters must not be interpreted as an argument in favour of the immediate stabilization of exchange at 1s. 4d.; *but it is a strong argument for waiting*" (*italics of 1926*, p. 83).

Wholesale Prices (Annual averages)

	India	United Kingdom	Holland	U. S. A.
Pre-war	100(*a*)	100(*b*)	100(*c*)	70(*d*)
1922	176	159	160	97
1923	172	159	151	101
1924	173	166	156	98
1925	159	159	155	104
1926	148	148	145	100
1927	148	141	148	95
1928	145	140	149	97
1929	141	137	142	95
1930	116	120	117	86
1931	96	104	97	73

(*a*) Calcutta series, July 1914=100; (*b*) Board of Trade, 1913=100; (*c*) 1913=100; (*d*) Bureau of Labour, 1926=100.

(Bombay Labour Gazette for March 1934)

In all four countries prices moved down. In India they fell from 148 in 1926 to 116 in 1930. If the average for 1926 is taken as 100, the fall of prices in 1930 amounted to 22 per cent in India, 19 per cent in the United Kingdom, also 19 per cent in Holland and 14 per cent in the United States. The fall continued in 1931. The heavier fall in our prices as compared with those of the other countries is explained by the greater extent of the fall in the case of raw materials and food-stuffs than in that of manufactured goods. This is shown by the following statement:

Calcutta Index Numbers. Prices in July 1914=100

	December, 1930	August, 1931
Cereals ..	84	76
Pulses ..	96	96
Sugar ..	128	131
Tea ..	115	65
Other food articles ..	116	108
Oil-seeds ..	99	79
Oil mustard ..	85	65
Jute raw ..	45	46
Jute manufactures ..	74	68
Cotton raw ..	69	71
Cotton manufactures ..	125	118
Other-textiles (wool and silk) ..	70	63
Hides and skins ..	79	62
Metals ..	109	106
Other raw and manufactured articles ..	107	98
Building materials (teak wood) ..	154	146
All commodities ..	100	92

At the end of December, 1930 raw cotton had fallen to 69, but cotton manufactures were still 25 per cent above the pre-War level; raw jute had fallen to 45 but jute manufactures to a smaller extent—74; metals were 9 per cent above the pre-War average.

The evidence of index numbers shows that our prices fell with world gold prices between 1926 and 1930. And throughout this period 18*d.* gold was the *de facto* and the *de jure* rate.

In September 1931 we went off the gold standard. The course of prices in India and certain other countries between September 1931 and December 1933 is shown by the following Table.

Wholesale Prices (Index Numbers)

	Calcutta	United Kingdom	France	Holland	Italy	Germany
1913 ..	100 (a)	100	100 (a)	100	100	100
1921 ..						
September	91	99	89 (437)	91	87 (319)	109
December	98	106	84 (413)	85	87 (319)	104
1932 ..						
March ..	94	105	87 (427)	82	86 (315)	100
June ..	86	98	83 (408)	78	81 (297)	96
September	91	102	81 (397)	76	82 (300)	95
December	88	101	79 (390)	76	81 (296)	92
1933 ..						
March ..	82	98	78 (385)	72	77 (281)	91
June ..	89	102	80 (396)	73	77 (281)	93
September	88	103	78 (386)	75	75 (276)	95
December	89	103	79 (389)	77	75 (275)	96

(a) July 1914=100. (*The Statist*).

British prices are sterling prices. Sterling having depreciated in terms of gold, our prices ceased to be gold prices when we linked the rupee to sterling. The other four countries have throughout this period maintained the link with gold. But while Holland and Germany maintained the value of their currency at the level of pre-war parity, there was devaluation in Italy and France. The new relation of paper francs to the gold franc is 4·92 paper francs to 1 gold franc and in Italy 3·66 paper lire are equal to 1 gold lira. The index numbers of prices in devalued currency in France and Italy are given in brackets under each country. By dividing the French index numbers by 4·92 and the Italian series by 3·66 we obtain gold index numbers for these countries comparable with the pre-war average, 100.

A comparison of our index numbers with those of France yields a remarkable result. Our prices rose from 91 in September, 1931 to 98 in December of the same year, while during this short period French prices fell. As we know already, the rise of our prices was due to the expansion of the currency. But after rising to 98 in December 1931 our prices fell steadily till June 1932. They rose in the next quarter, fell to 88 in December 1932, and were fairly steady in 1933 around 88. The French index number rose to 87 in March 1932, fell to 79 in December of that year and was fairly steady around 79 in 1933.

If one did not definitely know that India abandoned the gold standard in September 1931, the evidence of these index numbers would lead one to think that the rupee, throughout this period was linked to the gold franc.

We have seen that before September 1931 our gold prices were falling in sympathy with world gold prices, exchange being 18d. gold. And under the paper standard, in spite of the fall in the gold value of the rupee, paper prices are still behaving like gold prices. Our going off the gold standard has introduced no change in the movement of prices.

As the rupee is linked to sterling, the depreciation of the rupee in terms of gold may be measured by the gold exchange index of sterling. This is given below:

Gold Exchange Index, showing the Fall in the Gold Value of Sterling

Month	1931	1932	1933	1934
January	.. ..	70·70	69·12	65·53
February	.. ..	70·16	70·22	62·76
March	.. ..	74·58	70·39	62·39
April	.. ..	77·11	70·27	..
May	.. ..	75·35	69·04	..
June	.. ..	74·94	69·45	..
July	.. ..	73·08	68·49	..
August	.. 100·15	71·55	67·32	..
September	.. *	71·54	64·54	..
October	.. 79·74	69·99	64·45	..
November	.. 76·76	67·50	65·89	..
December	.. 69·52	67·54	67·28	..

*September 1—19, 100·18; September 21 (gold standard suspended)—30,82·63 (*The Statist,* April 7, 1934).

Roughly the rupee has lost a little more than 30 per cent of its gold value. Rupees prices under the gold standard were in equilibrium with world gold prices, and rupee prices, when the rupee has lost 30 per cent of its gold value, or more, are still in equilibrium with gold prices.

The situation is puzzling. Let us try to understand it with the help of the theory of purchasing power parity.

Before we abandoned the gold standard Rs. 13-5-4 were equal to one pound (gold) which was equal to 124·21 francs. Thus one rupee was equal to 9 1/8 francs. As the gold value of the rupee was steadily maintained at 18d. gold, according to the theory of purchasing power parity, the purchasing power in terms of goods and services of one rupee was equal to that of 9 1/8 francs.

Then we go off the gold standard, and the gold value of the rupee is reduced to about 6 francs. Prices in India and France again being in equilibrium, as shown by the movement of index numbers of prices in the two countries, the purchasing power in terms of goods and services of one rupee in India is now equal to that of about 6 francs.

How can that be true?

If rupee prices had become adjusted to gold prices under the 18d. gold rate, when the rupee depreciated in terms of gold, rupee prices should have risen to an extent corresponding to the fall in the gold value of the rupee. A fall in the gold value of the rupee of 33 1/3 per cent should have produced a rise of 55 per cent in paper prices in India. But not only have our prices not risen, but they have fallen with gold prices.

We are driven to the conclusion, and it is a conclusion from which there is no escape, that at 18d. gold our rupee was much over-valued. It was over-valued not only immediately before the abandonment of the gold standard, but also in 1927 when it was claimed that the *de facto* rate, which was stable, was an incontestable proof that prices in India had adjusted themselves to world gold prices.

The meaning of over-valuation may be explained by an example. When, before 21st September 1931 a cultivator sold goods worth 12,421 francs in France, he earned Rs.1,333. With this sum he had to cover all his costs of production (including wages of labour and profits of enterprise). Now suppose methods of agriculture undergo a revolution in the West, so that costs of production there fall heavily. The same products may be offered to France by one of our foreign competitors at a cheaper rate—or for less than 12,421 francs. If our costs of production do not fall, and if we do not lower the gold value of the rupee, we may lose the French market. For we want Rs.1,333 to cover our costs, and their equivalent in French money at 9 1/3 francs to the rupee is 12,421 francs. Exports from India would decline first slowly, and then rapidly, if costs proved inelastic.

In such circumstances the foreign market can be retained only by selling at a lower price in foreign money. That may wipe out the whole of the profits in rupees. If the cultivator in our example lowers his price to 10,000 francs, he would receive 1073 rupees at 9 1/8 francs to the rupee (18d. gold), or suffer a loss of approximately Rs. 260.

It should be clear that an over-valued rupee imposes the heaviest sacrifices on those who produce for export, particularly when, as in the case of the Indian peasant, the main items of expenditure possess little elasticity.

Now suppose we go off the gold standard and the gold value of the rupee falls. If one pound buys only 77·21 francs, and if prices in France do not change, 12,421 francs will give our cultivator Rs. 2,144, or Rs. 811 more than before. A fall of the price to 10,000 francs would still give him approximately Rs. 393 more than before.

Such is the present position. For produce of the gold value of 12,421 francs the Indian cultivator receives Rs. 2,144, or Rs. 811 more than the equivalent of 12,421 francs at 18d. gold (Rs. 1,333).

Similarly the British exporter will receive about £161 for goods sold in France at 77·21 francs to the pound, instead of £100 at the rate of 124·21 francs. Some of the gain may be reduced by the fall of prices in France, or a rise in cost of production in England (increased cost of raw material imported from gold standard countries). But the British exporter will be still substantially better off than before. His power of competition will increase, and British exports will begin to expand.

Such indeed has been the effect of the depreciation of sterling on British exports.

The course of sterling prices has generally been the same since September 1931 as that of gold prices. It is admitted that England's return to the gold standard in 1925 was a mistake. When the gold value of the pound rose, internal costs and prices failed to adjust themselves to world costs and prices. Writing on the subject of "Depreciation of the pound and movement of internal prices" in the

Wirtschaftsdienst for April 27, 1934, Dr. E. von Mickwitz says that already in 1926 there existed in many countries a considerable difference between world and internal prices, which increased in the following years. It was this difference which led to currency depreciation, which became a means of adjusting internal prices to the level of world market prices without deflation. Dr. E. von Mickwitz regards England as a classical example of this. England abandoned the gold standard apparently under the pressure of withdrawal of loans by foreign countries, but her real object in going off gold was to bring about the adjustment of her costs and prices to world costs and prices.

The stimulus to British exports through the depreciation of the pound is yet undiminished. Dr. Mickwitz divides the process of adjustment of paper to gold prices into three stages. In the first stage costs of production in depreciated paper rise in so far as it is necessary to import raw material from gold standard countries; other costs remain unaltered and there is a premium on exports from the paper standard country to gold standard countries. In the second stage internal prices begin to rise, though cost of living and wages do not. In the third or final stage wages also go up, and the export premium disappears.

Prices are slowly beginning to rise in England. In February 1934 the Board of Trade index number stood at 105. As compared with April 1933 English prices had risen 8 per cent in February 1934. Prices rose 5·5 per cent in Germany during the same period, and 5·5 per cent in France between April 1933 and January 1934. The rise of prices in England is largely in sympathy with that in gold prices. If there was a substantial rise in English prices while gold prices remained stable, there would be definite evidence that the process of adjustment in England had entered the second phase.

The British cost of living index number is still below the level of September 1931.

Cost of living Index Numbers for England (food, fuel and light, clothing, rent and miscellaneous):

	July 1914-100
September 1931	145
„ 1932	141
„ 1933	141
February 1934	141

The adjustment of British costs to the new external value of the pound has not yet entered the second stage. British exports are still enjoying an export premium, and they may continue to enjoy it for a long time.

The Case of India

In the final phase in England wages will rise. If prices go up while wages are stationary, the gain of the exporter is at the expense of the wage-earner. When all elements of cost are higher than before (including interest), the stimulus to export in the shape of currency depreciation will have exhausted itself.

The case of India presents a few peculiarities. As in the case of the United Kingdom our exports to gold standard countries are at present enjoying a premium. Our prices, as we have seen, have not risen. British exports are chiefly manufactured goods, and British costs of production are affected by the depreciation of the pound in so far as the raw material for British exporting industries has to be purchased from gold standard countries. Our exports consist of raw materials and food-stuffs whose cost of production is a rupee cost, which is not affected by the depreciation of the rupee in terms of gold. Then, as we have seen, hired labour is used to a very small extent in crop production in our country. Wages are a deduction from profits in British industries. In Indian agriculture, *wages are profits*. The rise of wages in England will be the cause of the disappearance of the export premium. But the rise of wages has no meaning in Indian agriculture. The danger to our export premium lies not in any rise of wages, but in a rise in the cost of bullock labour, or increase in Government dues. A rise of prices will somewhat increase the cost of upkeep of bullocks, but Government dues are already high and a further rise may be avoided, when prices rise, by readjustments in taxation, or economies in Government expenditure. The rate of interest can be controlled. The cultivator borrows from Co-operative Credit Societies and the money-lender, and in both cases regulation of the rate of interest directly and indirectly, is feasible. The net result is to show that our grower of primary products will enjoy the benefits if the export premium were much longer than the British manufacturer.

Sterling Exchange Standard

We are at present under the sterling exchange standard. Sterling is the basis of our monetary system, and the continuance of this basis has been provisionally assumed in the Reserve Bank Act. When the international monetary position becomes more clear and stable, the question of a permanent basis for our monetary system will have to be considered.

The Reserve Bank Act provides for the buying and selling of sterling by the Reserve Bank, at 18 $^{3}|_{16}$d. and 17 $^{49}|_{64}$d. per rupee respectively. Until a permanent basis for the Indian monetary system has been found the 18d. sterling rate will be maintained.

The rupee has no fixed gold value at present. But since the rupee is linked to sterling, when England returns to the gold standard, our sterling rate will automatically acquire a fixed gold value.

England's return to the old parity is impossible. Sooner or later the British pound will be devalued. If we may assume that the British pound is established at a rate, say, 35 per cent below the old parity, the extent of devaluation of the rupee in terms of gold will be exactly the same.

The meaning of 35 per cent devaluation of the £ is that a pound will buy 60·1 Italian lire (parity 92·46), 80·7

French francs (parity 124·21), 7·87 Dutch florins (parity 12·107) and 13·28 German marks (parity 20·43). 35 per cent devaluation of the £ will mean a 35 per cent decrease in the purchasing power of the £ in terms of gold or currencies linked to gold. At the moment of writing (June 1934) the depreciation of the £ in relation to gold exceeds 35 per cent.

In choosing the rate of stabilisation for sterling England will be guided by two chief considerations: interest of her exporting industries, and the interests of London as the world's financial centre.

In returning to her pre-War gold parity in 1925 England sacrificed the interests of her exporting industries to considerations of financial prestige. This mistake is not likely to be repeated.

India is vitally interested in the devaluation of the £, but she will not be consulted when that momentous decision is taken. The gold value of the £ will be determined (quite naturally) in accordance with the requirements of British industry and finance.

It does not follow that devaluation which suits England must also suit India. Our financial responsibilities are not the same as those of England, and the conditions under which our exports compete in world markets are also different from those of British exports. The devaluation of the rupee is a separate problem.

In currency matters we have been slavishly following England during the past ten years, forgetting that the economic and financial position of India is not the same as that of England. In post-War years a policy of deflation was adopted in England with the deliberate object of raising the gold value of the £ to the pre-War parity. We followed the same policy, and succeeded in raising the gold value of the rupee 12½ per cent above the pre-War parity. England's excuse for desiring to return to the old parity was her position as the leading financial country of the world. No such considerations compelled us to raise the gold value of the rupee above its pre-War gold value. The whole of India protested against that mistaken policy, but the protest was ignored. Then, on September 21, 1931, England decided to go off the gold standard, and we waited till the same day to make the discovery that the rupee was over-valued at 18d. gold. The discovery would have been made much earlier if India had a currency policy of her own.

At present the Government of India again seem to be waiting for the decision of the Government of Britain. Till then the 18d. sterling rate is to be maintained.

This is no Indian currency policy. And, if it can be called a policy at all, it does not inspire confidence.

The interests of the two countries are different and it is desirable that India should have a currency policy suited to her needs.

Take Australia as an example. She suspended the gold standard in December 1929, and some time later depreciated her currency 25 per cent below sterling. We are not concerned with the exact amount of benefit that Australia has derived from this depreciation; the point is that Australia is free to adopt a currency policy which she conceives to be in her interests. Incidentally, even if Australia has failed to materially benefit by depreciating her currency below the sterling level, it would be difficult to show that she would have gained by maintaining its value 12½ per cent above the sterling level.

Adjustment of Costs and Prices

Eventually the rupee would be stabilised in relation to gold. In determining the ratio of stabilisation account must be taken of the new conditions of international competition in regard to agricultural products.

The situation has changed materially since the examination of the question by the Hilton Young Currency Commission. We have seen that the agricultural revolution has lowered the cost of cultivation in Western countries. We have also seen that costs of production in Indian agriculture are comparatively inelastic—it is impossible for India, under existing conditions, to adjust her costs to world costs by developing large-scale farming with power-driven machinery. In these circumstances it will be suicidal for us to stabilise the gold value of the rupee at a high level.

The level chosen by England may be too high for India, for our power of international competition is less than that of England.

It will be admitted that where costs in a country are higher than world costs, a lower rate of exchange is an important means of bringing about the necessary adjustment. The abandonment of the gold standard was such an attempt.

Is the adjustment complete?

If this adjustment had already been attained, the problem of exchange stabilisation would be simple—the rupee might be immediately stabilised at its present gold value. It has been argued that the revival of exports in 1933-34 and the maintenance of the 18d. sterling rate show that Indian costs and prices have become adjusted to world costs and prices.

One year is too short a period as a test of such adjustment. The Hilton Young Commission thought that the adjustment was complete in 1925 when, as subsequent events were to show, there had been no adjustment. And yet the statistics of foreign trade strengthened the assumption in favour of adjustment. It may be recalled that between 1920-21 and 1924-25, net imports of gold into India amounted to 143½ crores.

At the present time India is exporting gold. On an average we have exported 6 crores of gold per month since the abandonment of the gold standard.

The exports of gold, as we have seen in a preceding chapter, have materially helped in the maintenance of the 18d. sterling rate. It is impossible to doubt that but for gold exports exchange would have fallen. It is not at all improbable that if gold exports suddenly ceased, the maintenance of the 18d. sterling rate would become difficult.

The 18d. sterling rate has thus been produced by trade conditions *plus* gold exports, and more by gold exports than by trade conditions. The 18d. gold rate was described as a 'natural rate' by the Hilton Young Commission, when, as we know now, it was a rate artificially produced and artificially maintained. The 18d. sterling rate is still more artificial as it depends on gold exports. So long as gold exports continue, it is impossible to talk of adjustment of Indian costs and prices to world costs and prices at the 18d. sterling rate.

Wanted a lower rate

A lower rate of exchange would be beneficial from the point of view of the agricultural population. As has been explained above, the larger number of rupees obtained for produce sold abroad at a lower rate of exchange represents a real gain to the cultivator.

The 18d. sterling exchange has had a sufficiently long trial. It is associated with exports of gold on an unprecedented scale, and that is enough ground for condemning it.

We shall be forced to abandon the 18d. sterling rate—it is only a question of time. If we abandon it now, the stimulus to exports of merchandise may lessen the outflow of gold.

A strong case exists for depreciating the rupee below the sterling level up to 25 per cent. Stabilisation in relation to gold will come later.

A lower rate of exchange will not solve all the difficulties of the Indian cultivator, but it will give him relief to which he is justly entitled.

PART II

THE CRISIS

CHAPTER VI

THE CRISIS: INTRODUCTORY

The flow of trade and production is not uniform—it is subject to rise and fall of a cyclical nature.

The more important crises in the 19th century occurred in England in 1825, 1837, 1847, 1857, 1866, 1878, 1890, and 1900. Each year formed the middle point of a cycle, being preceded by a period of expansion leading to over-trading and followed by a period of contraction, more or less prolonged and more or less painful.

The years 1843 to 1910 saw eight major trade cycles in Germany: 1843-51, 1852-61, 1862-68, 1869-79, 1880-87, 1888-94, 1895-1902 and 1903-10. Each cycle began with a boom, which was followed by a depression lasting from 2 to 6 years.

A new upward cycle in world production and trade was in progress when the Great War broke out.

Production in an agricultural country also revolves in a cycle. But crises in a country where credit is less developed are chiefly Nature's crises.

When, for example, we examine the course of food-grain prices in India we are at once struck by the cyclical nature of the price fluctuations. Taking the retail prices of food-grains in 1873 as 100, we find that the index number rose from 81 in 1862 to 137 in 1866, and after falling to 116 in 1868, rose to 149 in 1869. The next great rise took place in 1878 when prices rose 74 per cent as compared with the base year. Between 1881 and 1884 prices were below 100, but they rose in 1892, and more sharply in 1896-97 and 1899-1900.

The explanation of this rise and fall of prices is simple. Prices rose on account of famine or scarcity, and they fell with the return of favourable seasons. It is only after 1905 that food prices rose to famine levels without famine in the country.

Crises in the West are of a different character. It is probably true that every crisis has its roots in physical, objective events, but the course of trade and production in the West is materially influenced by the supply of credit and various other factors which are concerned more with men's psychology than changes in the physical volume of production.

Credit and states of mind are so intimately connected with the expansion and contraction of business activity in the West that attempts have been made to evolve theories of crises which almost completely ignore physical factors. The psychological theory attributes crises to errors of pessimism and optimism. Monetary theories ascribe trade cycles mainly to defects in monetary, financial and banking organisation.

The recent crisis has led to a re-examination of these theories, for it contains features which are difficult to explain in monetary or psychological terms. What is particularly inexplicable is the extraordinary persistence of the crisis. The crises of the past came and went. There took place a contraction of credit and a fall of prices, followed by gradual recovery and re-expansion. The worst phase of a crisis of the past was over within a year. The acute phase of the present crisis began in 1929, and even in the middle of 1934 it is impossible to say in India whether the worst is over.

Fall of Prices 1929-33

The chief feature of the crisis is a heavy, continuous and universal fall of prices. The course of wholesale prices in India is shown below:

	July 1914=100
1929	141
1930	116
1931	96
1932	91
1933 (March)	82

Between 1929 and March 1933 the fall in our prices amounted to 42 per cent. The percentage decline in prices in the more important countries between the peak in 1929 and March 1933 was as follows: United Kingdom 30·4; U. S. A. 37·6; Germany 34·7; France 40·9; Japan 22·2; Italy 42·5; Netherlands 51·0; Canada 34·4. Of 32 countries, for which price statistics are available, only 2 (Greece and Chile) show a rise of prices[1]. As regards the remaining 30, the fall of prices in no less than 18 exceeded 30 per cent in this period.

The fall of prices has not been uniform. It is much greater in the case of food-stuffs and raw materials than in that of manufactured goods. For example, in March 1933 the index number for raw jute in India stood at 38, and for jute manufactures at 68; raw cotton had in the same month fallen to 79 but cotton manufactures showed a rise of 12 per cent above the pre-War level. Cereals had fallen to 61 but metals only to 94, while building materials (teak wood) stood at 124. The experience of other countries has been similar.

Percentage decline in agricultural prices in certain countries[2]:

JANUARY 1929 TO MARCH 1933

	Decline in national currency	Decline in gold prices
Argentine ..	51·4	70·5
Australia ..	35·9	65·5
Canada ..	53·2	61·0
India ..	38·3	56·4
U. S. A. ..	59·6	59·6

Agricultural countries have suffered not only on account of the greater fall in the prices of their products as compared with those of manufactured goods, but on account of the

[1] League, Depression, p. 39.
[2] *Ibid*, p. 57.

agricultural protection that has greatly increased in industrial countries. Terms of foreign trade have moved against agricultural countries and in favour of manufacturing countries. Of this a few examples may be given. In 1929 the index of import prices in the United Kingdom (1927=100), was 99, and of export prices 97, export prices being thus 99 per cent. of import prices. In 1932 import prices fell to 65 and export prices to 76, with the result that export prices were 19 per cent. above import prices. The percentage excess of export over import prices for other countries in 1932 was as follows[3]:

France	18
Germany	41
Italy	3
Switzerland	19
U. S. A.	46

It is evident that agricultural countries, have suffered grievously on account of the heavier fall in the prices of foot-stuffs and raw materials.[4]

The facts relating to the origin of the crisis and its development are fairly clear and, thanks to the excellent publications of the League of Nations on this subject, they are widely known. It is the explanation of the crisis that is difficult. Is the crisis merely a conjunctural crisis, that is of a cyclical nature, such as those of the past, or one due to

[3] *Ibid*, p. 59.

[4] Manufacturing countries have their own difficulties. While the prices of imported food-stuffs and raw materials have fallen more than those of exported manufactured goods, export prices are lower than those of goods retained in the country for home consumption. Protection has added to the difficulties of manufacturers. They have been compelled, in order to sell anything at all in foreign countries, to continuously lower the prices of exported articles. This has meant heavy sacrifices for those who produce for export, in view of the fact that many items of cost of production (i.e., wages and taxes) are inelastic. The internal prices of same goods have remained relatively high. "Such is the sacrifice", remarks Sig. Vincent Porri, "now necessary for conquering tariff barriers, erected everywhere for shutting out foreign competition; such are the efforts made for maintaining relations with the foreign clientele". (Economic Essays in Honour of Gustav Cassel, pp. 523-25).

structural changes, bringing in their train alterations of a fundamental nature in the relations of supply and demand, of production and consumption. The answer to this question is important, for the discussion of remedies must depend on the view taken of the causes of the crisis.

Wilhelm Roepke, a leading German economist, has given an interesting analysis of the crisis. In its nature and first stage the crisis was a conjunctural crisis, that is, it represented an inevitable reaction to the preceding period of credit expansion and over-investment in the whole world. But in that case, after a painful period of liquidation, extending over not more than a year, a new equilibrium should have been established. Not only did that not happen, but many circumstances conspired to cause a 'secondary' crisis to emerge from the first, to which Roepke gives the name 'primary'. The emergence of this secondary crisis dates from the year 1931[5]. This 'secondary' crisis is marked by deflation of an altogether new kind, in which the fall of prices is of wholly subsidiary importance. Declining prices are only a weak reflection of the general process of economic contraction. "As a matter of fact the process of contraction, is, in the first place, a process of contraction of quantities produced, and only so far as the adjustment through the quantities produced (*i.e.*, their reduction in relation to demand) is incomplete, there is also a process of price-contraction". The chief features of the 'secondary' crisis are, therefore, contraction of income, contraction of demand, and contraction of production. Complications were introduced in this process of adjustment by other factors, *e.g.*, reparations and other political and commercial debts, short period loans, the rise of nationalism, and an 'orgy of protectionism' which may be regarded as a product of *Bellizisumus* (growth of war-like feeling) and nationalism[6]. The agricultural crisis made matters worse, and, finally there was superadded the

[5] Economic Essays in Honour of Gustav Cassel, pp. 556-57.
[6] W. A. Jan. 1933, p. 27.

international credit-crisis of the year 1931, which might have been avoided by timely united action on the part of the leading countries[7].

Roepke's remedy for the present situation is the adoption of a policy of 're-expansion'. He makes it quite clear that 're-expansion' does not mean a demand for raising the general price level. "The essential thing is not fighting price-contraction but fighting demand—, production—, and thus finally also income-contraction." As to how precisely the war against demand—, production—, and income-contraction is to be waged, he tells us nothing.

Other writers, while recognising that a return to 1928 prices is impossible, still advocate a policy of 'reflation'[8]. At the same time the State is asked to follow a vigorous policy of assisting industry, and of saving such businesses as can be saved.

If, in its essential nature, the crisis is a conjunctural crisis, it will find its own remedy in due course. But the State may help in mitigating the suffering and reducing the losses which the process of deflation inevitably brings with itself.

But if the crisis is due to structural changes which have upset the old relations between agriculture and industry, and between demand and supply, it may be necessary to make a deliberate attempt to adjust production to consumption. Even in this case, if no action is taken, an adjustment will take place automatically in time, but uncontrolled and unregulated action of economic forces, which produced this crisis, may produce others still worse. It will be seen that the question of the real causes of the crisis demands a definite and unequivocal answer.

The Conjunctural Explanation

Keeping in view the catastrophic fall of prices, the universal character of the depression, its intensity, and the

[7] Economic Essays, loc. cit. p. 562.
[8] *Ibid*, p. 615.

extraordinary persistence of its worst features, we inquire: was the crisis preceded by an extraordinary inflation of credit and abnormal boom conditions throughout the world, so that when the brake in the shape of stiffer money rates was applied, a crisis of unprecedented magnitude was precipitated?

There is not much evidence to support this view. *The Course and Phases of the World Economic Depression* of the League of Nations thus summarises the economic situation in the world in the years 1920-29:

"The general impression conveyed is that there was very little uniformity in the movement of business conditions in the different countries during the last decade, especially before 1927. Only in a few countries—such, for instance, as the United States, Great Britain, Canada and Czecho-Slovakia —can a cyclical movement with a period of 3 to 4 years be observed, and even in these cases the movements did not synchronise"[9].

A few examples may be given to illustrate this. There was a crisis in 1921-22, but it was felt severely only in countries which were pursuing a policy of deflation. In other countries, where there was no deflation, 'prices, after a temporary setback, resumed their upward movement'. The year 1923 was one of recovery, but improvement had begun earlier in Canada and the United States, and these countries "entered upon a brief phase of declining activity" in the latter part of the same year[10].

The recession of 1924 in North America was not felt in Europe.

Monetary deflation depressed business conditions in many countries in 1925, but in the second half of the year, Canada, Spain, the Argentine, Japan and India "were still in the upward phase of the cycle"[11].

[9] League, Depression, p. 110.
[10] *Ibid*, p. 106.
[11] *Ibid*, p. 107.

England's loss in 1926 on account of the coal dispute and the general strike was her rivals' gain. Germany, Belgium, Sweden and other countries profited by the decline of business activity in England. But production in France, Spain and Italy suffered on account of monetary troubles.

The year 1927 saw currency stabilisation in most countries and "there was a clearly marked tendency towards expansion of production and trade"[12]. But conditions were unsatisfactory in some countries (France, Italy, Denmark, Norway, Rumania, Brazil and Japan), chiefly on account of monetary difficulties.

In the year 1928 industrial activity and stock exchange transactions and quotations in some countries "attained boom proportions". But in Germany and certain cereal producing countries there was no boom, only "on the whole the level reached was maintained". In Australia, on the other hand, conditions were adverse on account of the bad crop in the winter of 1927-28. There was 'a certain recession' in Finland, and "industrial production in England declined in the first half of the year" (1928) .

In the year 1929 production remained stationary or slightly declined in Poland, Hungary, the Argentine, Canada, Czecho-Slovakia and Switzerland, but in other countries (*e.g.*, United States, England, France, Germany and Sweden) it increased, and in some branches of industry "hitherto undreamt of levels were attained"[13].

All this does not furnish evidence of any extraordinary or universal boom. What we actually find is an improvement in some countries, and a recession in others, and the degrees of improvement or recession in different countries are different.

Boom conditions did exist in the United States in 1928 and 1929. "In other countries, there was also an increase in production during these years, but boom conditions were felt

[12] *Ibid*, p. 107.
[13] *Ibid*, p. 108.

to a less extent"[14]. Unemployment, though declining, still "remained on a relatively high level". Agricultural countries experienced no boom, as the fall of agricultural prices (which commenced before the New York stock exchange crash of October 1929) had reduced the purchasing power of the peasant class.

Great Britain was adversely affected by the unsatisfactory conditions in certain over-seas markets. There was no boom even in Italy. The increase in business activity in this country marked a revival of trade after the depression, due to deflation, of 1927.

Having noted the fact that there was no real boom throughout the world in 1927-29, or preceding years, let us follow the story of the crisis in the United States.

American Boom

The signal for the outbreak of the crisis was given by the stock exchange crash in New York in October 1929. The collapse was preceded by the usual boom.

Authoritative figures show that between 1926 and 1929, prices were rising very slowly in the United States. Taking prices in 1926 as 100, the index number rose to 103 in 1928 and 105 in 1929. There was a slight reduction in the quantity of money in circulation (3 per cent in 1928 and 1929; 1926=100) and a small increase in the amount of deposits subject to cheque (4 per cent in 1928 and 3 per cent in 1929; 1926=100). The clearing index of business, prepared by the Federal Reserve Bank of New York, rose from 100 in 1926 to 102 in 1928 and 106 in 1926, while industrial production, after falling 2 per cent in 1927 (1926=100) rose to 103 in 1928 and 110 in 1929[15].

These figures do not show any sensational growth of business activity. And yet, in spite of almost stationary

[14] *Ibid*, p. 123.
[15] Facing the Facts, pp. 16-19.

prices, and on the basis of a slowly expanding industrial production, business profits in the United States were increasing at an abnormal rate.

The increase of business profits was due to the fall in costs of production made possible by technical progress; wages did not rise much.

The very high profits earned in the automobile industry led to over-investment in that field, "and the capacity of the industry reached the most amazing proportions"[16].

With the growth of industrial profits speculation grew and prices of industrial stocks leapt up. Kemmerer thus describes the situation:

"Prices of stocks on our exchanges rose to figures out of all proportion to the earnings, actual or prospective, of the respective companies........ From September 1924 to September 1929 the mean of the monthly high and low daily averages of prices of 351 industrial stocks, as given by the Standard Statistics Company, rose from 70·7 to 216, and for 33 railroad stocks from 79·3 to 168·1. The volume of monthly sales on the New York stock exchange increased during the same period from 18 million shares to 100 million shares"[17].

It may be noted that the boom in the United States "was rather a typical investment boom than a consumption boom"[18]. The increase in the production of articles of consumption such as leather goods, shoes and textiles was much less than that in the production of iron and steel. The consumption of food products remained unchanged. The increased purchases of automobiles or the products of the radio industry "required investment of savings no less than the purchase of machinery".

Credit conditions in the first 12 months after the summer of 1927 were easy in the United States and other

[16] *Monetary Policy and the Depression*, p. 7.
[17] Facing the Facts, p. 7.
[18] League, Depression, p. 124.

countries. The credit created in the United States in this period was largely utilised for speculative purposes.

The conditions of easy credit changed both in the United States and other countries in the summer of 1928. To counteract the speculative movement, discount rates were raised by the Federal Reserve Banks, and commercial banks in New York were persuaded not to lend money to the stock market. The high money rates and the contraction of credit attracted foreign funds and caused a reduction of American short term investments abroad. This created difficulties for debtor countries. From January to October 1929 the gold stocks of the United States rose by 260,000,000, dollars.

At about the same time France also attracted some gold, on account of the improvement in her balance of payments. "The high rates on call money in the United States (8-9 per cent.), the fear that the stock exchange boom there would end in a sudden crash, and to some extent the strain on gold supplies, induced Central banks elsewhere to raise their rates and restrict credit"[19].

The restriction of credit in the United States led to a collapse which meant the ruin of millions. Between June 1929 and June 1932 the prices of 351 industrial stocks fell from 191 to 34 (1926=100), of 33 railroad stocks from 145 to 14 and of 37 public utility stocks from 233 to 55[20].

Speculators had over-reached themselves and were punished heavily for their sins[21].

[19] *Ibid*, p. 128.

[20] Facing the Facts, p. 8.

[21] The fate of speculators in America, and the fact that the stock exchange collapse plunged the United States into chaos and precipitated a violent crisis in the rest of the world, have led many writers to emphasize the danger of speculative activities divorced from production. Speculation, we are taught in text books of economics, tends to steady prices. The speculator does not add to existing supplies, nor does he substract from them, but these activities result in a better adjustment of supply to demand as between the present and the future.

But this is true of speculation which has some relation to actual life. As Sir Arthur Salter says:

Debtor and Creditor Relations

Reference has been made above to reduction in American short time investments abroad, which created difficulties in debtor countries. Debtor and creditor relations next claim our attention as they are intimately connected with the development of the crisis in 1929-31.

Before the War the chief creditor nations were England and France, and of less importance, Belgium, Holland and Switzerland. The United States borrowed more than she lent and the net sum that she owed to other countries in 1924 is estimated at 3,000 million dollars[22].

The economy of a debtor country is different from that of a creditor country. For example, India must export more goods than she imports. A decrease in the amount of our favourable balance of trade is a matter of grave concern to us, for to be able to meet our foreign obligations, we must have a surplus of exports over imports at least equal in amount to our annual external obligations. A creditor country, on the other hand, can afford the luxury of an unfavourable balance of trade. In fact, creditor countries must have an

"Speculation based on economic realities may be beneficial but 'speculation on speculation' is definitely injurious" (*Recovery*, pp. 37-38).

Speculation has been described as the salt of industrial and commercial activity. Accepting the gastronomic comparison as true, says an Italian writer, it may still happen, that the same palate may reject equally food without salt as food which contains too much salt.

In the United States, in the years immediately preceding the collapse, speculation became an 'end-in-itself'. What happens when speculation becomes an 'end-in-itself'?

"But it is certain that when this happens, and the hope of gain is more and more isolated from productive activity, and comes to rest exclusively on the game of a probability of a rise or fall of prices or the hope of profit arising from the difference between the purchase and the sale price......there is a transference of activity from the field of work to that of play: from the factory to the stock exchange, from the field of production to that of distribution or redistribution of wealth; and thus the easy enrichment of one at the expense of another comes to mean a transfer of wealth from the one to the other, without any increase in the amount of the wealth—which must, in the end, impoverish the country" (Fabio Luzzatto in Giornale degli Economisti e Rivista Statistica for Feb. 1934, p. 84).

[22] H. W. B. Supplement, p. 629.

unfavourable balance of trade, for that is only how, normally, debtors can pay interest on loans or return the principal sum.

In the year 1913 imports of merchandise into England were valued at £ 659 millions and exports at £ 525 millions, or England had an adverse balance of trade amounting to 5,134 millions. Imports and exports in 1930 had increased to £ 958 millions and £ 571 millions respectively, or the amount of England's adverse balance had grown to £ 387 millions. How did England pay for this huge total of surplus imports?

In the first place she earned about £ 160 millions as banking, insurance and other commissions and in shipping freights. Secondly, her income from overseas investments in the shape of interest amounted to £ 235 millions.

The mechanism of international lending and borrowing is intimately connected with that of credit and exchange.

When we raise a loan in England, exchange will tend to move in our favour, for the loan places us in funds with which we might reduce our foreign indebtedness. In pre-War years and till recently when the Government of India adopted the practice of making remittances to England through sterling purchases in India, these remittances were made through drawings of the Secretary of State for India, or by the sale of Council bills. If a loan was raised in England, the Secretary of State was able to reduce the amount of the sales and use the proceeds of the loan to meet the 'Home charges'. Reduction in the sale of Council bills tended to raise the exchange value of the rupee. At present reduction in the sterling purchases of the Government of India has the same effect on the rupee exchange.

A loan raised abroad increases the purchasing power of the borrowing country. If gold is imported, it may be used for creating additional credit. In our case, a part of the loan, in the shape of gold or British securities, may be added to the Paper Currency Reserve in England, permitting the issue of more notes in India.

The creation of additional credit in debtor countries would stimulate trade and industry. Prices would tend to rise, imports would increase, new industries may be founded, old industries strengthened and enlarged and large public works may be undertaken. Thus a steady stream of gold flowing into debtor countries may give rise to boom conditions.

Interest would be paid by exports of produce which is in demand in the creditor country. If, on account of famine or scarcity, the necessary exports are not forthcoming, against which bills may be drawn on importers in the creditor country, difficulties arise. A new loan must be arranged or gold must be exported.

Foreign capital has played an important part in the development of colonies and backward countries. India imports both foreign capital and the foreign capitalist.

A part of the capital borrowed is generally spent in the creditor country on machinery, railway material and other goods. Employment is thus created in the lending country and the industries concerned are enabled to expand. A country, then, which exports capital on a large scale would be industrially prosperous, with high wages and a high standard of living. The increase in her purchasing power, due to the expansion of constructional and other industries would enable her to buy more food and raw materials from debtor countries.

But the whole mechanism of international investments is a delicate one. When it is suddenly subjected to a severe strain, it may break.

During 1924-29 the United States and England, respectively, made loans to South America approximating 1,200,000,000 dollars and £50,000,000, of which the small Republic of Columbia received 170,000,000 dollars. "There was a great boom. Competitive railway building and other public works sent up wages by leaps and bounds; imports vastly increased; food was imported where before it had been produced locally. When the gold stream ceased, there was a collapse. Imports ceased and Columbia thus added its small quota to depression in the industrial countries"[23]. The same thing happened in Brazil, Peru, Chile, probably in the Argentine and "certainly in Australia"[24].

But why should the gold stream cease to flow?

Suppose on account of technical advance in agriculture, production increases so much that food-stuffs and raw materials, the products of debtor countries, cannot be sold at remunerative prices. Prices come down, profits vanish, the credit of borrowing countries contracts and the golden stream ceases to flow. Not only would the creditors not make fresh loans to agricultural countries, but insist on the payment of old debts. Under such conditions foreign capital becomes 'home-sick' (*Heimweh* des Kapitals).[25] The sudden recall of foreign capital may throw the currency system of debtor countries into confusion.

The creditor countries themselves cannot escape injury. If the purchasing power of debtors shrinks, their demand for imports from creditor countries would fall. First the constructional industries would be affected and gradually the depression would spread to other industries. The figures of the unemployed would mount up. As the situation grows worse, more countries would become involved in the general chaos and ruin.

This is precisely what happened in 1928—31. During and after the war there was an enormous addition to the debt of the world. The total amount of the world's Government debts in 1924 was officially estimated in Germany at 190,600,000,000 Marks (20·43 Marks=1 £ gold). This includes inter-Allied debts but excludes Reparations

[23] Macmillan Report, p. 80.
[24] Macmillan Report, p. 80.
[25] W. A. April, 1933, p. 323.

imposed by the Treaty of Versailles. The German Institute fuer Konjuncturforschung estimated the political debt of the world at the end of 1931 at 541,600,000,000 Marks. The private debt of the world about the middle of the year 1932 is put at 252,628,000,000 Marks.[26]

The leading creditor country is now the United States, followed closely by England and at a respectable distance by France and Holland:

World's Debt in Million Marks[27]

	Private	Political and Private
Europe without Germany	91,942	125,893
Germany	18,582	18,582
Other countries ..	127,104	147,733
China	3,000	3,000
British India	12,000	12,000
Total ..	252,628	307,208

Of the total political debt amounting to 54,580,000,000 Marks the amounts lent by the United States and England respectively are 29,248,000,000 Marks and 22,200,000,000 Marks. The private investments of creditor countries are shown below:

In Million Marks[28]

U. S. A.	73,148
Great Britain	72,100
France	33,956
Holland	14,900
Switzerland	14,000
Scandinavian countries	5,382
Germany	..
Japan	15,000
Other countries	22,142
Total ..	252,628

[26] W. A. April, 1933, pp. 326-27.
[27] *Ibid.*
[28] *Ibid.*

It was the War that turned the United States into a creditor country. France began to export capital in 1921 and soon after the War England assumed her old role of an international lender on a large scale. Germany had lost all her foreign assets and became an importer of capital.

Between 1923 and 1929 about equal amounts were invested abroad by the United Kingdom and the United States —about 3,000 million dollars. The leading borrowers were Germany and Australia.[29]

About 1928 the net foreign assets of the United States reached a total of 6,500—8,500 million dollars (excluding War debts). British long term investments were valued at 20,000 million dollars. Germany, apart from Reparations, owed at the end of 1928 about 1,900 million dollars on long term account and 1,000 million dollars on short term account.

The income of the United States earned abroad in the form of interest in 1928 has been estimated at 5·7 dollars per head of the population, and of England no less than 29 dollars. The obligations on account of interest of some debtor countries, particularly those exporting food-stuffs and raw materials, were as shown below:

Net interest owed abroad per head of the population in 1928.[30]

	Dollars
New Zealand	27·6
Australia	27·5
Canada	22·3
Argentine	17·4
Union of South Africa	9·8
Norway	6·7
Denmark	3·8
Hungary	3·0

[29] League, Depression, p. 31.
[30] League, Depression, p. 36.

It can be easily understood that agricultural countries with heavy foreign obligations found themselves in a position of great difficulty when the prices of their products began to fall. Gold imports declined and ceased, and finally, gold began to flow in the direction of creditor countries. Between 1928 and 1929 capital movements from the United States fell by 561 million dollars and the total overseas issues on the London market declined from £143 millions to £94 millions. As a consequence of an adverse balance of payments, the surplus of gold, or gold stocks over legal minimum gold requirements in debtor countries began to decline:

Surplus gold in million dollars[31]

	End of 1928	June 1930	June 1931
Argentine	147	65	..
Australia	167	71	..
Germany	300	292	34
Spain	159	146	57
United Kingdom ..	178	269	336
U. S. A.	1420	1967	2245
France	139	520	831

Between 1928 and 1930 there was a fall in the gold reserves or foreign assets of the following countries, all of which had been hit hard by the fall in the prices of foodstuffs: Argentine, Australia, Brazil, Canada, Columbia, and Hungary. The crisis in raw materials affected the following countries: Bolivia, Egypt, Eucador, India, Mexico, Dutch East Indies, Peru, Uruguay, and Venezula. Gold stocks of the United States increased from 4,332 million dollars in December 1928 to 4,787 million dollars in December 1930, and those of France from 1,271 million dollars to 2,099 million dollars in the same period.

[31] *Ibid*, pp. 96 and 230.

Before the abandoment of the gold standard by England towards the end of September 1931 the following countries had already suspended the gold standard officially: Uruguay (December 1929), Argentine (December 16, 1929), Australia (December 17, 1929), and Mexico (July 25, 1931). In addition, the currencies of the following countries had depreciated in relation to gold before September 1931: Turkey, Spain, Paraguay, New Zealand, Venezula, and Bolivia. New Zealand and Uruguay had reverted to *de facto* gold parity, but there had been no return to the gold standard in Spain and Turkey.[32]

The heavy losses suffered by debtor countries in consequence of the fall in prices, the weakening of their financial position and the breaking of their exchanges had created a situation which was bound to react on creditor countries. The chief cause of the trouble, was the fall in prices. The League of Nations Economic Survey for the year 1931-32 refers to the steady and continuous fall in the prices of raw materials and food-stuffs and says: "The financial crisis which followed made it abundantly clear that it was the plight of the debtor countries, at once a main cause and the consequence of falling commodity prices, that was the darkest spot in the almost universal depression".[33]

As the economic situation in debtor countries grew worse, their demand for manufactured imports heavily decreased, which led to a further fall in commodity prices. The plight of the debtor countries was thus both a main cause and the consequence of falling prices.

The Financial Crisis of 1931

The story of the financial crisis of 1931 may be thus summarised.

The Creditanstalt, a large Austrian bank, had suffered heavy losses in 1930. In May 1931 it was found in

[32] League, Economic Survey, 1932-33, pp. 222-23.
[33] *Ibid*, p. 70.

difficulties again. The Austrian Government came to its help, assisted by substantial advances by the Bank of England and the Bank of International Settlements. For the time the situation was saved, but on August 7 the Austrian Government requested the League of Nations "to proceed to an examination of Austria's economic and financial difficulties and to seek the means of remedying them".

At the end of 1930 Germany's short-term indebtedness was estimated at 103,000 million Marks. The weakness of Austria, revealed in May 1931, created a panic which spread to Germany and a run started on the Reichsbank, which lost 250 million dollars of its gold and foreign exchange in four weeks. On June 23, the President of the United States proposed a year's moratorium of reparation and war debt payments. Later the British Government announced that it would not require the payment of its share of the reparations due on July 15. The Bank of International Settlements also rendered assistance in the shape of rediscount credit. An expert committee declared in the first week of August that withdrawal of short term balances from Germany was "not justified by the economic situation of the country" and a "Standstill Agreement" was reached in the middle of August by which arrangements were made for the "continuation of credits to the German debtors" under certain conditions. But in the first seven months of 1931 Germany lost 2,900 million Marks, of which 2,100 million marks came from the short term liabilities of the banks. However, as the result of international effort, the situation in Germany improved and the Bank rate was reduced from 15 per cent on August 1 to 10 per cent on August 12 and 8 per cent on August 19.[34]

When the run started on the German banks, the Bank of England began to lose gold. The Bank rate was raised but the drain continued. In the last fortnight of July the Bank lost over £30 millions. The uneasiness increased when it became widely known from the Report of the Macmillan

[34] League, Economic Survey, 1931-32, p. 76.

Committee, published on July 13, that London had a large volume of short-term indebtedness. Its own short-term claims on Europe were smaller in amount and of little value on account of the financial situation of Europe.

The Bank of England borrowed £50 millions from French and Amercian banks at the beginning of August and a further £80 millions was borrowed by the government from the same sources. Still the drain continued. In the two months preceding September 20 the London money market lost over £200 millions. Between Wednesday morning (September 16) and Saturday mid-day (September 19) London lost over £43 millions of short-term foreign funds. On September 21 came the suspension of the gold standard.

The immediate cause of the breakdown of the gold standard in England was the drain of gold. But England's return to gold in 1925 was a mistake, and in view of her declining exports, quite apart from the drain of gold in 1931, it would have been impossible for her to remain on the gold standard much longer.

The Macmillan Committee rejected devaluation. They thought that the lowering of the value of the £ as a deliberate measure, after the return to gold in 1925, would mean the adoption of 'an entirely new principle' which would shock the entire financial world.[35] The events of the two months following the publication of the Report showed that the Macmillan Committee had over-rated England's financial strength and under-rated the strain of falling prices and declining demand on debtor countries and the reaction of this on creditor countries.

[35] p. 111.

CHAPTER VII

CAUSES: MONETARY AND NON-MONETARY

Reference has been made in the preceding pages to the fall of prices which made debtor countries bankrupt and which ultimately led to the breakdown of the gold standard.

Why did prices fall?

In attempting an answer to this question we shall begin with the monetary theory of the crisis. Among others Sir Henry Strakosh (England) and Prof. Gustav Cassel lay emphasis on the monetary causes of the crisis.

The gold standard works automatically, provided gold is permitted to move in and out freely. Let us assume a given distribution of monetary gold among the nations of the world, which has produced a given level of world prices. Prices in different countries are never precisely the same, but a tendency to equality in the case of commodities which enter into international trade always exists. Suppose the general level of prices suddenly begins to rise in some countries. These countries will become a good market to sell in, and a bad market to buy in; they will begin to import goods heavily, while their exports of goods will decline. The equilibrium will be restored by the export of gold. On the one hand, the export of gold will tend to bring about a fall of prices (through the contraction of the gold basis of credit) in the countries where prices had risen, and on the other, it will raise prices, by enabling credit to expand, in the countries which import the gold.

This is the classical theory of distribution of the precious metals throughout the world through the mechanism of changing prices. It is assumed that when gold is imported, it does not disappear into hoards. If it does, prices will not be affected. India imported gold and silver on a large scale in the 16th and 17th centuries, but this import led to no considerable rise of prices, as the precious metals were used in India chiefly for hoarding purposes. Similarly, if gold received by a country, say France or the United States, is not used for the expansion of credit, and simply locked up in the reserves of Central banks, prices will remain unaffected.

The mechanism of the gold standard is delicate and it may be easily thrown out of balance by a 'mal-distribution of gold', which fails to correct itself. For example, let us assume that one or two countries, somehow, acquire a strong pull on the world's stocks of monetary gold. Gold begins to flow to these countries, and it is hoarded by them. Their prices fail to rise, and may even fall. While the acquisition of gold by these creditor countries has in no way augmented their prosperity, the reduction of gold reserves in other countries may produce dire consequences. A process of wholesale liquidation may set in in the gold-losing countries. Suppose England is one of these countries. To guard its gold reserve the Bank of England will raise the Bank rate and take steps to induce joint-stock banks to raise their rates of discount. Borrowers will find it increasingly difficult to obtain accommodation, and will have to pay more for it. To meet their obligations some borrowers may be forced to sell securities and goods. This is the beginning of a period of deflation—of the contraction of money and credit and fall of prices.

Distinguished economists, whose names command respect both in the scientific and the business world, assure us that it was precisely thus that the fall of prices started. It is argued that the fall of prices was not due to the scarcity of gold. It is estimated that between 1913 and 1931 the world's stock of gold increased at an annual average rate of 4·7 per cent, while the demand for gold, as represented by growth in the production of 'basic physical commodities', from 1913-14 to

1929-30 increased at the rate of 1·86 per cent per annum.[1]

Between January 1, 1929 and June 30, 1931 the gold holding of France increased 74 per cent and of the United States 19½ per cent, while monetary gold in the possession of the rest of the world decreased 16 per cent.[2] During the same period the total gold stock of the world increased from 10,962 million dollars to 11,817 millions dollars, or 8 per cent.

How did it become possible for France and the United States to draw gold from the rest of the world?

The answer is reparations and War-debts. The War made them creditor nations. They might have saved the world's gold stock from the strain which their creditor position imposed on it by agreeing to have the debts owing to them paid in commodities. But this they refused to do. On the contrary, they raised high tariff walls to keep out foreign goods.

Between January 1925 and January 1931 France and the United States received, on account of reparations and War-debt payments, 2,262 million dollars. In the same period their gold reserves grew by 1,520 million dollars. The connection between the import of gold by France and the United States and reparations and War-debts is clear.[3]

"The breakdown of the gold standard must therefore be regarded as the combined result of the obligation to pay reparations and War-debts on the one side, and the unwillingness of the receiving countries to receive payment in the form of goods and services on the other" (Sir Reginald Mant and Sir Henry Strakosh).[4]

The breakdown of the gold standard might have been

[1] *Facing the Facts*, edited by J. G. Smith (New York, 1932), p. 14.

[2] *Report of the Gold Delegation of the Financial Committee of the League of Nations* (Geneva, 1932). Minute of Dissent by Sir Reginald Mant and Sir Henry Strakosh, p. 67.

[3] *Ibid*, p. 67.

[4] *Ibid*, p. 67.

avoided if France and the United States had re-invested their favourable balances in debtor countries. Before 1928 Germany paid reparations with the help of loans from the United States. But after 1928 the United States wanted all her capital for her own use. Boom conditions existed in American industry, and capital was required both for investment in American industry and for speculative purposes. It also seems that Germany had exhausted her borrowing capacity.

Again, the collapse of the gold standard might not have occurred if the gold imported by France and the United States had led to a rise of prices in these countries. Their imports of goods would have increased and exports declined, and gold would have flown out. But they did not use the gold in a monetary way. It "was simply buried in the vaults of the Central Banks. Not only was the level of prices of these countries not raised but was actually lowered as the price level fell in the rest of the world". (Mant and Strakosh).[5]

With this opinion Prof. Gustav Cassel is wholly in agreement: He says: "The payment of War-debts in conjunction with the unwillingness to receive payment in the normal form of goods led to unreasonable demands on the world's monetary gold stocks; and the claimants failed to use in a proper way the gold that they had accumulated".[6]

This situation is described as the 'sterilisation of gold'. Sir Arthur Salter says:

"But as France and America did not need this extra gold it became in part 'sterilised', that is, it was not used as the basis of as much money as in the countries from which it had come. The net result of this mal-distribution of gold was therefore to reduce the total amount of money in the world, and thus to exert a depressing influence on the general level of prices".[7]

[5] *Ibid*, p. 67.

[6] *The Crisis in the World's Monetary System* by Prof. Gustav Cassel (Oxford, 1932) pp. 71-2.

[7] *Recovery* (G. Bell, 1932), p. 39.

The whole blame for the breakdown of the gold standard thus rests on France and the United States.

If this view is accepted, the crisis would appear to be a monetary phenomenon. Something went wrong with the world's money, and the whole system of production collapsed. Prof. Gustav Cassel insists that in dealing with the crisis what we have to explain 'is essentially a monetary phenomenon"[8]. According to Prof. Verryn Stuart, the general fall of prices was caused 'by a shrinking of the quantity of money, particularly by a decrease in the velocity of circulation of money"[9]. A decrease in the velocity of circulation of money and credit is also a monetary phenomenon, and an inevitable consequence of deflation. When the process of liquidation sets in, there is loss of confidence, and money circulates less rapidly.

The view that the crisis is 'essentially a money crisis'[10], or wholly due to a breakdown of the machinery of exchange, deserves closer examination. Agreeing with Sir William Beveridge that "there is a flaw in our machinery for making and unmaking purchasing power" and that it is not under control[11], we ask whether this is the whole account of the crisis. And then why did the machinery of exchange break down so suddenly? Are France and the United States really the villains of the piece? The world has not been able to avoid alternate inflation and deflation: it has failed to manage credit properly. Assuming that the failure to manage credit caused the crisis, to what extent must France and the United States be held responsible for what has happened?

FRANCE

France has been accused of deliberately attracting gold to herself, of accumulating a huge gold and foreign exchange

[8] Note of Dissent to the Gold Delegation Report, p. 74.
[9] *Economic Essays in Honour of Gustav Cassel* (George Allen, 1933), p. 605.
[10] *The World's Economic Crisis* (George Allen), p. 163.
[11] *Ibid*, p. 175.

reserve "which was to play a predominant part in International politics during the subsequent years" (Paul Einzig).[12]

The causes which led to the import of gold into France were the following: (1) a favourable balance of payments, (2) reparation receipts, (3) return of French capital from overseas. During the depreciation of the franc capital had fled from France. Before M. Poincare took charge of the French finances in 1926, the franc had fallen to 240 to the £, which led many Frenchmen to sell francs. The flight from the franc resulted in the accumulation of foreign balances by France. Confidence in the franc returned on the restoration of budgetary equilibrium in France and the stabilization of the franc, and French capital abroad returned to France.

The influx of gold did not lead to inflation, but the charge of deliberate 'sterilisation' made against the French authorities is unfounded. "It appears" says T. Balogh, "that those who make the charge of wilful hoarding mistake for conscious tactics the shortcomings of the French banking system and of the gold standard in general".[13]

But France has a much better case than that. M. Rist says:

"One may assert, as does Sir Henry Strakosh, that the actual crisis is solely due to monetary factors, in particular to an insufficient utilisation of credit. It is difficult to prove it".[14]

M. Rist shows that between June 1927 and June 1929 there was an increase in the reserve of the Bank of France of 9,338 million gold (francs), but it was accompanied by an increase in bills and advances of 5,916 million gold (francs). After the autumn of 1929 till October 17, 1930, bills and advances decreased from 10,443 million gold (francs) to 7,832 million gold (francs), under the influence of the world depression started by the banking crisis of New York.[15]

[12] Quoted by H. Withers in *Money in the Melting pot*, p. 38.
[13] *Economic Journal* for Sept. 1930.
[14] *Essais sur quelques Problemes Economiques et Monetaires*, Paris 1933, p. 109
[15] *Ibid*, pp. 107-8.

"Normally a bank of issue", says M. Rist, "limits its action to meeting the demands for credit addressed to it; in a period of depression these demands do not arise".[16] In the two years following the *de facto* stabilization of the franc the growth of general prosperity increased the demand for credit on the Bank of France, and the Bank met it. After 1929 this demand decreased and the Bank's bills and advances fell. The reserves of the Bank increased "under the influence of causes which have nothing to do with its credit policy".

A further point may be considered. The flow of gold to France and the United States had reduced the monetary gold at the disposal of the rest of the world. The gold-losing countries might have met the situation by economising the use of gold. They might have lowered the legal proportion between gold and paper, thus enabling a larger credit superstructure to be raised on a smaller gold basis. In the words of Mr. Hartley Withers, it was necessary to "slim the Golden Calf".[17] The Golden Calf was not slimmed. The gold-losing countries, on the other hand, raised their rates of discount and thus deliberately started the process of liquidation.

If the Bank of France had pursued an erroneous monetary policy in not forcing the French business community to take advances when it did not want them, the monetary policy pursued by gold-losing countries was not less erroneous.

The charge of wilful sterilisation against France must be dismissed as not proved. We may accept M. Rist's conclusion that the re-distribution of the world's gold reserves was not the result of "any policy of governors of banks of issue, but of a group of circumstances which it was not in their power to control".[18]

[16] *Ibid*, p. 107.

[17] *Money in the Melting Pot* by Hartley Withers (London, 1932), p. 43.

[18] *Rist. Loc. cit.* p. 115.

United States

A high authority like Irving Fisher declares the charge of sterilisation of gold by the United States a 'myth'.

France, he says, "doubtless became possessed of surplus gold." This was only "partly true of America".

America imported gold during the War. "But upon this gold", says Fisher, "we speedily built such a credit structure and raised the price level so high as to require almost all of this gold as a base". Prices reached their high water-mark in 1920; they fell in 1920—22. Fisher admits that then there was temporarily an excess of gold in the United States, but "soon both our business structure and our credit structure expanded so much as to make our unused or so-called 'sterilized' gold more or less of a myth".[19]

The United States had a considerable amount of gold, but much of it was ear-marked as belonging to Europe. The gold that was free "was not great enough to justify much more than the credit currency created upon it".[20]

In 1924-25 the Bank rate was raised in England to prepare the way for England's return to the gold standard, and the Federal Reserve authorities 'obligingly cooperated' by lowering the interest rates in New York. From 1925 to 1928 America lost 422 million dollars of gold. During the same period gold in the United States ear-marked as belonging to Europe increased from 13 to 35 million dollars.

Lower interest rates in New York not only drove gold out of the United States but stimulated stock exchange speculation. Fisher says:

"In a word we dismissed some of our gold foundation and at the same time built a debt structure over the place where the gold had been.

"Billions of debts and a gold base that was slippery—

[19] *Booms and Depressions* by Irving Fisher (London, George Allen), p. 83.
[20] *Ibid*, p. 83.

these two conditions had now set the stage for the collapse of 1929".[21]

Gold went to the United States and France because of reparations and War-debts. It is useless to blame these countries for not receiving payment in goods. The claims of national industry cannot be disregarded to please foreigners.

Non-monetary Causes

Is it permissible to speak of non-monetary causes at all?

Prof. Gustav Cassel's answer is 'No'. Whatever be the causes of the rise or fall of prices, the problem always remains a monetary problem.

Suppose there is an increase in the volume of production. Then the supply of money should be increased at the same rate. Prices will then neither rise nor fall.

Technical progress as a cause of the trade depression thus means nothing. It is primarily a question of money. "From 1895 up to the War", Prof. Gustav Cassel argues, "the general level of commodity prices actually rose in spite of the unusually high rate of technical progress in that period".[22] Prices rose because the supply of means of payment increased more rapidly than that of goods. If the supply of money had not become scarce in 1925—29 prices would not have fallen, and no trade depression would have occurred.

Prof. Gustav Cassel is willing to admit that non-monetary causes may disturb the monetary equilibrium, and thus bring about changes in prices. "This only means that monetary policy has not been strong enough to offer a sufficient resistance to these disturbing factors".[23]

There are others who attach considerable importance to the psychological factor. They regard the depression as a

[21] *Ibid*, pp. 83-4.
[22] *The Crisis in the World's Monetary System*, p. 50.
[23] *Ibid*, p. 50.

crisis of confidence of gigantic dimensions. It is pointed out that the capitalistic system rests on phychological foundations:

"A considerable measure of general optimism is the psychological pre-requisite without which a capitalistic world economy, widely extended and dynamically progressive, cannot live".[24] Prof. Gustav Cassel's answer to this would be that 'confidence', or optimism is not an independent factor, any more than demand and supply: "Monetary policy ought to be able, in spite of adverse psychological conditions to control the purchasing power of the currency".[25]

The Gold Delegation Report attributed the crisis to various causes—partly monetary and partly of a financial, economic and political character. It attached considerable importance to 'economic maladjustments and instability in the post-War world' (para. 42).

Can all these maladjustments and causes of instability, financial, political and economic, be interpreted as monetary phenomena?

The Report draws attention to irregularity in international capital movements, which was due to a complex group of factors: (*a*) violent fluctuations of prices discouraged direct investments in productive enterprises in debtor countries; (*b*) instability of currencies had the same effect; (*c*) stabilization of currencies at levels which in some cases did not correspond to the domestic price levels, caused speculative movements of short-term capital; (*d*) the growth of short-term investments was an important cause of financial instability—French investors, particularly, preferred this form of investment; (*e*) there was a reduction in England's share in international capital investments, and (*f*) lending by the United States was irregular in volume. The Report of the Gold Delegation next referred to profound changes in the structure and localisation of industries, both primary

[24] Dr. E. Wiskenmann in *Weltwirtschaftliche Archiv* for March, 1934, p. 240.

[25] *The Crisis etc.*, pp. 51-2.

and manufacturing. Beet-sugar had again started competing with cane-sugar, and there was growing competition between European wheat-areas and those of North and South America and Australia. The industrial organisation was becoming more elaborate and more rigid, and the processes of manufacture more complex. There was evidence of over-investment in certain industries, and over-investment "rendered production more difficult of adjustment to changing demand". As a result the free adjustment of supply to demand had become much restricted: "The cartellisation of industry and various forms of price control, pools and control boards of primary products, valorisation schemes and their like have all tended to render the economic system unduly rigid".[26] Another cause of the increasing rigidity of the economic system was the comparative inflexibility of wages, and the heavy cost of the 'semi-fixed' charges for unemployment benefits and social services. Increasing rigidity in production and distribution implied 'loss of tensile strength'—an important source of various maladjustments.

On the side of demand, the Gold Delegation Committee noted that with the growth of production and wealth, consumers wanted more of non-essential commodities and services, so that demand tended to become more capricious.

This array of arguments did not impress Prof. Gustav Cassel and Sir Henry Strakosh. The years from 1925 to 1929 were years of progress. How could this progress have been achieved if all the maladjustments mentioned above had been accumulating in an intensified form? The answer to this naive question is that the maladjustments were there, and that sooner or later their combined action was bound to check progress. The check came in 1929.

[26] Para. 55.

OVER-PRODUCTION

Prof. Gustav Cassel characterises the belief that the capacity for production may develop faster than that for consumption as 'superstitious' arising from "a very defective understanding of the mechanism of uniform economic progress". In the 'normal state of development', we are told 'consumption grows at the same pace as production', which is also supposed to be true of saving and the creation of fresh capital. "It is very deplorable", says Prof. Gustav Cassel, "that a great part of the world's financial press is ignorant of such an elementary truth".[27]

It is also an elementary truth that even in a planned economy, mistakes may be made in estimating demand or supply, and production may therefore exceed or fall short of effective demand. A capitalist economy is not a planned economy. When a capitalist economy is of world-wide extent, and producers and consumers are separated by enormous distances, all forms of maladjustments are theoretically conceivable and actually possible.

We have no right to assume that as productive capacity increases effective demand must automatically increase at the same rate.

Suppose that technical advance relating to agriculture leads to a considerable increase in food production. New lands are brought under cultivation, and the yield of old lands increases, while the cost of production per unit falls. There is nothing inherently impossible in such a supposition. If demand for food was expanding less rapidly, producers whose costs of production were comparatively inelastic would be undersold by their rivals. Exports from less advanced agricultural countries would decline, and they would begin to complain of depression. As agricultural production is difficult to curtail, stocks would accumulate, and prices fall.

[27] *The Crisis etc.*, p. 57.

It is seen that over-production in relation to effective demand can occur. It is with effective demand alone that we are concerned. In view of the enormous unsatisfied demand in the world for everything, over-production in the absolute sense is impossible. But over-production that causes crises—and it is with such over-production alone that we are here concerned—is over-production in relation to purchasing power. The masses of India could very well use all the products of Indian hand-looms and cotton mills, 3,000 million yards of British cotton goods, and an equal amount of Japanese piece-goods. Nor is there lack of hunger in India. But it is a question of effective demand or purchasing power, not of need.

When over-production occurs, prices fall because of supply exceeding demand.

Soon after the annexation of the Punjab prices of food-grains and raw materials fell heavily throughout the Province, which made revenue collections very difficult. The causes of agricultural distress are thus analysed in the Punjab Administration Report for 1849-50 and 1850-51:

"For the three first years after annexation the harvests, with a few isolated exceptions, were remarkably favourable. For twenty years, the agriculturists declare, they have never witnessed such crops of wheat and barley. Not only did the unirrigated lands usually under cultivation yield a particularly large return, but cultivation was greatly extended. Lands which in ordinary seasons were seldom sown, gave large returns. These circumstances, joined to the general peace and security of the country, and the fact that large bodies of disbanded soldiers and discharged employees had to turn attention to agriculture for a subsistence, all contributed to cause so great an increase of produce as to reduce prices to an unprecedented extent. The result of these different causes has doubtless been that production has exceeded consumption, and hence that while an abundance of food exists, there is not a sufficient market to secure its sale at remunerative prices."

Here was an agricultural crisis in the Punjab about 85 years ago which embarrassed both the Government and the people. Is it possible to interpret it as a monetary phenomenon?

The writer of the first Administration Report of the Punjab did not interpret it thus. He described the crisis simply as one of over-production of food. But suppose by a remarkable feat of clairvoyance, this writer had acquired a knowledge of monetary theory as expounded in our times by Prof. Gustav Cassel and Sir Henry Strakosh. How would he have explained the crisis?

"An extraordinary scarcity in the means of payment suddenly revealed itself during the first three years after annexation, so that prices of agricultural produce fell heavily. Decrease in the rapidity of circulation also contributed to the same result". That would be the monetary explanation, on approved lines, of the agricultural crisis of 1849-50. It strikes one as a little absurd.

From the point of view of wheat and cotton growers in the Punjab (and other parts of India) the present situation is more or less the same as that which arose in the Punjab 85 years ago. Since 1849-50 great developments have taken place in the means of communication and transportation. India is now a part of world economy, which it was not 85 years ago. But at the present time, as 85 years ago, while there is an abundance of food "there is not a sufficient market to secure its sale at remunerative prices." World production has exceeded world consumption.

In monetary language it would be said that there is not enough money to buy what has been produced at the old prices. If 85 years ago, when we had super-abundant harvests in the Punjab, somehow more money had been created prices would not have fallen either.

The question of over-production is a question of fact about which there should be no dispute. But over-production is alleged by some writers and denied by others.

Prof. Gustav Cassel considers it "a mistake to believe

that production in these years (after the war) showed an abnormal rate of progress".[28]

It is estimated that the average rate of progress in post-War years was 3 per cent per annum, which was approximately the average pre-War rate of progress. "The whole idea," says Prof. Gustav Cassel, "that the rate of progress was exaggerated and that the exaggeration must necessarily be punished by a crisis finds no support in actual facts. No doubt there was an expansion in some branches. But that is a very common occurrence which usually does not seriously disturb the world's economy"[29]

Irving Fisher argues similarly:

"Over-production can scarcely be itself the lasting force which keeps depression going year after year. Were it merely a matter of over-production, it would seem to me to be likely to correct itself more promptly and almost automatically.

"But it may still be true that over-production may precipitate liquidation of debts".[30]

Prof. Jean Lescure, on the other hand believes that the American stock exchange crash came at a time of "agricultural over-production (corn, sugar)"[31]. He says:

"To tell the truth, the fall of prices cannot be effectively mastered except by an increase of demand and consumption or by a restriction of supply".[32]

M. Rist explains the reduction of consumption by referring to the fall in the price of silver which reduced the purchasing power of certain Eastern countries, and the difficulty in finding a market for cereals "due to super-abundant harvests of 1929-30 and the extension of cultivation since the War".[33] The same was true of coffee. He insists again and again that the price level of 1925 was artificial. It was an American price level, produced by American conditions,

[28] *Ibid*, p. 55.
[29] *Ibid*, p. 56.
[30] *Booms and Depressions*, p. 66.
[31] *Essays in Honour of Gustav Cassel*, p. 389.
[32] *Ibid*, p. 389.
[33] *Rist Loc. cit.* p. 336.

which twenty countries of Europe also sought to maintain on their return to the gold standard. "The idea", continues M. Rist, "that this artificial level of prices could be maintained when, under the influence of peace, world production was bound to increase very rapidly, was an idea devoid of rational basis, and events were soon to show its impossibility".[34]

Evidence for Over-Production

In discussing the evidence for over-production we shall first describe the technical changes which have transformed agriculture in the West, and which are so important as to be called an agricultural revolution.

As Prof. Gustav Cassel says, there was technical progress also in the whole period from 1896 to the outbreak of the War. But there was no such revolution in agricultural methods as has occurred in post-War years.

This revolution consists in the use of power-driven machinery in agriculture, and fruits of biological research in application to agriculture.

The industrial revolution began in England; the agricultural revolution began in the United States.

First, America learnt to use machines on a large-scale in large-scale farming, and then she started making them for other countries. The export of Combined Harvester-Threshers and Threshers, and of Tractors from the United States from 1925 to 1930 is shown below:

	Combines	Tractors
1925 ..	1,720	45,946
1926 ..	4,444	51,242
1927 ..	4,705	58,279
1928 ..	7,317	57,869
1929 ..	10,887	60,155
1930 ..	6,573	49,896
	35,646	323,387

[34] *Ibid*, p. 167.

The principal exports were to four countries: Canada, Australia, Argentine and Russia.

In 1914, 270 combine harvesters were manufactured in the United States, and in 1929 about 37,000. In 1916 about 30,000 tractors were manufactured in the United States; in 1928, about 853,000 tractors were in use in that country.[35]

It is estimated that the value of the equipment per farm labourer in the United States was 2,000 dollars in 1925 as compared with 36 dollars in 1870.[36]

The use of the combine harvester saves time and labour. "The combine harvester cuts the heads of wheat, leaving the straw standing, it carries the heads into a threshing drum, threshes, winnows, and bags the grain; it weighs the bags, and they are then removed ready for despatch to the railway-siding. Machines are made to cut a 10- to 15- foot swathe, and with their aid two men can complete the harvesting of 50 acres of wheat per day. Grains need not be man-handled at all from the field right through to the bake-house. For the most effective use of the combine harvester, the standing crop must be completely ripe and sufficiently dry to allow the wheat to be bagged within a minute of its being cut; moreover, the machine is only economical in use where large areas of wheat are harvested".[37]

It is stated that in the United States a combine harvester thresher usually harvests and threshes wheat at a cost of about 3—5 cents a bushel; the cost of threshing alone with the header or binder is more than 10 cents a bushel. As for the saving in time, it is found that a combine harvester would harvest and thresh an acre of wheat with a yield of 15 bushels in three-quarters of an hour; with the sickle and the flail, for the same amount of work 35-50 hours of labour would be required.[38]

The area ploughed per day in Europe with a single

[35] *World Agriculture* (Royal Institute of International Affairs). Chapter III (Oxford, 1932).

[36] *The Agricultural Crisis* (League of Nations, 1931). p. 17.

[37] *World Agriculture*, p. 37

[38] *Ibid*, p.39.

furrow plough driven by a pair of horses or a team of oxen varies from three acres to less than one acre. The average in England is probably less than ¾ acre. In the Punjab a pair of oxen will plough about one acre in a day. One man with a 50 horse-power tractor can plough up to 20 acres per day. "The tractor-drawn seed drill can sow from 70 to 80 acres as against 10 to 15 acres with a horse-drill in England". With the ordinary drill about one acre is sown in the Punjab in a day, and with the automatic drill 3-4 acres.

We further learn that in certain cotton States in the United States each worker can look after 10 to 20 acres of cotton, but in Texas and Oklahoma, with the use of large machinery, 100 acres per man can be cultivated.[39] In the Punjab 2 pairs of oxen and 3 men can, on an average, manage 28 acres of cotton.

Biological improvement has proceeded side by side with mechanical progress. New types of wheat have been evolved which have enormously extended the area under wheat. It is estimated that through this means 100,000,000 acres have been added in Canada alone to the world's possible wheat fields. Certain types of wheat enabled the wheat belt of Canada to be extended west to the Rockies and then north up to the Peace River District. Further:

"The work initiated by Farrer in Australia has certainly doubled the potential wheat belt, and similar work has resulted in opening hundreds of thousands of square miles in the semi-arid acres of Russia and of Russian Asia. The gigantic farms of the U. S. S. R. are indeed mostly in areas which could not, in normal years, have produced wheat until the plant-breeders evolved the new types".[40]

The researches of Dutch plant-breeders in Java have increased the yield of sugar there more than three-fold.[41]. The meaning of biological and mechanical progress as affecting agriculture is not fully realised by those who insist that the present crisis is due solely to monetary factors.

[39] *Ibid*, pp. 41-2. [40] *Ibid*, p. 45. [41] *Ibid*, p. 46.

The average growth of production at the rate of 3 per cent per annum does not bring out the significance of the much more rapid rate of growth in the production of wheat, other cereals and coffee. As we shall see later, important consequences may flow from the over-production of a limited number of important agricultural products, even when the rate of growth of production in general is not very remarkable.

"There can be no question," says *World Agriculture*, "but that the improvement of methods and systems of production have already much complicated the serious problem of adjusting agricultural output to market requirements".[42]

Reference has been made above to Russia. Her reappearance as a seller of cereals and other products also contributed to the downward tendency of prices.

WHEAT

We are particularly interested in Wheat. It is also the most important cereal.

"The depression in agricultural products is at the bottom of the general crisis; the depression in cereals is at the bottom of the agricultural depression".[43]

The depression in wheat, we may add, is at the bottom of the depression in cereals. The prices of coarser grains rise and fall with the price of wheat.

The following tables, borrowed from *The Agricultural Crisis* show the world production of wheat:

World Production of Wheat Average 1909-13=100.

	Average 1925-30
Europe (excluding U. S. S. R.)	98
Canada	214·8
U. S. A.	119·7
Argentine	165·0
Australia	172·0

[42] *Ibid*, p. 18.
[43] *Ibid*, p. 22.

Annual World Production of Wheat
Average 1909-13=100

	Production in millions of quintals	Per cent
Average 1909-13	.. 1,029·6	100
Average 1921-25	.. 1,018·7	99
Year		
1926	.. 1,182·3	115
1927	.. 1,191·2	116
1928	.. 1,280·9	124
1929	.. 1,129·0	110
1930	.. 1,276·7	124

Production has exceeded consumption: "It is a fact that, at the present time, the equilibrium between supply and demand has been destroyed. Consumption naturally increases with the growth of the population; it is, however, only rising slowly and is not keeping pace with production".[44]

Cotton

The World Production of Cotton is thus estimated:

	Millions of quintals	Per cent
1913	.. 48·5	100
1921-25, average	.. 46·4	96
1926	.. 61·5	127
1927	.. 51·9	107
1928	.. 56·9	117
1929	.. 56·4	116
1930	.. 56·0	115

Between 1926 and 1930 production was from 7 to 26 per cent higher than in 1913. The heavy fall in the price of cotton in 1929-1931 (in August 1931 the United Kingdom index number of the price of cotton—American middling, had fallen to 41·1 as compared with 100 for 1925-29), and

[44] *Ibid*, pp. 25-6.

the growth of stocks suggest that there was an over-production of cotton. The same is true of sugar, coffee and rubber. The world stocks of these commodities and wheat are shown below:

Commodity and Unit	Month	1925	1929	1930	1931
Wheat (millions of quintals).	August	114	233	220	246
Sugar ,, ,,	December	37[1]	57	71	87
Coffee ,, ,,	March	5[1]	9	16	17[2]
Cotton (millions of bales)	December	5,635	7,234	9,396	10,709
Rubber (thousands of metric tons)	March	..	243	367	556[3]

[1] Statistics for 1926.

[2] Stocks at February 29, 1932 were 205,000,000 quintals.

[3] Stocks at February 29, 1932 were 654,000 metric tons.

(World Agriculture, p. 89)

Inter-action of Monetary and Non-Monetary Factors

It is impossible to deny the fact of agricultural over-production. Given this over-productions, prices of agricultural products were bound to fall. And it is important to note that they began to fall before the stock exchange crisis in New York in October 1929.

The fall of agricultural prices reduced the income of agricultural countries. In view of the growing competition in the supply of agricultural products, some countries, as, India, found it difficult to maintain their position in world markets. This further reduced their purchasing power.

Even when the fall of prices and the diminution in the quantities exported are limited to a comparatively small number of commodities, the effects may be serious if large numbers of people are concerned in their production. For example, the disappearance of wheat exports, the fall in the exports of cotton, and the heavy fall in the price of these staples, have literally brought agriculture in the Punjab and other parts of India to the verge of ruin.

The agricultural depression has affected over 70 per cent of the population of India. The total population of the world in 1930 is estimated to be 2,013 millions, of whom 1,301 millions, or about 65 per cent, were dependent on agriculture.

The impoverishment of such large numbers inevitably reduced the demand for the products of industrial countries.

Stanley Jevons connected depressions in the Lancashire trade with famines in India. But from the point of view of the agriculturist, agricultural over-production has the same serious effects as a famine. In a famine agricultural income falls, though prices go up, because less is produced. At the present time plenty is the cause of poverty.

INDUSTRY

We have seen that technical progress has profoundly altered the relation of world supply to world demand in the case of primary products. Such changes are called structural.

Side by side with the transformation of agriculture the structure of world industry has also changed.

Technical improvements and rationalisation have enormously increased the producing capacity of mining, metallurgical and manufacturing industries. Great as was the waste caused by the War, recovery was rapid, thanks to applied science and organisation. Of this, the ship-building industry is a striking example.

The gross tonnage of world shipping in 1914 was 49·1 millions. The destruction of shipping during the War caused an abnormal rise in freight rates, but as soon as the War ended the ship-building industry, aided by subventions began to expand, and ignoring a slight fall in 1924, the tonnage increased steadily till 1931. Already in 1919 the gross tonnage of world shipping amounted to 50·1 millions, or 3·6 per cent more than in 1914. In 1931 it rose to 70·1 millions—an increase of 43 per cent as compared with 1914. It may be thought that this increase was called forth by the growth of foreign commerce. But in that case freights should have risen, or at any rate, not fallen. But during this whole period, excepting one year, freights steadily moved downwards, the index number (1913=100) falling from 427 in 1920 to 106 in 1929 and 82 in 1930. As Moretti in a brief but excellent study of the subject says, we find ourselves confronted with a singular phenomenon, which is that ships were launched annually in numbers which form a strong contrast to ships demolished (which means that it was not merely a question of replacing old vessels), to the downward movement of freights and to the state of profound depression which has characterised in these past few years the navigation of the world (*Annali di statistica e di Economia,* Vol. I).

It would not be incorrect to speak of over-production of ships in this period, over-production in relation to the total mass of goods to be carried.

The ship-building industry is of national importance and non-economic motives have played an important part in the expansion of world shipping.

There is keen competition among the main shipping lines, but that does not prevent the existence of rings, pools and agreements in the shipping industry whose object is to soften this competition.

Non-economic motives have played an important part also in the development of other industries. In India the decline in manufactured imports during the War subjected the people to great hardships and acted as a stimulus to industrialisation. The rise in the price of manufactured goods during the War encouraged the foundation of new and the expansion of old industries. Later the fiscal needs of the Government led to the imposition of higher tariffs on imports, and after the adoption of the policy of discriminating protection in 1924 the pace of industrialisation was accelerated.

The War directly and indirectly stimulated industrial production, but even before the War forces were in operation which would have in time profoundly modified the structure of the world's industrial economy. The Industrial Revolution had made England the workshop of the world, but gradually British methods of manufacture were copied by other countries, which began to compete with England in their own and foreign markets. By the end of the 19th century England's advantage over other countries had grown substantially less and at the time of the outbreak of the War England, though still maintaining her lead, was compelled to fight for her markets in a way she had not done before. The growing commercial rivalry between England and Germany is regarded as one of the pre-disposing causes of the War.

The industrial development of the United States, Germany and Japan may be easily traced through the growth of imports from these countries into India. In 1875-76 not less than 83 per cent of our total imports came from the United Kingdom, the share of Germany being 0·05 per cent, of the United States 0·5 per cent and Japan 0·01 per cent. By 1905-06 Britain's share in our imports had fallen to 68·6 per cent of the total. In 1913-14, 2·6 per cent of the total imports came from Japan, also 2·6 per cent from the United States, 6·9 per cent from Germany and 64·2 per cent from the United Kingdom.

The growth of Indian production in post-War years was remarkable. A new iron and steel industry had been founded with a producing capacity of 600,000 tons of finished goods. The growth of the cotton mill industry was steadily reducing the demand for British piece-goods. In the year 1913-14 over 3,000 million yards of piece-goods were imported from the United Kingdom, Indian mill production in that year amounting to a little over 1,000 million yards (422 million yards in 1900-01). In 1927-28 we imported 1,541 million yards of British piece-goods, while Indian mill production amounted to 2,356 million yards (over 3,000 million yards now). The progress of the match industry has rendered India independent of foreign sources of supply and considerable progress has been made in the production of soaps and other toilet requisites, cement, paper, boots and shoes and other leather goods, sugar and other industries.

The industrial progress of the world in recent years may be judged from the following table of index numbers:

Index Numbers of Industrial Production.* 1913=100

	1919	1920	1928	1929	1930	1931
Industrial						
Europe ..	..	77	115	120	111	98
U. S. A. ..	123	126	161	171	137	115
Canada ..	128	121	213	234	196	166
Australia ..	103	116	143	150	154	133
New Zealand ..	..	..	137	148	..	..
India ..	140	124	161	182	211	200
Japan ..	200	162	294	323	300	303
Argentine ..	110	97	149	143	148	..
Brazil ..	..	76	270	235	..	..
Chile ..	..	..	130	153	160	132

The percentage increase in 1929 in the case of India, Japan, Canada and Brazil was heavy. It may, however, be remembered that excepting Japan, the total volume of industrial production in agricultural countries like India, Brazil, the Argentine and Canada is small. According to estimates of world production made by the League of Nations the percentage share of the more important countries in the total is as follows: U. S. A. 31·3 per cent, Great Britain (weighted index) 12·9 per cent, France 10·1 per cent, Japan 5·9 per cent and Belgium 2·2 per cent. Still the growth of industrial production in agricultural countries is of some significance from the point of view of world economy. It will also be noted that in 1929, as compared with 1913, there was an increase of 20 per cent in the industrial production of industrial

*A. W. April 1933, p. 345.

Europe and no less than 71 per cent in that of the United States.

Both in 1919 and 1920 the industrial production of the world was below the pre-War level:

Industrial Production of the World in 1919 and 1920.*
1913=100

	1919	1920
Europe:		
Belligerent countries ..	63	69
Neutral countries ..	99	101
Total ..	66	72
Non-European countries ..	114	118
World ..	90	97

But in 1925 the pre-War level of industrial production was reached and thereafter progress continued till 1929:

National Indices of Industrial Production. 1925=100

	1926	1927	1928	1929
France ..	116	102	119	130
Germany ..	95	120	120	122
Poland ..	98	123	138	138
Sweden ..	103	108	104	127
United Kingdom ..	77	111	105	113
U. S. S. R. ..	139	164	198	223
Canada ..	117	125	138	154
U. S. A. ..	104	102	107	114

As compared with 1925 the estimated increase in the population of Europe was 5 per cent, North America 6 per cent, rest of the world 3 per cent. There is little doubt that industrial production was increasing in the years immediately preceding the depression at a more rapid rate than demand.

But demand does not necessarily depend on numbers. It is perfectly conceivable that demand for finished goods should increase when the population is stationary or even declining. That may be so if the standard of living rises and the

* *Ibid*, p. 344.

purchasing power of the people increases sufficiently to enable them to maintain a higher standard of living.

Let us take an example. Between 1913-14 and 1927-28 the total consumption of cloth in India increased from 5,146 million yards to 5,444 million yards, or by something less than 6 per cent. Allowing for the growth of numbers in this period, per capita consumption probably fell, or increased very little, if at all. But India can consume more cloth. The masses are not so well provided with cotton goods that an additional ten yards per head in the shape of two or three dhoties and two or three shirts or upper cloths would be considered a superfluity. Consumption, however, is limited by purchasing power.

The purchasing power of the people remaining the same, suppose Indian mill production suddenly doubled. The result would be the accumulation of stocks and a large drop in price, for even if imports of foreign cloth ceased altogether, the output of Indian mills and hand-looms would be in excess of the demand as determined by the present purchasing power of the people.

It is in this sense that the term over-production is to be understood, particularly when it is applied to finished goods. In the case of crude food-stuffs, such as cereals, there is a physical limit to human consumption, and even a slight excess of supply may bring about a collapse of prices.

Income and purchasing power set the limit to the demand for industrial goods. Our review of industrial production (incomplete as the figures are) shows a rapid growth and suggests the conclusion that the world's purchasing power did not increase at the same rate.

We may conclude that structural changes in industry (including under this expression improvements in organisation and technical progress on the one hand and the rise of industrialism in agricultural countries on the other) in post-War years were of a nature calculated to upset the relation of production to consumption. The actual point of time when the crisis broke out is a matter of less importance.

CONJUNCTURAL EXPANSION AND STRUCTURAL OVER-PRODUCTION

Such over-production as we have been considering has nothing whatever to do with conjunctural expansion which is a characteristic feature of the trade cycle. A trade cycle begins with a state of quiescence, which is followed successively by improvement, expansion, feverish activity, decline and collapse. A comparatively low rate of discount encourages borrowing, and as the rise of prices makes it profitable to borrow, there takes place a general expansion of trade. Finally, when the rate of discount is raised and credit contracts, liquidation begins, which results in the elimination of unsound businesses. Trade returns to the state of quiescence from which it started and the whole cycle begins anew.

These are the well-known phases of conjunctural expansion and contraction.

But the expansion of industrial and agricultural production since the War is of a different order.

Let us recall the case of wheat. The mechanical and biological progress which has increased the area and yield of wheat in the principal wheat-producing countries of the West, as we have seen, began long before 1929. Its causes do not lie in the favourable conjuncture of the years 1927-29.

Not merely the supply but the demand for wheat has undergone profound changes. Italy, France, Germany and Czecho-Slovakia were considerable importers of wheat. Now they are 'autark' or self-sufficient, and it is not improbable that they may appear in the role of exporters in the near future.

With the growth of civilization there is a tendency in European countries to consume less wheat but more meat, fruits and vegetables. While production is increasing, demand tends to contract. It is estimated that between 1916 and 1928-29 the production of wheat flour in the United States increased only 5·5 per cent, while the population increased 20·5 per cent. In spite of growing prosperity, rather because of it, the consumption of wheat flour per head of the population in this period in the United States fell by 15 per cent.

Dr. Guenter Keiser describes this interesting situation as a 'tendency towards a structural aversion from the use of bread', and says that this tendency is observable in all countries.[45] Not in India yet. Our masses have not yet become so highly civilised as to regard bread with aversion.

The development of wheat production in European countries which formerly imported wheat, has, as has been stated above, taken place behind tariff walls. The result has been to change the character of the world wheat market, the existence of which was never questioned before. A world wheat market may still be said to exist, but it is a market in which domestic prices are different in different countries, the differences being due, not to cost of transportation, but heavy import duties. Dr. Guenter Keiser may well ask: *Gibt es noch einen Weizenweltmarkt?* (Does a world wheat market still exist?). In the *World Economic Survey, 1931-32*, attention was called to the wide variations in wheat prices in different parts of the 'world' market, and their inharmonious rise and fall. For example, between January 1929 and January 1932, the price of wheat, reckoned in United States cents per bushel of 60 lbs., fell in Argentine from 113 to 44 cents (61 per cent) and in India from 158 to 60 cents (62 per cent), but it rose in Germany from 135 to 147 cents, and in France from 164 to 179 cents. The lowest price in the same month (January 1932) was 44 cents in Argentine and the highest 179 cents in France—the French price being four times the price of the same cereal in the same month in Argentine.

In November 1933 wheat prices ranged from 34 cents in Buenes Aires to 130 cents in France.

[45] *Laesst sich der Weizenpreis steigen, by* Dr. Keiser, in Wirtschaftsdenst, May 11 and May 18, 1934.

All this meant a change in the structure of the market, which inevitably reacted on the price of wheat.

The growth of production owing to technical improvements in the methods of production, the decline in demand owing to changes in the habits of consumption, and, finally, non-economic factors which have created national wheat markets and national wheat prices—these are structural changes having no connection whatever with cyclical oscillations of trade.

We are not unfamiliar with structural changes. There was one such change when the opening of the Suez Canal opened the markets of the world to our wheat. Before India began to export wheat, the price of wheat in India was uninfluenced by world factors. The development of railway construction, which linked the internal markets with the ports and the linking of Indian ports with foreign ports through sea communication, transformed the Indian market. The price of wheat began to rise and fall in sympathy with the world price; very often the price rose, in spite of increased production, because of increase in foreign demand, and very often the price fell, when production had declined, because of a reduction in the foreign demand.

Manufacturing industries furnish many examples of structural changes. The transition from hand-work to factory production is a structural change. India is still in a stage of economic transition in this sense, and we are witnessing not one but bundles of structural changes in industry. Hand-made paper has entirely disappeared (excepting such paper made in Indian jails). Paper made from Sabai grass in modern factories is one change; paper made from bamboo pulp, when this can be successfully done, will be another change. Even the world paper-making industry is undergoing changes which are described as 'structural'.[46] Another example is furnished by the market in cotton piece-goods.

[46] See Strukturwandlungen am Weltmarkt fuer Paper, Pappe, Holzschliff und Zellstoff, by Dr. W. Twerrdochleboff, in W. A. for May, 1934.

Its structure has changed since the War, and it is still in a state of flux. We may expect to see in the future the gradual elimination of imports, a decrease in the proportion of hand-woven stuffs, and a steady growth of mill-production.

It is clear that such changes are independent of rhythmical expansion and contraction of business which is so largely influenced by the supply of credit money. But can monetary policies be so framed as to counteract the effect of structural changes in production on prices?

The question may best be answered by putting another. Suppose there is a famine and food cannot be imported from outside. Is it possible to devise a monetary policy which will prevent the price of food from rising?

The answer is 'No'. Money is no substitute for food. If people could eat rupees in a time of famine, scarcity of food might be relieved by the consumption of silver. But if it is food that is wanted, and food in quantities sufficient to relieve every one's hunger is not available, price must go up. The problem is not a monetary one. It is a question of demand and supply, and so long as the forces of demand and supply have free play, the result of their action must be to raise the price of food. Price can be prevented from rising either by reducing demand or by adding to the supply.

Over-production is the converse of the same problem. Famines, as we have said above, are Nature's crises. Over-production at the present time is not so much due to the bounty of nature as to the genius of man in utilizing the forces of nature for his own purposes. But the problem is essentially the same as in a time of famine: to prevent prices from falling either supply must be reduced or demand increased. It is not a monetary problem.

Silver

What is the role of silver in the present depression? Sir Arthur Salter says:

"I will not say that silver counts for nothing at all in

this depression, but my own strong view is that it occupies a very small place indeed in it".[47]

But in *The Crisis in Agriculture* we read:

"Now it is certain that the purchasing power of hundreds of millions of inhabitants in certain large countries cannot develop normally on account of disturbed general conditions, aggravated in a part of Asia by the collapse of the silver currency".[48]

M. Rist attaches more importance to silver than Sir Arthur Salter:

"Another aggravating circumstance was the fall in the price of silver, low already in 1929, and which has fallen perceptibly since 1930, in reducing suddenly the purchasing power of countries of the Far East, where silver has remained the standard of value"[49].

In explaining under-consumption, Paul Einzig thus refers to silver:

"As a result of the depreciation of silver during the last few years, the purchasing power of China, India and other Eastern countries has been severely reduced. The price of silver declined from 36d. an ounce in 1924 to about 12d. an ounce in 1931, as a result of which the purchasing power of half the world's population has been greatly reduced".[50]

The report of the Macmillan Committee also refers to "the disorganisation of trade with China and India and many other countries resulting from political and other forms of disturbance, and to a large extent from the fall in the value of silver" (para. 111).

In India Mr. S. K. Sarma has been fighting the cause of silver for a long time. In the preface to his *Papers on Currency and the Reserve Bank for India* (1934), he refers

[47] *The World Economic Crisis*, p. 22.
[48] *The Agricultural Crisis*, p. 16.
[49] *Rist. Loc. cit.* p. 336.
[50] *The world Economic Crisis* (Macmillan, 1932) by Paul Einzig, p. 47.

to the 'original sin' of closing the mints to the coinage of silver; the effect of the fall in the price of silver in recent years on the people of India is thus described:

"The silver which they purchased at varying rates, at 40d. and 50d. and even 72d. an ounce, now sells at 20d. an ounce. The holders of silver are practically ruined and their hoards have become of absolutely no value. And yet the rupee is our legal standard and measure of value" (p. ii).

It may be admitted that the fall in the price of silver has reduced the purchasing power of countries like China, which use silver as their standard of value. The case of India is different.

The rupee is our unit of account. It ceased to be the standard of value in 1893. It may have been wrong to close the mints to the free coinage of silver, but once the silver mints were closed to free coinage India's purchasing power ceased to be influenced by fluctuations in the price of silver.

The price of silver was about 40d. per ounce in 1893. Between 1899 and 1914 it fluctuated between 24 $^{1}/_{16}$d. (1903) and 30⅞d. (1907). In spite of the fall in the value of silver India prospered in this period. Exchange was steady at 16d. gold, and the purchasing power of India increased owing to the growing world demand, at rising prices, for her food-stuffs and raw materials. So far as India's purchasing power for manufactured imports was concerned, it did not matter at all what the price of silver was. Of course the value of our silver hoards fell. Some of this silver may have been purchased before 1893 at more than 50d. per ounce.

The purchasing power of a country which does not produce silver, and whose currency has been given a fixed gold value above its intrinsic value, does not depend on the rise or fall in the price of silver. Such a country would lose by a fall in the price of silver only if she were compelled to part with her silver stocks, acquired at high prices, to pay for imports of goods and services.

Since September 21, 1931 India has exported a considerable amount of gold, but her imports of silver exceed exports of silver:

		Silver. In lakhs of rupees	
Averages		Imports	Exports
1909-10 to 1913-14	..	10,88	3,67
1914-15 to 1918-19	..	4,56	1,77
1919-20 to 1923-24	..	14,18	2,66
1924-25 to 1928-29	..	19,62	2,85
Year			
1929-30	..	13,36	1,47
1930-31	..	13,46	1,81
1931-32	..	4,42	1,83
1932-33	..	1,63	90
1933-34	..	..	..

The purchasing power of India should be measured in terms of commodities that she produces and sells abroad—not in terms of silver which she imports.

Under normal conditions a country's purchasing power is a function of her annual income, not of the hoarded value of her past savings in the form of ornaments and bullions.

It may also be pointed out that if, somehow, the fall in the price of silver has actually reduced India's purchasing power, this loss of purchasing power, has been more than counter-balanced by the sharp rise in the price of gold.

Wages Interest and Taxes

Reference has been made above to the failure of domestic costs and prices in certain countries which returned to the gold standard, notably in the United Kingdom, to adjust themselves to the rate of exchange. The lack of adjustment was due in part to the high level of wages and interest charges. According to the figures given by the Macmillan Committee, real wages in Great Britain, based on hourly time-rates of wages, in January 1930 were 13 per cent higher than in Holland, 23 per cent higher than in Germany, 42 per cent higher than in France and no less than 57 per cent higher than in Italy (para. 121).

The maintenance of the Bank rate in England at a level higher than in New York kept interest charges, as a burden on industry, high: "The significant fact is that adherence to the gold standard under these conditions prevented a fall in interest rates, which in its turn preserved the dead weight of past-obligations as a large factor in British costs".[51]

M. Rist refers to the high level of taxation, which retarded the adjustment of industry and commerce to the new conditions of competition.[52]

This has also an important application to Indian agriculture. The land revenue and water-rates form a considerable proportion of costs in Indian agriculture. While prices of agriculture products have fallen, these charges have not been sufficiently reduced. They constitute a heavy burden on agriculture in India.

Since September 1931 considerable additions have been made to both direct and indirect taxation. The income-tax is heavy, and the new excise duties on sugar and matches may tend to check the growth of these industries.

One important cause of high taxation is the fear of war and the need for 'preparedness'. In Europe disarmament is discussed every year, but no country is sincerely willing to disarm. In India the great increase in military expenditure came after the War. Military expenditure has been reduced in recent years, but it still absorbs a high proportion of central revenues.

Political reforms have led to the multiplication of departments and an all-round increase of expenditure. With the inauguration of the new constitution there will be a further increase in expenditure both in the Provinces and at the Centre.

[51] *Monetary Policy and the Depression*, p. 6.
[52] *Rist. Loc. cit.*, p. 339.

It may certainly be said that we have chosen the wrong time for trying costly constitutional experiments.

Rise of National Economies

The rise of national economies is largely an effect of the depression. It is an attempt by each country to 'safeguard' its own position.

When exports decline, imports have necessarily to be cut down. When home-producers lose their foreign markets, they naturally desire to exclude the foreigner from their home-market. Hence the growth of protection all-round.

Protection for agriculture is a new development. We tax foreign wheat ourselves, for having lost their markets abroad, our wheat growers are anxious to retain the entire home-market for themselves.

In European countries, like France, Germany and Italy, agriculture is protected as an industry of political importance. Between 1929 and 1932 while the price of wheat in India fell heavily, it was kept high in these countries by taxation of imports.

Germany has become self-sufficient in the matter of food-supply. She suffered terribly from the blocade during the War. The Allies taught her a lesson then, which she has not forgotten.

In Italy '*la bataglia del grano*' (battle of wheat) is being waged furiously. The object is to free Italy from the 'slavery of foreign bread' (*schiavitu del pane straniero*).[53] The 'Battle of Wheat', as Mussolini has said, 'responds to a fundamental necessity of the economic life of the nation'.[54] The population of Italy is increasing rapidly and Italy must grow more food—for the alternative is the 'slavery of foreign bread'. Large areas under swamps are being drained and rendered fit for cultivation. This *bonifica integrale*, as it is

[53] *Mussolini. Discorsi* (Alpes, Milano), 1922. p. 122.
[54] *Mussolini. Discorsi*, 1926, p. 327.

called, it is expected, will add 1,600,000 hectares (3,840,000 acres) of land to the cultivable area of Italy, and save an import of no less than 2,300,000,000 lire (about £40 million).[55]

As Mussolini said several years ago, Italian agriculture is entering an epoch of 'grande splendore'.[56] Unfortunately the 'splendore' of agriculture elsewhere means depression of agriculture in India.

Mussolini dislikes urbanisation. "The people who abandon the land are condemned to decadence".[57] He gives to agriculture the first place in the national economy, as he wants to see Italy inhabited by a numerous, healthy and virile population.

Attention is drawn in *The Agricultural Crisis* to the growth of agricultural protection everywhere. "While limitations of every sort are placed on imports, export bounties are granted in certain countries". The duties on cereals particularly have been increased. "Faced with the competition of imports from other countries, European producers are determined to ensure a profit from their harvest and to protect it".[58]

But, as we have seen, in certain cases, it is not a question merely of profits of agriculture: it is a question of national self-sufficiency and political power.

Tariffs and other aids to industry have tended to deepen the gloom by adding to the difficulties of marketing. As M. Rist says, tariffs have enabled new and vast countries "to create a large number of industries, which have only served to double the means of production which were more than sufficient already".[59] The tendency towards over-production thus becomes still more emphasized.

[55] *Mussolini. Discorsi,* 1929. p. 253.
[56] *Mussolini.. Discorsi.* 1925. p. 122.
[57] *Mussolini, Dicorsi* 1928. p. 288.
[58] p. 20.
[59] *Rist. Loc. cit.* p. 339.

Cartellisation

A remarkable feature of recent economic developments is the growth of cartels in the leading manufacturing countries. The object of these cartels is to regulate prices. Their rapid growth would lead one to suppose that productive capacity was increasing at a rate faster than demand so that remunerative prices could not be obtained unless competition was restricted by means of agreements among producers. In an article in the Wirtschaftsdienst for October 14, 1932 Dr. Udo-Horst Bychelberg, while reviewing the progress of cartels in different countries remarks that the free play of forces exists no longer in most of the spheres of our economic life. "In industries producing raw materials and half-finished goods", he says, "there is rising a proud edifice of associations and cartels", and manufacturing industries are taking care not to be left behind in this movement. The number of cartels in Germany which was 385 in 1905, rose to 500-600 before the War. For the year 1925 it is unofficially estimated at 1,500-2,000 and officially at 2,200-2,600. Of industrial raw materials and half-finished goods consumed in Germany the prices of about half are controlled (gebunden)—they are not determined by the free play of supply and demand. According to Liefmann, a recognised authority on cartels, cartels in Germany control about 400 commodities. The cartel has made its appearance in other countries as well *e.g.*, England. The British cotton industry has formed a cartel, and there is a marked tendency towards concentration in several other British industries. The branches of industry which are controlled or have an organised economy in England are mining, metallurgy, manufacture of iron and steel and other metallic goods and of machines and means of transportation, electrotechnical industries, building industries, chemicals, paper, leather, textiles, and food industries. Most of these industries are also controlled in the following countries where they are of any importance: Germany, Austria, Czecho-Slovakia,

Hungary, Switzerland, Holland, Belgium (including Luxemburg), France, Poland, Italy and Spain.

In Germany, of all prices paid for goods, those paid for the products of cartellised industries represent 10-20 per cent. The comparison of 'controlled' prices with the total value of foreign trade yields the following interesting result:

	Value of cartellised products as a percentage of the total value of foreign trade of each country
Germany	70—80
England	38·9—48·9
France	46·6
Italy	12·4—25·0
Hungary	46·2
Czecho-Slovakia	44·3
Poland	43·5
Spain	22·3
Rumania	25·0
Belgium	45·5

Perhaps these percentages (for which we are indebted to Dr. Bychelberg) give an exaggerated idea of the importance of cartels in the economic life of the countries concerned: a more reliable index of their importance would be the proportion of sales of cartellised products to total sales which, as we have seen, is 10-20 per cent in Germany. But this information is not available for other countries.

The fact, however, remains that in manufacturing industries and in those producing raw materials or half-finished goods, a 'controlled' economy is taking the place of free competition. This has some significance in the study of overproduction.

PART III

THE WAY-OUT

CHAPTER VIII

SOME SUGGESTED REMEDIES

Every one is agreed that for the return of prosperity it is necessary to raise prices. Sir Arthur Salter suggested the raising of gold prices to the level of 1929 and their stabilization at that level. "I believe", he wrote, "both are practicable, if the world really desires them".

As a method of achieving this aim Sir Arthur favoured monetary expansion in France and the United States, which would lead to greater imports of goods into these countries. At the same time commercial policies and tariffs were to be reformed, and an attempt made to restore foreign lending as soon as possible.[1]

The payment of reparations and War-debts has already been suspended.

Since the out-break of the depression each country, as we have seen, has sought to protect its position by means of tariffs. Currency depreciation and other methods have also been largely employed to restrict imports and stimulate exports. "But competitive currency depreciations and competitive tariffs, and more artificial means of improving an individual country's foreign balance such as exchange restrictions, import prohibitions and quotas", as Mr. Keynes says, "help no one and injure each, if they are applied all round."[2]

The attempt to raise prices by the restriction of supply is "worse than useless".[3] For the community as a whole it means a diminished, not augmented income.

[1] *Recovery.* pp. 36-8.
[2] *Means to Prosperity.* p. 19.
[3] *Ibid*, p. 17.

Prices would certainly rise if demand increased. The growth of demand is dependent on the growth of purchasing power. If now the burden of taxation was lowered everywhere, and at the same time there was an expansion of public works programmes in many different countries with the help of loans, new purchasing power would be created. Mr. Keynes says:

"I see no reliable prospect of a sufficient rise in world prices within a reasonable time, except as the result of a substantial and more or less simultaneous, relief of taxation and increase of loan expenditure in many different countries".[4] It is important that this action should be taken simultaneously by different countries. For the increase of loan expenditure would raise prices in a country and restrict its exports, thus exercising an unfavourable effect on the balance of trade.

"Isolated action may be imprudent, General action has no dangers whatever".[5]

In industrial countries of the West loan expenditure would create employment, reduce the number of the unemployed, and increase the purchasing power of a large section of the population. Prices would thus rise, and India would not fail to benefit by that.

A public works programme for India, which is sometimes advocated, has however, no meaning. It may burden India with a heavy load of debt, without exercising a perceptible influence on the demand or purchasing power of the Indian masses.

The construction of public works in a time of famine gives employment to idle agriculturists, and keeps their body and soul together. At the present time, however, there is no question of creating employment for the agricultural population. Men and women in the villages are not unemployed. They have such employment as agriculture offers—only they

[4] *Ibid*, p. 24.
[5] *Ibid*, p. 24.

have suddenly become poor, because the prices of their products have fallen.

Industrial labour in India is a very small fraction of the total population—about one per cent. And then there is no depression in Indian manufacturing industries. State expenditure may create employment for the educated unemployed, but an increase in the purchasing power of the educated unemployed will not raise the prices of food-stuffs and raw materials.

For us the real problem is that of persuading the world to buy more of our products, and at higher prices. An increase of loan expenditure will not help in the expansion of exports. Nor can such expenditure be expected to perceptibly increase the demand for raw materials by stimulating industrial development, or reduce the numbers dependent on agriculture.

Stable Prices or Stable Money Incomes

At present the United States is attempting to raise prices by means of an ambitious plan of public expenditure, accompanied by an expansion of credit. The American experiment is being watched with interest by the whole world. Will it succeed?

Socialist writers are sceptical. Mr. Cole says:

"I do not doubt the possibility, or even the probability of American reflation being able to bring about a temporary revival. But I still doubt very much the ability of any Government, under capitalist conditions, to control the revival when it has occurred, or to prevent a period of restored prosperity being so abused as to lead on to an unsound boom, which will engender in its turn a fresh, and even a worse depression".[6]

The remedy, then, is worse than the disease. We get over a crisis, or emerge from a trade depression, only to fall

[6] *What Everybody Wants to Know About Money* (Edited by G. D. H. Cole), p. 113.

again into the trough of another, and even worse depression.

Why? The explanation is as follows.

The fall of prices during the past four or five years has been due to technical progress, which has enabled larger quantities of all goods, particularly raw materials and foodstuffs, to be produced at very much reduced costs. If costs continue to fall, as they will, if progress continues, prices will fall also. If, now, prices are stabilised, while costs are falling, profits will most certainly increase. That must lead to an expansion of production and demand for more and more money to finance it. As Mr. Durbin says: "A general inflationary situation will therefore develop, although the price level does not rise by a single point".[7] This is more or less what happened in the United States between 1926 and 1929. At a time when a sharp contraction in agricultural prices had occurred owing to over-production, made possible by the growth of mechanisation and fall in the costs of production, American bankers attempted to maintain a stable general level of prices. The attempt failed. It led to a boom, which ended in the collapse of the whole system.

It is seen that when costs are falling prices cannot be kept stable without inviting ultimate disaster. Inflation, open or disguised, will be the only result of such a policy, and temporary boom conditions will be followed by a prolonged period of depression and readjustment.

Mr. Durbin does not attach much importance to a stable level of prices. Prices may and should be allowed to fall as costs fall. "There is", as Mr. Durbin says, "nothing disastrous in such a fall". The correct long term credit policy should aim at stabilising money incomes. This is the solution of the riddle of money—not stable exchanges, nor stable prices, but stable money incomes.

Prices, as Mr. Durbin says, "would only fall after and because of a previous decline in money costs, and the full

[7] *Socialist Credit Policy by E. F. M. Durbin* (New Fabian Research Bureau), p. 25.

output of consumption goods could be maintained at the lower prices. Everywhere more would be produced for the same total cost. Everyone would receive the same or approximately the same money income but the real income would continuously rise as the prices of finished products continued to fall".[8]

Again:

"Hence I conclude that the solution of the long period problem is to be found in the policy of constant purchasing power per head of the population. The socialised banking system must be required to change the criterion of its policy over the long period. The banking corporation must not look to prices, nor to the total of their liabilities, nor even to the unemployment problem, but to the general level of money incomes which their credit policy is in large part determining. They must construct some suitable index of the income position and seek to stabilise that".[9]

Similarly in his contribution to *What Everybody Wants to Know about Money* (Chapter VII) Mr. Durbin writes:

"The relation between money and prices should be such that money incomes are stabilised while accumulation proceeds by a slow and steady fall in the cost of living" (p. 339).

Neither in the *Socialist Credit Policy* nor in *What Everybody Wants to Know About Money* are we told by Mr. Durbin or any one else how money incomes are to be stabilised, or how constant purchasing power per head of the population is to be secured in a capitalist economy.

It simply cannot be done.

We agree that when costs fall, prices should be allowed to fall. But a fall of costs must necessarily reduce money incomes of large sections of the population. When costs and prices are falling, purchasing power per head of the population cannot remain constant.

[8] *Ibid*, p. 29.
[9] *Ibid*, p. 29.

Mr. Durbin thinks that when costs fall, more would be purchased for the same total cost, and therefore everyone would receive the same or approximately the same money income. When costs of production per unit are falling owing to technical progress, the total cost will remain unchanged only if demand increases sufficiently. Not otherwise.

Let us take an example. Suppose a unit of agricultural produce costs £5, including wages, rent, interest and the farmer's profit. Assuming that 100 million units are produced, the total cost amounts to £500 million. If now costs per unit fall from £5 to £2½, demand must double, so that the total cost remains the same—or 200 million units must be produced and sold.

Are we entitled to assume that when, *e.g.*, in the case of food-stuffs, costs per unit fall heavily, increase in demand will be such as to keep the total cost at the old level? And if the total cost falls, it is obvious that money incomes do not remain constant, or purchasing power per head of the population falls.

It will appear that at a time of falling costs of production, increase in demand is a vital factor in determining the stability of money incomes.

Stable money incomes presuppose a stable and unchanged relation of supply to demand. If, therefore, supply increases owing to reduced costs and prices fall, equilibrium between supply and demand can be restored either by the reduction of supply or growth of demand. It is not a question of credit policy.

Devaluation

In January 1934, the United States devalued its gold dollar. The old gold dollar contained 25·8 grains of gold $^{9}|_{10}$ fine, or 23·22 grains of pure gold. The new gold dollar contains 15 $^{5}|_{21}$ grains of gold $^{9}|_{10}$ fine, or 13·71 grains of pure gold. This represents a reduction of 41 per cent in the gold contents of the dollar.

The fineness of the dollar remains unchanged. Another method of devaluation is to leave the weight of the standard coin unchanged, but to reduce its fineness.

This is the proposal of Dr. Ernest Zucker, explained in his "*Standard Gold" and Silver* (1932).

For example, a franc (France) is equal to 0·0655 gram of gold 900 fine, or 1 franc is equal to 0·05895 g. of fine gold and 1 kg. of gold gives 16,963·528 francs. If the fineness of the gold franc were reduced to 60 per cent, (the present fineness is 90 per cent), 1 kg. of gold will give 25,445·292 francs, or 50 per cent more.

Forty pounds troy of "standard gold", 916 2|3 fine are coined into 1869 sovereigns in England. If the fineness were reduced to 60 per cent, the same amount of gold would give about 2856½ sovereigns, or about 53 per cent more.

Dr. Zucker's proposal amounts to a change in the meaning of 'standard gold'. Gold of 60 per cent fineness is to become 'Standard gold'.

It is seen that where the old fineness of gold was 90 per cent, the adoption of 'standard gold', 60 per cent fine, for coinage purposes, would increase the number of coins 50 per cent. The weight of the gold coins will not change, but each coin will contain more alloy.

Dr. Zucker does not suggest that such coins should be actually put into circulation. Paper money is used every where in the place of gold coins. Notes will now represent 'standard' gold coins of 60 per cent fineness.

It is obvious that a change in the definition of 'standard gold' will enable more paper money to be created on the basis of existing gold reserves. The proposal makes note inflation possible. But inflation may be avoided by altering the reserve ratios of Central Banks. Where a ratio of 40 per cent gold to notes is the law, a ratio of 60 per cent may be adopted. There will thus be no increase in the note circulation.

The advantage claimed for the proposal is that prices of commodities will rise 50 per cent.

When the new definition of 'standard gold' is adopted, if a given quantity of cotton cost £1 of gold of old fineness ($916\frac{2}{3}$) it will cost £1·53 of gold of new fineness (60 per cent). The grower of cotton thus gains immediately, to the extent of 53 per cent, on account of the rise in the price of his raw material.

Dr. Zucker assumes that the introduction of his 'standard gold' will not raise wages and salaries and other costs of manufacture. Taking these to be three times the cost of the raw material, and allowing for the 53 per cent rise in the price of cotton, the price of cotton manufactures will rise 13 per cent.

In $916\frac{2}{3}$ gold per 1,000 (old fineness)

Raw material	£1
Manufacture	£3
Total ..	£4

In 'standard gold' (60 per cent fine)

Raw material	£1·53
Manufacture	£3·00
Total ..	£4·53

The finished product has risen 13 per cent in price, while raw cotton rose 53 per cent.

The loss suffered by the peasant on account of the heavier fall in the price of cotton than in that of cotton goods is thus made good. According to this calculation there would be a net increase in his consuming capacity equal to 40 per cent.

We are assuming that the costs of manufacture, apart from the cost of raw material, do not rise. This assumption implies a reduction in wages and salaries, reckoned in gold of the old fineness ($916\frac{2}{3}$ per 1,000) of a little more than one-third (34·6 per cent). This is an important point. Dr. Zucker says:

"On the other hand, salaries and wages, if they remained unaltered, would be reduced by one-third, and since production costs consists for the most part of wages and salaries, the most important factor in production costs would be reduced by one-third, reckoned on gold of the old fineness.

"Thereby, we should remove one of the most important causes of the present crisis, which is to be found in the fact that the prices of raw materials are lower than in pre-war days, while costs of production have risen considerably. The producer of raw materials has therefore less capacity to consume than before the war, since he receives less for his raw materials and must pay more for the manufactured goods which he purchases" (p. 13).

Thus, it is claimed that by a purely monetary device, *i.e.*, without any increase in the demand for the raw materials which the peasant produces, a considerable increase in the purchasing power of the peasant can be brought about.

Are we justified in assuming that when the prices of food-stuffs and raw materials, reckoned in Dr. Zucker's, 'standard gold' rise 50 per cent, wages and salaries and other elements of costs of manufacture will remain unchanged? If they rise to the same extent, there is no change in the relative incomes or purchasing power of the different sections of the community. Only on account of the reduction of the unit of measurement, everything is 50 per cent higher than before.

Dr. Zucker's proposal is in substance the same as Irving Fisher's plan of stabilising the dollar, explained in Fisher's book bearing that title, published in 1920.

"Let it be granted, then", Fisher wrote, "that, according as the gold dollar is heavier or lighter, the more or the less will be its purchasing power. It follows at once that by adding new grains of gold to the dollar just fast enough to compensate for a loss in the purchasing power of each grain (and, of course, reversely, taking away gold to compensate for a gain), we can secure a stationary instead of a fluctuating dollar, in terms of purchasing power" (p. 91).

Fisher thought that variations in the purchasing power of money could be corrected by increasing or decreasing the gold contents of the unit of money. Money of stable value could be thus secured. He would not have countenanced the suggestion that relative incomes could be modified, or the purchasing power of some sections of the community increased and that of other reduced by varying the weight of the dollar.

It is reasonable to suppose that a reduction in the purchasing power of the pound in terms of cotton and wheat, or a rise in the prices of food-stuffs and raw materials in terms of the pound of 'standard gold', would mean a precisely similar rise in all wages and salaries and other elements of cost of manufacture.

If it is suggested that such a rise may be resisted, and wages and cost prevented from rising, which would place the grower of agricultural products in a favourable position as against the manufacturer, the same result may be brought about, without devaluation, by a reduction in wages, salaries and other costs of manufacture. The prices of manufactures will thus fall, and those of agricultural goods remaining the same, the purchasing power of agriculturists will increase.

Silver as Currency Metal

Dr. Zucker also advocates the use of silver in European countries for coinage purposes as the complement of gold at the ratio of 50·1. At this ratio, he thinks, the danger of a replacement of gold by silver on account of a fall in the price of silver is small. The present ratio of silver to gold is about 80·1.

As the result of the rise in the price of silver he expects the consuming capacity of India and China to increase:

"If one considers further that 700 million people in India and China have now a decreasing consuming capacity in consequence of the currency difficulties called into being because of the depreciation of silver, then it becomes evident that the currency problems are not only results of the world crisis but are also one of its greatest causes".[10]

When the price of silver is stabilized at a higher level, India and China, says Dr. Zucker, "will again become consumers. Furthermore, the stabilization of silver will bring political calm to these vast territories".[11]

Dr. Zucker does not seem to know that the rupee, in 1927, was re-stabilized in relation to gold. The fall in the price of silver is not a cause of currency difficulties in India.

The rupee is stable in relation to sterling. The fall in the price of silver has not affected the stability of the rupee exchange.

It has been said above that the rise in the price of silver will increase the value of our silver hoards. Mr. Sarma has argued that our mints should be thrown open to the free coinage of silver, for the return to the silver standard in India would, by increasing the demand for silver, raise the price of silver, and thus add a very considerable amount to the 'liquid capital of the country'.

"It is estimated that the stock of silver in this country is at least 3,000 million ounces hoarded in the form of vessels, ornaments etc. If the mints were opened to the free coinage of silver, there will be an immediate rise in the price of silver and the liquid capital of the country will have increased at least by a thousand crores".[12]

If Dr. Zucker's suggestion that silver be used as a complement to gold in Europe and America, both in the reserves of Central Banks and for coinage, is accepted, and if Indian mints are thrown open to the coinage of silver, the price of silver will certainly rise.

But Mr. Sarma very much exaggerates the increase in our liquid capital on account of the expected rise in the price of silver under the assumed conditions.

[10] "*Standard Gold and Silver* by Dr. Ernest Zucker (Manchester, 1932), p. 67.

[11] *Ibid*, p. 40.

[12] *Papers on Currency and the Reserve Bank of India* by S. K. Sarma (Trichinopoly, 1934), p. iii.

At the present time, the value of 3,000 million ounces of silver is something less than 350 crores of rupees (at 20d. per ounce). If silver were stabilized at 40d. per ounce, the increase in the liquid capital of the country would amount to about 350 crores. For an increase of 'at least' a thousand crores, the price of silver would have to rise to about 80d. per ounce. No one today seriously thinks such a rise in the price of silver possible and certainly no one would seriously suggest the stabilization of silver at such a high level.

At the most, then, taking the estimate of our stock of silver to approximately correct, the expected rise in the price of silver may increase the value of our silver hoards by 250-350 crores of rupees.

Between 1900-01 and 1930-31 net imports of gold into India amounted to about 550 crores of rupees. The total value of our gold stocks must be several times this amount. Since September 21, 1931, the price of gold has risen about 60 per cent, thus increasing the value of gold imports between 1900-01 and 1930-31 by 330 crores of rupees—or by an amount equal to the expected increase in the value of our entire stocks of silver when the mints are thrown open to the coinage of silver.

Gold exports since September 21, 1931 exceed 175 crores, which means that we have actually used some of the hoarded gold for the purchase of commodities and services, directly and indirectly. The very considerable increase in the 'liquid capital of the country' in the form of gold, on account of the rise in the price of gold, and the resulting increase in our purchasing power, have given India little relief. Only the peasants who have sold their gold, are poorer than before.

It may be desirable on other grounds to re-open the mints to the coinage of silver. But for India this is no way out of the depression. The increase in the value of our silver hoards would be comparatively small in amount, and the peasant could benefit by the rise in the price of silver only by selling his silver. No one is enriched by living on capital.

CHAPTER IX

FROM LAISSEZ FAIRE TO ECONOMIC PLANNING

The leading writers on the crisis may be divided into two chief groups: capitalist and anti-capitalist. Anti-capitalist writers regard the crisis as a crisis not within the capitalist system but one of the capitalist system itself. In their view the capitalist system has broken down, and the crisis marks the beginning of a new epoch in world economic history.

Wilhelm Roepke, a leading German economist of the capitalist school, dubs anti-capitalists "politico-economic desperados"[1].

Capitalist writers generally, as we have seen, look upon the crisis as purely one of conjuncture. They either ignore the changes in the structure of world supply and demand, or believe that the effects of such changes can be modified and controlled by a reorganisation of credit. The more reasonable among capitalist writers, however, recognise that the world's troubles are not entirely due to inflation and deflation, or the usual phases of a conjunctural crisis. Roepke says:—

"The present crisis has ceased more and more to be a mere conjunctural phase, and has more and more assumed the character of a structural transformation, or better still, of a bundle of structural transformations. One may even make a concession to the popular characterisation of the crisis in admitting that it is no longer a question of a crisis within the system, but of a crisis of the system itself"[2].

[1] W. A. Jan. 1933. p. 2.
[2] *Ibid*, p. 6.

But Roepke does not believe that the crisis marks the end of the capitalist system, or has invalidated the conceptions, hundreds of years old, on which the capitalist system is founded. "We require", he says, "neither a new social philosophy, nor a new national economy, nor a fundamental reconstruction of our economic system".[3]

It has to be admitted that the new economic world that is emerging from the crisis is different from the old. The old economic world was based on territorial division of labour; the principal article of its creed was freedom of trade. The new economic world that is emerging is autarkist—it is composed of a number of self-sufficient, undifferentiated units. But, argues Roepke, nothing has occurred to upset our faith in the old system. He is not impressed by national slogans such as 'Protect national labour', or 'Buy Swadeshi goods'. Protectionism rests on sentiment—hence its popular appeal. Free trade, on the other hand, implies earnest reflection, and the control of sentiment through reason. Roepke is an upholder of reason, freedom and individual responsibility, and an irreconciliable opponent of Bellizismus, Nationalismus and Egoismus. In concluding his contribution to *Economic Essays in Honour of Gustav Cassel* he expresses his firm conviction that the welfare of millions of Western people and the progress of Western civilisation depend on the maintenance of the economic system based on individual responsibility. Neither in the interpretation of the crisis nor in formulating proposals for fighting it is he prepared to make the least concession to anti-capitalist Romantik[4].

According to Roepke, then, there is no question of a breakdown of capitalism. There are others who agree with him. For example, Christian Eckert maintains that the capitalist system, in spite of the crisis, is still progressing, and that it will continue to progress until it has spread over the whole world. Only when capitalism has conquered all

[3] *Ibid*, p. 24.
[4] p. 567.

continents, or has at least conquered the greater portions of them, it might, perhaps, begin to weaken[5].

Another German writer, Karl Muhs, shares these views. It may be thought, he says, that the rise of the Soviet system points the way to a new world economy. But the case of Russia is different. The 'soul' of the Russian people is not the soul of Germanic and Roman races in capitalist countries[6]. Instead of any shrinking of capitalism Karl Muhs anticipates a further territorial expansion of old capitalism, which will help the growth of young capitalism in countries which are at present comparatively undeveloped[7]. Of course capitalism which is co-extensive with the whole world is a contradiction in terms. The capitalist system must break up then. But it will be long before the development of capitalism ceases because of its too wide extension.

Capitalism may last for hundreds of years, but not in its present form. All over the world there is a violent reaction against pure and undiluted capitalism.

Capitalism is based on freedom of initiative and enterprise—individual responsibility is the very life of the system. But everywhere a system of artificial control and regulation is developing which is the very antithesis of freedom.

The rise of national economies has been referred to above. It is a product of the crisis. We are forced to levy a duty on wheat because, having lost our wheat markets abroad, we do not wish to lose the home-market as well. Rice is not protected at present, but the crop-planning conference at Simla discussed the proposal (passed by the sub-committee) to levy a duty of Rs.1-4-0 per maund on rice and of annas 15 per maund on paddy.

The case for protecting manufacturing industries is not less strong. Progress is a good thing, but if progress threatens

[5] W. A. 1929 I, pp. 18-22.
[6] W. A. 1930 I, p. 7.
[7] *Ibid*, p. 12.

to rob millions of people of their bread, a little of retrogression is better than progress.

The theoretical advantages of territorial division of labour are unquestioned, but interests of national industry, safety and security have led all countries to restrict the freedom of importation.

Apart from the regulation of foreign trade, internal production in Western countries is in no sense free. The growth of Kartels has been noticed above. Trusts, kartels and other forms of combination, agreements and associations restrict freedom of enterprise. And, finally, every where the State is more actively interfering in business than ever before.

Planning

The transition from the present system of very much restricted, freedom and ever-increasing State regulation and control to a planned economy may be difficult in practice, but it is a natural transition. Sombart, the great German historian of capitalism, says:

"The present is characterised by planless control and regulation as the past was by planless freedom and individual choice; the future will be characterised by planned development of the economic system"[8].

State policy, under a system of State control and regulation, does not directly determine the quantity or quality of the goods produced—these ultimately depend on the decision of individual producers. For example, heavy duties imposed on imported sugar have created an Indian sugar industry, but the State has no control over the number of factories set up or the amount of sugar produced in them. Through the sugar excise it is now sought to diminish the incentive to sugar-manufacture, so that there is no over-production of sugar, as there was over-production of cement

[8] *Sombart, Zukunft des Kapitalismus*, p. 18.

sometime ago. Such intervention by the State may sometimes do more harm than good—in any case, it is essentially different from economic planning of which Sombart speaks.

Economic planning is winning adherents everywhere. Russian economy is a planned economy, as we shall presently see; economic planning, of a sort, is also a part of the Fascist creed. Both Italy and Germany decisively repudiate *laissez faire* as a solution of the difficult economic problems of the present time. A Fascist Party is being organized in England with economic planning as a plank of its platform. But it is not merely Fascists and socialists who advocate economic planning in England. Sir Basil Blackett, who is neither, in the course of his Halley Stewart Lecture (1931) said: "I wish to put before you this evening the view that conscious, corporative planning is not only a desirable means of progress but an unaviodable necessity if we are to save the economic structure of modern civilization from disaster, and that the immediate task to which we should bend all our energies is to prove to ourselves and to the world that planning is consistent with freedom and freedom with planning"[9].

Sir Basil Blackett expressed his thorough dissatisfaction with *laissez faire*. Science and invention by increasing enormously the size of the business unit have rendered invalid the assumptions on which the theory of *laissez faire* is founded. Mobility of labour and capital is not so great now as we are wont to assume. When huge businesses are created, with million of pounds sunk in them, and thousands of labourers employed in them, over-production causes havoc, because it is not possible to speedily convert specialised fixed capital to other uses, or to divert masses of skilled labour to other employments. When, at the same time, it is considered that there is a growth of industrial production, with modern appliances, all over the world, the danger of production outstripping consumption becomes still more real. Under such

[9] The world's Economic Crisis Halley Stewart Lecture, 1931, p. 98.

conditions, planned production, or deliberate adjustment of supply to demand, is a safer course than unregulated, un-co-ordinated production which results from the independent choice of individual producers. One has no difficulty in agreeing with Sir Basil Blackett that "the whole body of *laissez faire* doctrine, the undiluted individualistic philosophy of Bentham and his school, has broken down, is dead, and ought to be buried"[10].

But what shall we put in the place vacated by *laissez faire*? Sir Basil Blackett suggests a planned economy consistent with freedom of enterprise. The British people are to show to the world that a planned economy and freedom are consistent with each other.

India is not an industrial country, but economic planning, in the conditions created by the world crisis, is a necessity for us. In the course of a remarkable address delivered in Bombay on the eve of his departure from India Sir George Schuster "stressed the necessity for simultaneous attempts to regulate crop production for the whole of India on a definite plan". He referred to Java where sugar production had to be reduced from 3 millions to half a million ton, and said that a similar situation was arising in India in regard to wheat and rice. The general economic policy that India needs, according to Sir George Schuster, is not one aiming at complete economic self-sufficiency. "But", he added "the course of world development does indicate the need for a policy for India which must be something different from past policy both in being more consciously planned and in its general orientation."

Planning in India. Crop-Planning

The central idea of crop-planning is to prevent over-production of wheat and rice, and to find more remunerative crops to take the place of those which are no longer remunerative.

[10] *Ibid*, p. 97.

The crop-planning conference, which met at Simla early in June 1934, was attended by 13 officials of the Government of India and 28 representatives, chiefly agricultural experts from the Provinces. After a lengthy discussion the conference came to the conclusion that there was no over-production of rice or wheat in India and that the cultivation of these crops should not be restricted. But the rice cultivator has been warned against contemplating extended cultivation of this food-grain, while on the question of wheat many delegates felt that it was undesirable that the area under wheat in India should exceed 33 million acres.

Linseed as a partial substitute for wheat and rice has been suggested. The area under linseed in the whole of India fluctuates between 3-4 million acres. It is thought that this can be increased by about 2 million acres. Incidentally it may be mentioned that the phenomenal increase in the exports of linseed from India from 72,000 tons in 1932-33 to about 379,000 tons in 1933-34 was due to the failure of the Argentine crop. That was a piece of luck for India. It is difficult to say whether exports will be maintained at the high level of 1933-34 when the Argentine crop of linseed is normal.

The reader may be reminded that linseed can replace rice and wheat to an extent which is so small as to be negligible. The total area under rice in 1932-33 was 82½ million acres (over 84 million acres in 1931-32), and under wheat about 33 million acres in 1932-33, and about 34 million acres in 1931-32.

The Conference adopted the following suggestions:

"Madras could increase the area under Cambodia cotton by 50,000 acres and put in another 50,000 acres under sugarcane in three or four years to be self-supporting in the matter of sugar. Madras, which had already increased the area under fruit by 14 per cent, could further increase it if transport facilities were granted by railways.

'Bombay can increase the area under sugarcane, mangoes, plantains and pine-apples.

"Bengal had further scope for sugarcane production and could also increase the area under fodder crops.

"The United Provinces has room for high quality barley, suitable for malting, and could also increase the area under linseed with proper rust-resisting varieties.

"As for the Punjab a suitable substitute crop was soya bean. An experimental consignment of suitable soya bean should be sent to England.

"Sugarcane is the only alternative crop for Burma, which can be increased to 100,000 acres.

"Bihar and Orissa could increase sugarcane and could expand linseed and fodder crops.

"The Central Provinces could increase the acreage under linseed and ground-nut and also sesamum.

"Sind should have a programme of expansion of cotton, rice and linseed.

"Assam had a scope for expansion of the area under linseed and sugarcane."

Crop-planning is one aspect of economic planning—the agricultural aspect. The other aspect relates to manufacturing industries. While reviewing the measures adopted by the Government of India to fight the crisis, Sir George Schuster made a detailed reference to Government policy in regard to industries in his budget speech for 1934-35.

It must not be supposed that the Government did not have a definite policy in dealing with the crisis, or that it does not recognise its duty "at every point to assist the economic well-being of the country". "We have had such a policy," declared the Finance Member. When the crisis came, the first duty of the Government was naturally to maintain the credit of India. The first task of the Government was "to safeguard and restore the position as regards credit and revenue resources". Having safeguarded and restored that position, the Government adopted measures to encourage industrial development. The output of our iron and steel, cotton, cement and sugar industries has increased. New industries have been initiated. We have started making a wide range of articles, such as electric lamps, and all kinds of electrical appliances, rubber tyres, water-softening plant, coking stoves, asbestos, cement products, paints and enamels. In recent years there have been well-known developments in the Indian manufacture of railway rolling stock, bridge-work and heavy structures. "Now all this", said Sir George Schuster, "is in accord with a policy deliberately adopted by Government".

The second aspect of economic planning in India thus consists in the encouragement of industrial development by means of the tariff.

From Sir George Schuster's budget speech it appears that India is overcoming the crisis with far less difficulty than certain other countries. This may be attributed to the wonderful elasticity of our economic system. To deal with the crisis it was found necessary in the United States to control every phase of economic activity of the country. In India adjustment is taking place naturally and automatically.

"It is a remarkable fact", said the Finance Member, "and one that is not generally appreciated, that in India, so far, we have not had to resort to any production control of this kind, and yet our exportable products have somehow or other throughout the crisis found a market in the outside world. We have no dangerous accumulations of unsaleable stocks and we have escaped so far some of the worst problems which have afflicted other agricultural countries".

Still, the Finance Member admitted, we have some problems of our own. These may be grouped under three heads: (1) increase in the real burden of indebtedness owing to the fall of prices, (2) stimulating the internal demand for India's agricultural produce, and (3) improving the external demand.

The Finance Member approached these problems with a feeling of confidence.

"As to the first", he said, "there have been many alleviating factors which have resulted in the avoidance so far of any really urgent crisis. The various Provincial Governments have made substantial remissions in land revenue and water-rates. Landlords have not pressed for their full rents. India's ancient money-lending system has proved elastic and repayments of debts have not been pressed. As a result the great mass of agriculturists have had enough to eat and a sufficient margin in cash not only to pay taxes at the reduced level but also to maintain at a fairly reasonable level their purchases of necessities. The figures for the consumption of the main necessities of the poor, kerosine and cotton piece goods, demonstrate that in broad outline this is the position".

It would seem that conditions in India are almost idyllic—without our knowing it. Landlords do not demand their full rents—excepting over 80 per cent of the 'net income' from the land, as in the Punjab; money-lenders do not press for repayment of debts—they are murdered when they do; while the land revenue policy of the Government is marked by extreme leniency—only, as we have seen, the land revenue demand may exceed the 'net income' from the land, as it did in many cases in the Punjab in 1930-31. Then, in spite of the depression and the fall in agricultural prices, the population of India is consuming greater quantities of cotton goods than in 1920-30, and only slightly smaller quantities of salt and kerosine oil. We are a wonderful people! One may even say that the trade depression has not affected India!

One method of developing internal purchasing power is the development of our own industries. The growth of Indian industrial production may react unfavourably on our exports—foreign countries may buy less of our raw materials and food-stuffs, if we limit our purchases of their goods. But we may raise the general standard of living—we shall then be able to buy the products of Indian industries, and also continue the use of imported goods. "This", said the Finance Member, "opens out an interesting and intensely important field of work, and it is a field in which industrialists themselves ought to take an active part and not shift all the burden on to Government". Let us hope that our industrialists will willingly take this burden on themselves.

The hope of improving external demand lies in the development of Empire markets. The Finance Member made a powerful appeal for Indo-British co-operation in the field of commerce and industry. In conclusion he summed up the position thus:

"The sum and substance of what I have said is this. Great opportunities have been created in India for agricultural and industrial expansion, and that has been proceeding even in recent years. The economic machinery has worked steadily without break-down even through three years of unexampled difficulty. The worst that can be said is that it has worked at an unduly small margin of profit and that there may be an aftermath of special problems arising out of the changes in the relations between money and goods. What is needed now is carefully directed action to deal with these special problems, combined with planning to take the fullest advantage of India's potentialities of production, and in doing this we must recognise that India cannot thrive alone or independently of the prosperity of other countries. That should be our purpose rather than the construction of entirely new machinery or the imposition of Government control in every sphere of economic activity."

The word planning occurs in the extract given above. It does not mean 'planning' in the Russian or even the American sense, for Sir George Schuster has definitely told us that the machinery of the Government of India is not adapted to such 'planning'.,

Capitalist Planning

It is obvious that economic planning in India is capitalist planning—that is planning consistent with freedom of enterprise.

In regard to industries, planning in India means very little more than our protective tariff. In this sense economic planning started in India in 1924 when, for the first time, we adopted discriminating protection as our fiscal policy. It seems wrong to use 'planning' where 'protection' would be the more suitable word.

Our industrial development is proceeding without any plan or system. No attempt is made to create basic or key industries. No attempt is made to develop machine-making industries. Behind the tariff wall we are trying to manufacture such consumers' goods as we find it profitable to manufacture. As the general rate of the tariff is now higher than before, and protection has been granted to certain industries, the industrial output is expanding. But we are building from the top. The whole industrial super-structure will topple down if, for any reason, it became difficult to import machinery. Industrialism based on imported means of production and, to a large extent, on imported technical skill, is inherently unsound.

It is futile to hope that such industrial development as is taking place now will provide the means, within any reasonable period of time, of lessening the pressure of population on the soil.

What is the significance of 'crop planning'?

The utter futility of planning consistent with freedom is seen most clearly in the case of agriculture.

Suppose it is desired to restrict the area under wheat. How will the Government persuade the farmers to give effect to its wishes?

In the United States the Government granted compensation to peasants who signed a contract binding themselves to sow a smaller area with wheat. This cost the Government more than £100 million dollars in one year (1933-34). And yet the contraction of area effected was comparatively small. "The success hitherto attained by the American restriction policy", says Dr. Guenter Keiser (W. D. May 18, 1934) consists really in this that the reduction in area made by the farmers *of their own accord* in 1932 and 1933 has been conserved by spending considerable sums of Government money" (*Italics* Dr. Keiser's). The actual decrease was from 42·7 million acres to 41 million acres. About 80 per cent of the farmers had signed that contract—the remaining 20 per cent sowed a larger area than before hoping to benefit by the rise of prices resulting from the restriction of area by others.

India is a larger country than the United States, and that makes the problem of crop control here still more difficult. Where the Government of the United States has failed, the Government of India cannot hope to succeed. The Government may announce by beat of drum in every village (our peasants cannot sign contracts) that it is desirable to grow less wheat and rice, but there are no means of compelling the peasant to carry out Government orders. The grant of compensation, where restriction is effected, is out of the question.

Further, when the Government tells the peasant to sow more soya bean or linseed, what guarantee is there that the peasant will be able to dispose of the crop at a profit? If the foreign demand declines owing to more abundant and cheaper supply from other sources, will the Government make good the losses incurred by the peasant owing to Government's miscalculation? The grant of compensation, again, is out of the question. It would seem that when the loss or profit is made by the peasant, the choice in regard to what the peasant may or may not grow must also belong to the peasant. It is also clear that so long as the peasant exercises this choice, there can be no control over the area or yield of crops. The problem of planning, in a country of small peasants, each working on his own account, is insoluble except through nationalisation of production.

CHAPTER X

SOCIALIST PLANNING

Russia is the only country where economic planning on a most comprehensive scale has been deliberately undertaken and successfully carried out. Socialist planning in Russia has attracted world attention. It is profitable for students of economics to know both the aims of socialist planning and the methods adopted for realising those aims.

"At the beginning of the First Five Year Plan period, the U. S. S. R. was an agrarian country with a backward and partly mediaeval technique, with an industry whose level of development was far from being adequate for the purpose of reorganising industry, transport and agriculture on the basis of modern technique" (*The First Year Plan*, p. 9).

The position of the U. S. S. R. in this respect was not unlike our own. A high proportion of her total national income was derived from agriculture, and an over-whelming majority of the population was rural. In 1928 the urban population formed 17·9 per cent of the total (India 1931, 11 per cent). The number of industrial workers and employees was 142 per 1,000 persons of working age. In India, according to the census of 1931, the number of workers engaged in 'Industry' was 15,352,000 out of 153,916,000, the number of 'industrial' workers formed about 10 per cent of the total.

The aim of the First Five Year Plan was to transform Russia into an industrial State. The Plan as a whole was fulfilled, it is claimed to the extent of 93·7 per cent as far as the gross output of industry is concerned (p. 11).

Considerable progress has been made in India in recent years in the development of industry. But our industrial development, as we have seen, is based on imported machinery. For example, as home production of factory sugar has increased, imports have fallen, and in a year or two they may cease altogether. But sugar machinery is not made in India. With the grant of protection to sugar, imports of sugar machinery have increased. The total value of imports of sugar machinery was about 14 lakhs in 1930-31, 30 lakhs in 1931-32, 153 lakhs in 1932-33 and 3,36 lakhs in 1933-34. What is true of sugar, is also true of other manufacturing industries. We have a large railway system, but we do not manufacture locomotives.

The authorities in Russia had decided "to transform the U. S. S. R. from a country importing machinery and equipment into a country that manufactures machinery and equipment" (p. 14). This was considered essential for the reconstruction of national economy.

Russia now produces her own technical equipment. She occupied the second place in the world's output of machinery in 1931.

A new iron and steel industry has been created and great progress made in electrification.

Agriculture has been modernised. At the beginning of the First Five Year Plan period, 45 per cent of the grain crops in Russia, we learn, were reaped with scythe and sickle; 70 per cent of the sowing was done by hand, and not less than 40 per cent of the harvest was threshed with primitive hand-tools. The Plan has equipped Russian agriculture with tractors, harvest-combines, and reaping machines.

The following figures show the rapid progress of Russia in industrialisation during 1928-32, or at a time when the output of industrial countries was falling:

Index of quantity of industrial output in 1932
(1928=100)

Countries	1932
Capitalist world	67
U. S. A.	57
Great Britian	89
Germany	57
France	74
U. S. S. R.	218·5

The re-organisation of Russian agriculture deserves special attention. It has transformed Russia "from a small peasant country into a land of large scale agriculture."

	Total sown area (in per cent)		Average size of farm (in hectares)†	
	1928	1932	1928	1932
Collective farms ..	1·2	68·0	42·0	434·0
State farms ..	1·5	10·0	544·0	2,303·0
Individual farmers..	97·3	22·0	4·5	3·15

These figures show that in less than five years the Russian Government accomplished a miracle. Agriculture has been largely socialized, making it possible to create large farms, which are cultivated with power-driven machinery.

In my *Indian Economic Life, Past and Present* (1929) I wrote:

"Nationalisation means getting rid of a useless class of intermediaries and substituting for it an active partner in agriculture. Apart from increasing the income of the non-owner cultivator immediately and substantially, the nationalisation of agricultural land offers other material advantages to Indian Agriculture.

"(*a*) Nationalisation will not reduce the numbers dependent upon agriculture; for that we must depend upon the progress of industries. But it will greatly facilitate the

† One hectare=about 2½ acres.

process of consolidation of holdings, and make it possible for farms of convenient size to be cultivated jointly and more economically.

"(*b*) Nationalisation offers the only hope of modernisation of Indian agriculture.

"The improvement of agriculture under existing conditions is difficult. The small-holder does not possess the means of intensifying his agriculture, and he will never be able to substitute the more economical machine for the more expensive bullock labour. It will perhaps be said that human labour is cheap in India. This is so on account of the excessive numbers that agriculture has to support. But is it really economical to have ten men to work on the land when two or three, aided by a machine, will be sufficient?"

In this respect again, conditions in Russia were not unlike our own. But within five years, as we have seen, Russian agriculture has been transformed.

In 1928 tractors were used on one per cent of the cultivated area; in 1932 more than one-third of the cultivated land was ploughed by tractors. The old wooden plough has disappeared. The scythe and the sickle have been replaced by harvesting machines and combines. "Hundreds of thousands of tractors, complex tractor implements, harvesting combines—these today characterise the new technique prevailing in socialist agriculture" (p. 21).

The economic revolution in Russia—for the changes in Russian economy can only be described as a revolution—has been accompanied by a cultural revolution. In 1913 the number of people able to read and write was equal to 33 per cent of the total population; in 1932 this figure rose to 90 per cent (p. 32-33). In India we congratulate ourselves on the remarkable progress of literacy from decade to decade. But in 1931 the proportions per 1,000 aged 5 and over who were illiterate were as follows. Persons 905, males 844, females 971.

The proportion of illiterates in our population is as high as that of literates in Russia.

The foregoing summary of the achievements of socialist planning is based on an authoritative source—the official report on the fulfilment of the First Five Year Plan issued by the State Planning Commission of the Council of People's Commissars of U. S. S. R. But the Bolsheviks are excessively fond of propaganda, and their report may be only a part of their well-known tactics to mislead the capitalist world. We therefore turn for light to a well-informed and, on the whole, impartial criticism of the official report on the First Five Year Plan by Professor Dr. Wassily Leontief (Berlin), who, to judge from his article in the *Welt-Wirtschaftliches Archiv* (May 1934), is obviously not a Bolshevik. The article is based on a thorough study of the Report in the original Russian and other authoritative Russian sources.

Prof. Leontief indeed says that the Report is not unexceptionable, and that it is a diplomatic publication, not unlike publications meant for public consumption issued by large private undertakings. Its defects consist not so much in general incompleteness as in the failure to appreciate economic and social points of view, and in silently passing over the failure of the plan in important particulars.

The Moscow Government claims that as regards the gross output of industry, the plan was fulfilled to the extent of 93·7 per cent. Prof. Leontief subjects this claim to a lengthy examination, and reaches the conclusion that about 75 per cent is the more correct figure. This percentage relates to quantitative production: The results are less favourable when they are considered qualitatively and financially. However, even if the plan was fulfilled in regard to the gross industrial output to the extent of 75 per cent or even 64 per cent, that is no mean achievement. And Prof. Leontief admits it. Referring to his percentage (75) he says: "This figure is rather too high, for the arithmetic average of percentages is 64. Such is the conclusion regarding quantities produced. The qualitative and financial aspects, as we shall see later, are less favourable. And yet one must admit that it has been a notable achievement (*hervorragende Leistung*) of the Government and the people"[1].

Great success has been achieved in particular branches of industry, for example, electrification. Prof. Leontief says: "This building of ten stations, each of 100,000 KW power, represents a mighty piece of work (*eine gewaltige Arbeit*). Not a single station of this capacity existed in U. S. S. R. before 1929. One may be particularly proud of '*Dneprogres*', easily the greatest power-station of Europe, which possessed a capacity of 310,000 KW at the end of 1932, capable of being increased to 558,000 KW. The ten power-stations mentioned furnished, in the year 1932, one-third of the total electrical energy"[2].

In regard to coal production the plan was fulfilled to the extent of 85·3 per cent. The amount of coal produced in 1932 was 79 per cent greater than in 1927-28 and more than double (117 per cent) as compared with the pre-war figure. Still industries in particular regions suffered from want of coal. The lack of pit-coal (*Steinkohle*) has been partly compensated by the very greatly increased production of turf, but the quality of the turf has deteriorated.

In the naphtha industry the plan was fulfilled within 2½ years.

Prof. Leontief considers the statistics of machine-construction very inexact, but he admits that in this industry, which is of special importance for the development of the industrial system in the coming years, the achievements of socialist planning are quite 'mighty' (*ist ganz Gewaltiges geleistet worden*)[3]. And he adds: "For Russia these achievements are rather technical than economic achievements, still they may be described as an important success. At present, in the words of Friedrich List, it is only a question of developing

[1] W. A. May, 1934, p. 518.
[2] *Ibid*, p. 520.
[3] *Ibid*, p. 522.

productive powers; future will show whether these will be utilised to produce better exchangeable consumers' goods"[4].

In its last year (1932) the plan was fulfilled in regard to agricultural machines to the extent of 72·3 per cent. The percentage is higher if tractors are included, but not so high (99·7 per cent) as the Moscow Government claims.

In mining and metallurgy the success attained was more modest—about 50-60 per cent according to Prof. Leontief's estimate. The official report does not give these percentages in many cases.

In the chemical industry, Group A, which is concerned with non-consumable goods, the percentage of plan fulfilment is 73·6. The report does not comment on this modest result, but, describes in great detail the notable success achieved in certain branches of the chemical industry—the production of aniline dyes, rubber and asbestos. In the production of super-phosphates the plan was fulfilled only to the extent of 18 per cent (super-phosphates are used in agriculture).

Prof. Leontief draws pointed attention to the neglect of 'light' as compared with 'heavy' industry. In all branches of textile industries, the manufacture of boots and shoes, furniture, and other articles of daily use in the household, the achievements fell far short of the Plan. For example, it was planned to increase the production of cotton goods, which are the chief articles of clothing in Russia, from 2742 million metres before 1929 to 4700 million metres, or by 70 per cent. Production increased in the first year of the Plan, then declined. In 1932 it increased again, but the quality deteriorated. According to Prof. Leontief the population of Russia, in regard to clothing, is worse off today than before the war. "This is explained by the fact that this industry was neglected for the sake of 'heavy' industry; besides there was a lack of raw material, which they did not wish to import from

[4] *Ibid*, p. 523.

abroad, since imports were restricted to material required for industrialisation".[5]

The scarcity of articles of food was felt throughout the Five Year Plan Period. As compared with 'heavy' industry, 'light' industry and industries producing articles of food had been set easier tasks in the Plan, and yet less success was attained in their case.

Prof. Leontief takes exception to the statement made by Stalin in a recent speech that in 1933 the value of the product of industry represented 76·8 per cent of the total production. The product of industry would be thus three times as great in importance as that of agriculture, which would justify the claim of Russia to rank as a leading industrial country. Prof. Leontief points out that the town population in Russia is less than one-fourth of the whole, and that the great majority of the people are still dependent on agriculture "By counting things twice over and assuming higher prices one may very much over-estimate the value of industrial turn-over, but fundamental facts are not altered thereby"[6].

It is difficult for those who do not possess first-hand knowledge of facts to take a share in this controversy. The value of Russia's industrial output may not be 3 times but only twice as great as that of her agricultural output—or the two may be just equal. But we may remember two things: first, that Russia's industrial production rapidly increased while that of the rest of the world declined during the depression, and second, that her industrial organisation and technical equipment vastly improved during the First Five Year Plan Period. On these two points there is no difference of opinion. The exact proportion of her industrial to agricultural output at present is a matter of less importance. Even if Russia is not an industrial country now, she is certainly on the road to become one. She has laid the foundations of industrialism well and truly, and unless her progress

[5] *Ibid*, p. 526.
[6] *Ibid*, p. 528.

is cut short by internal disturbances or external war, in a very few years she will take a prominent place among the leading industrial countries—even if she is a back-number today.

Prof. Leontief shows that the position in regard to agriculture in Russia is unsatisfactory. The plan was fulfilled to the extent of 66 per cent in regard to food-grains. The quantity produced in 1932 was 14 per cent less than the pre-war figure, while the population has increased by about 20 per cent. The number of horses, cattle, sheep and goats, and pigs in 1933 was on an average a little more than half of that of 1916.

The progress of collectivisation is undisputed. In 1929, before the drive against the *kulaks* started (called 'Terror' by Prof. Leontief) there were only 57,000 collectives in Russia, comprising 1 million farms (3·9 per cent of the total number of farms). At the end of the First Five Year Plan, in 1932, the number of collectives had increased to 211,000, comprising 15 million farms (61·5 per cent of the total). Most of these collectives are situated in the South and the East which produce a surplus of food-grains. It is expected that the second Five Year Plan will see the completion of collectivisation.

The financial aspect of the Plan does not escape the criticism of Prof. Leontief. The cost was estimated at 70·2 milliard rubles, but it increased to about 128 milliard rubles. The budget for industry grew from 9·6 to no less than 31·1 milliard rubles. To finance the plan more paper money had to be put into circulation. Figures of paper circulation at the end of the Plan are not available, but there is, according to Prof. Leontief, little doubt that "Industrialisation has been financed to a certain extent with the help of the note- printing press".[7] The resulting rise of prices has diminished the real wages of workers. The Plan proposed to raise real wages by 66 per cent. It has not been made known how far the

[7] *Ibid*, p. 543.

plan has been fulfilled in this respect. The average nominal wage rose about 104 per cent, but the ruble has heavily depreciated. Generally speaking the supplies of bread, milk, butter, sugar and meat were insufficient, and in the last years of the Plan famine conditions existed both in the town and the country. In so far as improvement in the conditions of living is concerned, according to Prof. Leontief, the plan must be judged to have failed.

Critics of the Plan feared that the Plan might unduly stimulate consumption, so that the surplus available for investment or saving might be dangerously reduced. Just the contrary has happened. Prof. Leontief says: "A Russian economist has stated that the problem of saving on an adequate scale is one of the most difficult problems of a socialist economy. The policy of the Five Year Plan has, however, shown that, under certain conditions, such as exist in Russia, one may err in the other direction: the ruling classes have seriously neglected the immediate needs of the population for the sake of constructive work".[8] Saving in Russia has imposed the heaviest sacrifices on the whole population.[9]

Such is Prof. Leontief's criticism of the Report on the working of the First Five Year Plan. On the whole the criticism is less damaging than one was led to expect by the author's denunciation of the Report as a diplomatic publication. The chief objects of the Plan were industrialisation of the country, and collectivisation of agriculture. The Plan has brilliantly succeeded in achieving these aims. Let it not be forgotten that with the completion of the First Five Year Plan Period, socialist planning in Russia has not come to an end. The experience gained in the working of the First Plan will be helpful in further planning.

Russia is at present concentrating on the improvement of her technique of production. Hence the comparative neglect of consumers' interests. Heavy sacrifices are imposed

[8] *Ibid*, p. 540.
[9] *Ibid*, p. 545.

on the general public in the present so that production in the future may be placed on a secure and stable basis. One may compare the policy of the Soviet Government to that of a new wisely managed joint-stock company which, instead of declaring heavy dividends at the outset, decides to build up strong reserves. Socialist Russia is at present building up strong reserves of Productive Power in the shape of a wide diffusion of education, a highly-developed technical equipment, abundant supply of electrical energy, and a liberal provision of producers' goods of all kinds. The requisite command over Productive Power having been obtained, it would not be difficult to increase the supply of consumers' goods. One is reminded of the old paradox: a country where most of the people are engaged in the production of consumers' goods (as in India), has, in the end, less of consumers' goods than a country which has a higher proportion of the population employed in the manufacture of tools, implements and machines. The readiness to sacrifice immediate comfort and well-being for the sake of distant but nobler aims implies courage and foresight on the part of the Government, and patience and a great capacity for bearing hardships on the part of the people.

Chief Features of Socialist Planning

We are not interested in the exact percentage of the Plan-fulfilment. The Russian experiment is interesting in so far as it brings out the contrast between a planned and an unplanned economy. The chief points of contrast are noted below:

1. The State owns and controls the means of production, including land. A capitalist economy is based on private ownership of the means of production.

2. All production in a socialist economy is controlled and directed by the State. In a capitalist economy the final decision as to the quantity and quality of goods to be produced rests with individual producers. There is a centralisation of control under socialism in contrast with complete

decentralisation under capitalism. The formation of trusts, cartels and other forms of combinations is an attempt to remedy the defects of unregulated, decentralised production in the sphere of industry.

3. Competition is the chief regulator in the capitalist world, and the hope of profit its chief driving force. In a socialist economy the place of competition is taken by deliberate selection.

The difficulties of socialist planning must not be over looked. A German critic says[10].

"Any one who possesses practical knowledge of business conditions knows that each day brings new problems, and that it would be necessary for the Economic General Staff [under a socialist economy] to possess the divine power of omniscience in order to know and consider beforehand the possibilities that may arise in the course of the struggle for international markets. The apparatus that would be required to adjust the whole economy to the necessities of daily life, and always to do punctually just what has to be done, is so inconceivable, and is so calculated to separate the whole economic system from contact with reality (which is ensured only by the splitting up of the economic system into millions of individual businesses) that one may predict that German economic re-construction on these lines would end in disaster".

We may add that those who plan production and others who direct the execution of the plans in a socialist economy must be men of the highest intelligence and character. Corruption and inefficiency in the socialist bureaucracy, and impatience and lack of faith in the general public, would be fatal to the success of socialist planning.

The value of the Russian experiment consists just in this that it has demonstrated the practicability of planning. The State Planning Commission at Moscow would not claim to

[10] *Dic Zukunft des Kapitalismus* by M. Georg Solmssen, (Georg Stilke, Berlin, 1933), p. 28.

possess the gift of Divine Omniscience, but they have succeeded in U. S. S. R. in evolving a system which has enabled the Russian people to emerge from the world crisis unhurt, a crisis which has shaken the whole of the capitalist world to its foundations.

It is difficult to see why contact with reality can be maintained only through millions of independent producers, each working on his own account. It is more obvious that a system of unregulated and undirected production may more easily get out of touch with reality than a system in which supply is deliberately adjusted to demand. No one believes today that the individual in seeking his own interests necessarily and always promotes the good of the society. There is no universal harmony of interests any where: in the actual economic world in which we live it would be more correct to speak of individual conflicts of interests than harmony. This conflict ceases when competition is abolished.

Over-production and under-consumption.

We have seen before that the term over-production must be understood with reference to effective demand. There is no over-production if we consider the unsatisfied demand of the masses in every country for even the most essential commodities.

The crisis thus appears to be a crisis of purchasing power. While the supply of goods has increased, the purchasing power of the masses has not increased in the same proportion.

Socialist writers attach much importance to 'under-consumption' as a cause of the crisis. This under-consumption is a direct result of the capitalist system in which the greater portion of the profits of enterprise goes to enrich a very small section of the community. The purchasing power of the masses is small because the masses earn so little. If wealth were more equally distributed in India the total purchasing power of the people would be undoubtedly greater. "There seems to be no reason", says a writer, "why the concentration of income in the hands of the producing class should not result in as much consumption as if that income flowed to the poorer classes: possibly more luxuries would be bought than necessaries, but, as we have seen, the demand for the latter is not very elastic and consequently cannot fall very much"[11]. If this reasoning is correct, growing inequality in the distribution of wealth does not affect the general demand for goods—there is only a change in the classes of goods demanded (more luxuries instead of necessaries), and the demand for necessaries, owing to its inelasticity, does not fall very much. In a country like India even the demand for necessaries is elastic, but let us assume that conditions in India are exceptional, and that in the rest of the world the masses are so well-provided with necessaries that any increase in their purchasing power would not cause the demand for necessaries to expand. Well, then, if the demand for necessaries remains unchanged, whatever the manner of distribution of wealth, and if the concentration of income in the hands of a small class increases the demand for luxuries, the total demand for goods must tend to increase. Why should crises occur then? And if they do occur, the mal-distribution of wealth, it would seem, is not responsible for them.

Let us develop this argument further, for it is interesting. Suppose wealth tends to concentrate into the hands of a class which tends to grow smaller and smaller, until, finally, not more than a dozen individuals come to own the great part of the wealth of a country. Will that have any effect in reducing the demand for goods in general? Conceivably the demand for necessaries may be as great as before, and the demand for luxuries on the part of these dozen Croesuses may expand indefinitely. But there are physical limits to the expansion of demand on the part of the most extravagant Croesus. One is reminded of a saying of Mussolini that "it is possible to accumulate wealth *all 'infinito,*

[11] *Elements of Economics* by S. E. Thomas, 6th Ed. p. 577.

but the possibility of enjoying it is limited"[12]. If that is so, doubling and quadrupling of the wealth of our Croesuses would result in a smaller increase of demand than a rise in the income of the masses by a few rupees per head.

It is perfectly ridiculous to suggest that under-consumption has nothing to do with the crisis. The concentration of wealth in the hands of a small capitalist class limits the purchasing power of the masses and keeps their standard of living at a low level. Hence under-consumption at a time when the world's productive capacity has increased enormously.

How can the purchasing power of the masses be increased? Is it a question of credit policy or a better distribution of wealth?

Socialism and Purchasing Power.

The Socialist State controls distribution as well as production. All incomes in a socialist economy are not equal, but there is no concentration of wealth in the hands of a small class of producers. All workers are producers and wealth is widely diffused among the masses. The Socialist State may produce a small amount of wealth, and every one may be poor, but, under socialism, the contrast between the non-working rich and the working poor does not exist, as the non-worker has been eliminated. The Socialist State may be likened to a joint-stock company working the industrial and agricultural resources of a country, of which the whole population is the proprietor. The net profits, after deducting the cost of working and setting apart sums required for re-investment, are distributed among the whole population in the shape of goods and services. The greater the production, the greater the share of every one in the wealth produced.

That is how socialism solves the problem of purchasing power—not through the creation of artificial purchasing

[12] *Discorsi*, 1926. p. 91.

power by means of credit inflation, but by greater production of wealth and a better distribution of it.

DESTRUCTION OF WEALTH

When inventions increase productive power faster than consumption, equilibrium may be restored by stimulating consumption. A better distribution of wealth is the means of raising the standard of living of the masses. When their purchasing power increases they will buy more and consume more. A rise in the standard of living also reacts on productive efficiency—it leads to greater production.

Growth of production should be a matter for universal rejoicing, but in a capitalist economy it becomes a curse. The Dutch in the 17th century used to destroy crops of pepper in order to keep up its price, and their methods are being widely copied at the present time. There is a Persian saying:

اے روشنئی طبع تو بر من بلا شدی

"My intelligence has become a source of my misfortune!" The inventive genius of man, which has made it possible to exploit Nature more effectively in the interests of production, has become the source of the world's misfortune!

Surely there is something wrong with the world's economy when, with increased production of wealth, the world is growing poorer! Surely the capitalist system has broken down if it cannot find any other remedy for the crises than the destruction of wealth, or restriction of production. To grow less wheat and rice, tea, coffee and sugarcane when the demand for them is almost indefinitely extensible, is to compel the masses to continue to live in poverty and want. In effect a policy of restriction of production means that the masses are prevented from enjoying the benefits of progress because greater production would reduce the profits of the capitalist class. It has just this and no other meaning.

Over-production is a cause of terror in a capitalist economy. Over-production has no meaning in a planned socialist economy, because the purchasing power of the people is determined by the wealth that they produce: with the growth of production the purchasing power and consuming power of the masses must increase. Secondly, when a point is reached where every one is surfeited with his or her real income in the form of goods and services (it will be long before this happens), the whole population may buy more leisure—that is, working hours may be shortened.

OTHER ASPECTS OF ECONOMIC PLANNING.

Economic planning is not patch-work. It must be comprehensive, embracing all fields of economic activity, the whole of production and the whole of distribution.

Economic planning cannot be sectional because economic life is not sectional. It is not possible to plan for industries, leaving agriculture alone, or to plan for agriculture neglecting industries. The various aspects of our economic life are so closely intertwined that a national plan of reconstruction cannot neglect any without deforming the whole structure.

Economic enterprise has many forms, for example, hand-work and machine-work, small and large scale production, individual and State enterprise. Should economic planning aim at preserving all this variety of form?

No less an authority than Werner Sombart, while accepting the idea of economic planning, has argued in favour of retaining the complexity of economic forms, structures and systems which we see around us. A planned economy, according to him, should not be confounded with Monism of economic forms, or identified with public economy, as distinguished from private economy, or State Capitalism, or Collectivism. *Khaddar* may therefore have a place in a planned economy side by side with the products of textile mills, and the *charkha* side by side with the spinning-machine. Some hand-work has survived even in advanced industrial countries; if capitalism itself has not been able to destroy the variety of economic forms, asks Sombart, why should a planned economy undertake to accomplish such a hopeless task? (*Die Zukunft des kapialismus*, p. 27). As regards private and public economy, it is not a question of "*either-or*", but indeed of "*also*". "Private property *and* communal property, private economy *and* social economy will exist side by side, nay, they *must* do so". ('p. 29). This is Sombart's idea of a planned economy, an idea which is acceptable to fascism, so far as economic planning has any place in the fascist scheme of thought at all.

Socialist planned economy is of a unitary character. In the domain of industry attention is concentrated on machine-making and development of the sources of power. In agriculture collective farming with power-driven appliances is the distinguishing feature. Production is on a large scale, or economic planning in the socialist State is on the basis of the machine, whether in agriculture or industries.

There is urgent need in our country for reducing the growing pressure of population on the soil. There is surplus agricultural labour in the villages for whom non-agricultural occupations have to be found. Russia is rapidly solving this problem for herself.

We want industrialisation of India because it is the only solution of under-employment in the villages. It is an old problem; 50 years ago a Famine Commission pointed out that there were too many people on the land—more than were required for the thorough cultivation of the land. Our industries are progressing, and we are now producing a wide range of articles which we never produced before. But as we have seen, we do not manufacture means of production: machine tools, steam engines, boilers, oil and gas engines, hydraulic presses and heavy cranes. We do not even manufacture agriculturists' and planters' tools such as ploughs, spades, shovels and pickaxes, or hand-tools of improved character used in most cottage industries. Bicycles, motor-cycles, motor-cars and busses are all imported. Scientific apparatus is mostly imported and so also machinery and technical equipment of mills. Sometime ago it was proposed to develop ship-building in India, but that talk has ceased.

India cannot be industrialised until the 'key' industries have been created, and we have learnt to manufacture means of production.

In the last year of the Five-Year-Plan the value of output of means of production in Russia rose to 18 billion rubles as against 6.96 billion rubles in 1928, or 158 per cent. The share of heavy industry in the total industrial output was 52.5 per cent in 1932. The same proportion for Germany in 1925 was equal to 54·5 per cent and in 1931, 45·2 per cent; in England in 1924 it was equal to 54 per cent (*The First-Five-Year-Plan*, *p.* 121).

There is need in India for industrial reorganisation on a new basis. The manufacture of means of production would necessitate the initiation of many new and important industries.

In the second place, there is need for modernisation of agriculture. This is a necessity imposed upon us by the structural changes in agriculture in the West.

Finally, there is the problem of increasing the purchasing power of the masses, which cannot be solved by waving the magic wand of Inflation. The right means are growth of production and a more equitable distribution of wealth, guaranteeing to the worker the whole fruits of his toil.

Such are our problems. We may refuse to face them as we have refused to face them in the past. We may continue to drift, imagining that everything will be all right in the end. Or, if we choose to be sentimental, we may talk in terms of *khaddar*, *charkha*, 'temple-entry' and 'Council-entry', as we have been doing in recent years.

Is the socialist organisation of industry something fundamentally opposed to Indian instincts or tradition? We are told that the masses of India look upon the Government as their *mai-bap*. Government is the political *mai-bap* of the people, and it had that character even in pre-British days. Socialism will make the Government also our economic *mai-bap*. It is emphatically not true that the common man in India is such a hardened individualist as to be unable to understand this new conception of the State. It will prove a popular conception, once it is realised that it stands for the economic regeneration of India, for social justice and for the greater well-being of all.

CHAPTER XI

FASCISM

We have made a study of socialist planning as a way out of the Crisis. The fascist solution of the problems created by the existing political and economic conditions next claims our attention.

The idea that Fascism has no message for the world is mistaken. Paul Einzig in his *Economic Foundations of Fascism* says: "While Soviet Russia is anxious to spread Communism all over the world and has spared no effort to make it known abroad, Fascist Italy has directed her propaganda inward, and has made no serious effort to gain converts abroad. As Signor Mussolini stated recently, "Fascism is not an article for export"[1].

This is incorrect. Mussolini denies that he ever said that fascism was not an article for export. Speaking in 1930 he said: "The statement that fascism is not an article for export is not mine . . . I affirm today that fascism in regard to idea, doctrine, realisation is universal. Italian in its own special institutions, it is universal in spirit; it cannot be otherwise. The spirit is universal in its own nature. One may therefore look forward to a Fascist Europe, a Europe whose institutions derive their inspiration from the doctrines and practice of fascism"[2].

Thus spoke Mussolini in October 1930. In less than three years Germany turned fascist. Fascist influence on the Continent of Europe and in England is steadily growing. A

[1] p. 3.

[2] *Discorsi* 1930, pp. 211-12.

British Union of Fascists under the leadership of Sir Oswald Mosley has come into existence; Sir Oswald is striving for the establishment of a fascist Government in the United Kingdom. Fascist ideas are also spreading in India. Incidentally, an Indian poet has sung: "It is the mission of Italy to rejuvenate the world"[3]. Whether Italy succeeds in rejuvenating this old and decrepit world or not, India is interested in fascism.

Mussolini claims that fascism is "the only new thing" which the first 30 years of the present century have brought in the political and social domain. Another, and perhaps a more important new thing which the past decade has brought is economic planning, with the State as the sole producer. A more important claim is that fascism has solved the threefold problem of the relation of the State to the individual, of the relation of the State to groups of individuals living under the protection of the State, and of the relation of groups which are not organised to those which are.[4].

It is beyond question that fascism has changed Italy. Speaking in February 1922 as a member of the Italian Parliament Mussolini declared that Fascism meant "a profound economic transformation of Italy"[5] Seven years later, in 1929, as head of the fascist Government he spoke of "the immense panorama of material and moral transformations which we have accomplished"[6] Fascism has given to Italy a strong, centralised Government, which exacts obedience from the Italian people, and which commands the respect of the world. It has ended the war between labour and capital which, before the rise of Mussolini to power, threatened to plunge Italy into chaos. The past ten years

[3] Vincenzo Meletti's *Civilita Fascista* bears the inscription: "*L'Italia ha la missione di ringiovanire il mondo*" (It is Italy's mission to rejuvenate the world)—Srijut V. A. Senduram, poeto Indiano".

[4] *Discorsi* 1930, p. 212.

[5] *Discorsi dal Banco di Deputato*, p. 154.

[6] *Discorsi* 1929, p. 283.

have also seen a vast development of Italy's industrial and, specially, agricultural resources. And, finally, fascism has taught the meaning of nationalism to Italians, and inspired them with a new faith in new ideals.

Lack of Theory

It has been often stated that fascism has no philosophy behind it, like socialism. This is true of the beginnings of fascism—Fascism began without a theory. Fascism began as a protest against the political and economic confusion in Italy in post-War years. But the theory of fascism is being developed now. A fascist University has been established at Peruggia, and a stream of fascist literature, dealing with the theoretical aspects of fascism is pouring forth from the University.

Fascism is irreconcilably opposed to socialism. This may be judged from the following condemnation of socialism by Mussolini: "All that is pompously called scientific socialism is nothing but rubbish (*un rottame*); the mighty, theatrical and grotesque conception of humanity divided into two irreconcilable classes is rubbish; the idea of growing misery, and concentration of capital is rubbish, for we see precisely the contrary process; rubbish, finally, is the idea of social palingenesis"[7]. This is what Mussolini thought of scientific socialism in 1925. But once upon a time he was a socialist himself, like Hitler (German fascists are known as National-socialists). At the outset of the fascist movement the distinction between fascism and socialism was not very clear. This was because fascism had no theory. Nor had the fascists any cut-and-dried programme[8]. They

[7] *Discorsi* 1925, p. 206.

[8] In view of the actual development of fascism it is interesting to read the programme proposed by Mussolini in 1919 for the creation of his Fasci:

1. A National Constituent Assembly, as the Italian section of the Internation Constituent Assembly, of peoples, to proceed to a radical transformation of the political and economic bases of community life.

2. Proclamation of the Italian Republic. Decentralisation of the executive power autonomous administration of regions and communes by means of their own legislative organs. Sovereignty of the people, exercised through a universal, equal

could therefore permit themselves the luxury of being both aristocrats and democrats, conservatives and progressives, reactionaries and revolutionaries[9]. Mussolini himself wrote in 1920 that life was not linear, for which reason there was no one solution of the problems of life. "*LET US RETURN TO THE INDIVIDUAL*", he said. "We shall support all that exalts, amplifies the Individual, gives him greater liberty, greater well-being, greater latitude in life; we shall fight against all that suppresses, mortifies the Individual"[10] As for socialism, in March 1921 Mussolini wrote that it mattered very little if the fascist programme, as was alleged by an Italian journal, "was not opposed to, and was rather convergent with that of socialists in regard to all that relates to technical re-organisation, administrative or political, of our country"[11].

and direct franchise of citizens of both sexes, the people to reserve to themselves the initiative of referendum and veto.

3. Abolition of the Senate. Abolition of the political police. Magistrates elected independently of the executive power.
4. Abolition of all titles of nobility and of all orders of knighthood.
5. Abolition of compulsory service.
6. Liberty of opinion and of conscience, of religion, of association, of the press.
7. An education system of schools, general and professional, open to all.
8. The maximum of attention to social hygiene.
9. Dissolution of industrial and financial limited companies. Suppression of every kind of speculation, of banks and stock exchanges.
10. Census and taxation of private wealth. Confiscation of unproductive revenue.
11. Prohibition of labour for children under 16 years of age. Eight hour day.
12. Reorganisation of production on a co-operative basis and direct sharing of all the workers in the profits.
13. Abolition of secret diplomacy.
14. International policy open to, and inspired by, the solidarity of peoples and their independence in a confederation of states.

(Contemporary Review, Sept. 1931. Article, Fascism and Bolshevism: A Legend, by Court Sforza).

Count Sforza may well describe this programme as that of "a youthful Red". Mussolini's fascism in 1919 was little different from socialism and it was international in outlook.

[9] *Diuturna*, p. 243.

[10] *Diuturna*, p. 224.

[11] *Diuturna*, p. 243.

It is surprising how a movement which was akin to socialism in the beginning, later developed into its most formidable opponent. It is also surprising how a movement which started without any definite aims or method, later came to grip the whole Italian people as Fascism does to-day. At the outset the great founder of Fascism had no perception of the economic and political system with which his name is now associated. The vague desire to exalt the individual was no philosophy. And if Fascism has succeeded in exalting the individual to-day, it is certainly not by giving him greater liberty or greater latitude in life.

The initial success of fascism in Italy was not due to any peculiar appeal that its intellectual concepts made to the Italian people, for a study of the writings of Mussolini before the historic March on Rome reveals no such concepts. Its initial victory over the minds of Italians was not an intellectual victory—Fascism has acquired an important intellectual content now, but it had none them. And yet it succeeded.

Nationalism

Mussolini succeeded because Italy was weak and he wished to make it strong; because Italy was torn by economic strife and he promised to end that strife; because Italy was despised by the Great Powers, and he was resolved to make it respected, even feared. Mussolini's appeal was a national appeal. His movement was a national movement for making Italy great, and it caught the imagination of the Italian people. Even to-day nationalism and Imperialism are the two great bulwarks of the movement. It is through sedulously preaching nationalism and Imperialism that Mussolini has succeeded in re-organising the economic and political life of Italy. The aim that Fascism has set before the Italian people is national aggrandisement through a revision of the Treaty of Versailles, through peaceful colonial expansion, and, if necessary, even through war and conquest.

The Treaty of Versailles.

The Great War taught Italians the meaning of the word 'nation'. Mussolini fully exploited the dissatisfaction of Italy with the Treaty of Versailles to strengthen Italian nationalism. The iron discipline of the Fascist regime, the military or dictatorial form of the Italian Government, the enforced collaboration of labour and capital—all derive their inspiration from Italian nationalism, whose object is the recognition by the world of Italy's 'just claims'. Italy wants her place in the sun, or as Il Duce has said, she wants to "make for herself a little place in the world"[12].

Mussolini does not regard peace treaties as 'eternal'. Nations arise, grow, decline and sometimes die. "Eternity of a treaty would signify that humanity, at a given moment, by a monstrous prodigy, had undergone a process of mummification, or in other words, was dead"[13].

Peace treaties "are not the result of Divine justice". They are the work of man, and therefore not perfect.

Mussolini gave expression to his dissatisfaction with the Peace of Versailles as a Deputtee of the Italian Parliament. Speaking on December 1, 1921, he referred to "events which are maturing and which are destined once more to transform the map of Europe"[14]. The world was on the horns of a dilemma. "Either a new war or the revision of treaties."

Why is Italy dissatisfied with the Peace of Versailles? She fought on the side of the Allies and won the War. Why should she demand a revision of the Treaty of Versailles?

This is because Italy won the War but lost the Peace. *Vincemmo la guerra, ma perdemmo la pace*—"We won the War but lost the Peace". How did Italy 'lose the Peace'?

600,000 Italian soldiers were killed in the War, and about 1 million wounded. In addition, there was the heavy money cost of the War, reckoned in milliards of Lire. What

[12] *Il Fascismo*, pp. 284-5.
[13] *Discorsi*, 1928, p. 167.
[14] *Discorsi, dal Banco di Deputato*, p. 128.

did Italy get as compensation for her 'enormous sacrifices'?

The victory was of all the Allies, and to win the War the Allies pooled their resources in men and money. Italy, therefore, expected that the Colonial booty would be equally divided among the principal victors.

What happened was entirely different. The victory enriched those who were already rich[15].

Let us consider the actual division of the spoils.

England got in Africa 2 million sq. KM. of territory with a population of 5 millions. Not counting Egypt and Sudan, England's possessions in Africa amount to 7 million sq. KM. with a population of 42 millions. In Asia England got Palestine, Transjordania and Irak—436,000 sq. KM. with a population of 4 millions. In Oceania she had New Guinea, Naum and Western Samoa, a total of 243,000 sq. KM. with a population of 441,000. In all, the British Colonial Empire, which Meletti calls 'mastodontico'[16] or huge like the pre-historic mastodon, comprises 47,360,678 sq. KM. with a population of more than 450 millions.

France, which already possessed vast territories out of all proportion to her numbers, became the master of almost the whole of Northern, Central, and Western Africa. In Asia she got Syria and the Great Libano. Her total colonial possessions amount to 12 millions of sq. KM. with a population of 47 millions, while the colonial possessions of Italy amount to 2 million sq. KM. of land with a population of a little over 2 millions!! (the two marks of exclamation are Meletti's). Even Portugal secured 100,000 sq. KM. of African land by the Treaty of Versailles. Italy was treated worse than Portugal—she was given only 90,000 sq. KM. of infertile land in Africa!!! (marks of exclamation Meletti's).

That is how Italy 'lost the Peace'. "Such acts of

[15] *Verso la Meta by Fatini*, p. 74.
[16] *Meletti, loc. cit.*, p. 112.

injustice" adds Meletti, "make the heart of every Italian quiver with rage"[17].

Now perhaps it will be said that it is wrong to call the Mandates 'possessions', or to look upon them as 'Colonial booty' (*bottine coloniale*). Germany, we are told, was deprived of her colonies because she misgoverned them. In a covering note addressed to Germany, dated June 16, 1919, the following explanation was given of the Allied decision in regard to the German colonies: "The Allied and Associated Powers have finally convinced themselves that the natives of German colonies strongly object to being placed again under German rule. And the history of German dominion, the traditions of the German Government, and the manner in which the colonies were used as a base for attacks on world trade, make it impossible for the Allied and Associated Powers to return the colonies to Germany, or to entrust the German Empire with the responsibility for educating and civilising the native population".

England and France shouldered the main responsibility for educating and civilising the natives of Africa and Asia who had suffered so grievously on account of mis-government by Germans and Turks. Italy should have accepted this decision in the spirit of the Allies. But she did not. This is because her conception of a colonial Empire is different from that of England and France.

The Italian view of colonies is an integral part of Fascism, and it deserves our careful attention.

Mussolini attaches considerable importance to the growth of numbers. Italy is one of the densely inhabited countries of Europe. Belgium has a density of 267 per sq. KM., England 264, Holland 231, Germany 137, Italy 133 and France 74. The population of Italy is 40 millions and it is increasing rapidly at the rate of 400,000 per year. But even this is not enough for Mussolini. Sometime ago he said:

[17] *Ibid*, p. 113.

"Let us talk clearly. What are 40 millions of Italians as against 90 millions of Germans and 200 millions of Slavs? Let us turn to the Orient. What are 40 millions of Italians as against 40 millions of the French, who have more than 90 millions of natives in their colonies; or against 46 millions of the English with a colonial population of more than 450 millions?

"Gentlemen, Italy, in order to count for something, should have, at the commencement of the second half of this century, a population of 60 millions"[18].

And Il Duce is practical. In matters of employment, under his orders, preference is given to those with a numerous family, with 7 children or more. Bachelors are subjected to heavy taxation in Italy.

If numbers continue to grow at the present rate, Italy will want room for expansion. She wants it now[19].

The Italian view of colonies is frankly selfish. The colonies exist for the mother-country. Politically, they increase the prestige of the mother-country, and are also otherwise useful because, in a time of war, they furnish troops to fight the battles of the mother-country. Economically, they provide room for settlers and employment for the unemployed at home, render the mother-country independent of foreign sources of raw material, and give to the home producer new markets, and to the capitalist new fields of investment.

Nationalism and Internationalism

The nationalist-Imperialist outlook of Fascism is fundamentally opposed to the international character of socialism.

[18] Quoted by *Fatini, loc. cit.* p. 82.

[19] In an article written to eulogise "the soul-expanding energism of Hitler" (!) Prof. Benoy Kumar Sarkar characterises Hitler's problems as "chiefly external" and says that with Mussolini "the chief problem is internal". Italy has precisely the same interest in the revision of the Peace Treaty as Germany. (The article appeared in the "*Insurance and Finance Review*" and has been reprinted in pamphlet form under the title "*The Hitler State*", C and M. Gazette, Lahore).

Socialism stands for the solidarity of the international proletariat. Whatever be the other defects of socialism, it seeks no conquests abroad and no Colonial expansion. Internationalism promotes peace, while aggressive nationalism, which is little different from unbridled Imperialism, must lead to war. A war-like feeling is growing in Europe, and Fascism has materially contributed to bring about this result.

Internationalism is a higher ideal, but Mussolini is right in saying that the masses in every country are national, not international in their outlook. Addressing the Socialist group as a member of the Italian Parliament Mussolini said in June 1921: "We repudiate your internationalism because it is an article of luxury of use only to the higher classes, while the people are desperately attached to their native soil"[20]. Referring to internationalism again in 1926 he said that it was the highest classes of society in Italy which imitated the French, the English and the Americans. It was they who adopted "the style of dress of other peoples, often their psychology and most often their defects". The humbler classes remained "attached desperately to the country of their origin", as they were "still so barbarous as not to appreciate all the advantages of the so-called modern comfort"[21]

Internationalism means much more than community of dress and tastes. It is based on the community of interests of the workers of all countries. The socialist idea is a world society under one Government, political as well as economic.

It will be said that this is a wholly impracticable ideal —a Utopia. But for important spheres of economic life, even non-socialist thinkers have suggested schemes of world-management and control. Sir Arthur Salter, for example, dreams of "a new world order", in which the world's monetary system and the world's credit system would be so

[20] *Discorsi, dal Banco di Deputato*, pp. 43-4.
[21] *Discorsi*, 1926, p. 89.

managed, and he says: "Mine is no distant or ideal Utopia, beyond either the vision or reach of the pedestrian"[22]. The world needs a stable level of prices and stable rates of exchange. Without abandoning national currencies, stability of exchange and prices may be secured through international co-operation. Rates of exchange may be once fixed, and different Governments might enter into binding agreements not to alter them. Short-term fluctuations in the price level, so far as they are due to monetary causes, may be removed by united action of Central Banks working under the direction of the Bank of International Settlements. If gold was becoming too scarce or too plentiful, the situation might be met by "a simultaneous change in the legal reserve ratios and, in case of necessity, a simultaneous change in the gold content of the currency standards"[23]. At present each country acts in its own interests—there has been devaluation of currencies but at different rates, and in different degrees in different countries. The result is confusion, mis-understandings, suspicion and hatred.

Conceivably the Bank of International Settlements may develop into a Central Bankers' Bank. Sir Arthur says: "It could save unnecessary movements of gold, arrange temporary aid where it was needed, and in time exercise the same salutary influence on national Central Banks, as the latter do on the general banking policy of their own countries. It might even, in time, if given the requisite resources and powers, issue its own notes based on gold; and these notes might be included in national currency reserves, or ultimately, even constitute the legal standard for these currencies".

Such is Sir Arthur Salter's conception of a managed world currency. A world Central Bankers' Bank, whose notes were accepted as the legal standard for national currencies, would be a means of realising this ideal. The world

[22] *Recovery*, p. 290.
[23] *Ibid*, p. 291.
[24] *Ibid*, pp. 291-92.

may then have one monetary policy, stable money, stable prices and stable rates of exchange. The war of currency depreciation would then definitely come to an end.

The credit policy of the world may also be directed from one centre, or, at any rate, an attempt may be made to co-ordinate and control national credit policies. Sir Arthur Salter says:

"The next requirement of world order is a reformed system of credit. Foreign investment must be within a secure frame-work of world policy; and home investment within a similar frame-work of national policy; while each is, within this frame work, free to adapt itself responsively to the myriad needs of economic enterprise and activities"[25].

If international regulation of money and credit is possible, production in different countries may also be internationally controlled. Attempts have been made recently to restrict the cultivation of tea, sugarcane, wheat and other crops by unofficial international agreements. We have seen that the world's troubles are not wholly of the monetary order, and that if prices are to be kept stable, it will be necessary to control world supply. Conceivably such control may be exercised through a central world organisation. As in the case of money and credit, different countries at present pursue independent policies in the sphere of production, without regard to the effect of their policy on the world situation. Under such conditions, the effect of restriction in one country is neutralised by expansion in another. When the world's producing capacity has increased so enormously there will be an obvious advantage in regulating and co-ordinating national productive efforts, through a central world organisation. If such an organisation ever came into existence, endowed with necessary powers and enjoying the confidence of the world, the entire world production might be subjected to scientific planning.

[25] *Ibid*, pp. 291-92.

Such is the meaning of internationalism in the economic sphere. Nationalism is a formidable obstacle to the creation of a new world order in which national interests would be sub-ordinated to world interests. And so long as there is economic war among the nations, the danger of political conflicts will always exist. To realise their national economic aims, nations will arm themselves and fight.

Mussolini may argue with perfect truth and sincere conviction that the proletariat is not international. But that does not alter the fact that internationalism is the way to peace, greater production, and greater well-being of humanity. The ethics of internationalism is infinitely superior to the ethics of nationalism, just as nationalism is a higher ideal than petty communalism, which regards a people as divided into a number of communities with divergent and conflicting interests.

Italy, in spite of winning the war, is dissatisfied with the Peace of Versailles. Germany has better reasons to desire a revision of the Peace Treaty. As in Italy, the aims of Fascism in Germany are national. Addressing a mammoth audience of 2 million workingmen on the 1st of May 1933 (which has become in Germany the Day of National Work) Hitler said:

"Germans! You are not a second-rate nation, even if the world should a thousand times wish it to be so. You are not of second-rate worth. Germans! Think of yourselves, of the deeds of your forefathers, yes, of the deeds of your own generation. Forget the 14 years of ruin. Arise and make 2000 years of German history".

With Germans preparing to make 2000 years of German history and Italians prepared to make 2000 years of Roman history, the prospects of a lasting world peace do not seem very bright. We are not directly concerned with this; but attention had to be drawn to the national aspirations of Germany and Italy, as they throw a flood of light on the fascist movement, and explain its phenomenal success in these two countries.

The Fascist State

The fascist State is the product of fascist nationalism.

The fascists are inordinately proud of their conception of the State. In fact they claim that at the present time there is no other theory of the State worth talking about except the fascist theory, for no State exists to-day except the fascist State. In the leading countries of the world the State is struggling with a crisis, and as for the Russian State and the theory of Soviet Government, they are mere names"[26].

The fascist theory of the State is simple—the State is all-in-all. It is *Stato forte ė soverano*—a strong and sovereign state[27]. It has the right to interfere in all spheres of life, whether economic, moral or religious. Civil life begins with the State—therefore all are in the State and no one outside the State. The State will tolerate no opposition. It commands all—it is of the essence of the State to govern.

The liberal State is a weak, timid State and fascists regard it with contempt. Is the socialist State, which is in the process of formation, any better?

There is no such thing as a socialist State! The real State is *lo Stato-impero, lo Stato-governo*—the State which rules and governs. The Socialist State is like a private business undertaking—it is all administration, management and commercial book-keeping—the State is reduced to an Accounts and Statistical office. Why so? we ask. The answer is that the main function of the socialist State is to organize production. Panunzio explains that fascism had no difficulty in Italy in conquering socialism—its victory was certain from the beginning—because socialism had misconceived the State. Far from developing the idea of the State, socialism destroyed the State, denied the State, and what is the

[26] *Il Sentimento dello Stato by Sergio Panunzio*, p. 20.

[27] *Panunzio*, loc. cit. p. 72.

same thing, reduced and degraded the State to administration and management"[28].

But is it possible for the State to be reduced to administration, management, book-keeping and accounts? The State, in order to exist at all, must govern. A socialist State, in order to carry out its economic policy in regard to production and distribution, must exercise political authority. That the socialist State devotes its chief attention to economic matters does not mean that it has abdicated its political power.

A socialist State may endeavour to educate the people, and raise their cultural level. In so far as it does so, it is not merely a commercial undertaking. And socialism can never succeed unless the masses have been taught to understand the aims and methods of socialist organisation. A socialist State must actively fight ignorance and superstition, or it will be short-lived. Mass education of a fairly high standard is an essential requisite of socialism.

No State can be managed as a purely business concern, whatever be the theory of the socialist State. We agree that the State is essentially *Imperium*[29], and that it is nonsensical to think that the State can cease to govern. But a State which governs and does nothing else is not less nonsensical—it has no right to exist. It is possible to over-emphasize the functions of the State in regard to governing a people.

The fascist State is superior to the old liberal State, whose chief functions were the maintenance of law and order, and external defence. But this conception of the State passed away many decades ago.

The fascist State endeavours to manage and regulate economic life while maintaining individual responsibility and freedom of enterprise. If the State goes a step further, and takes over production and distribution, why and how does it cease to be a State? Conceivably, that may be a means of

[28] *Ibid*, pp. 36-37.
[29] *Ibid*, p. 141.

enabling the masses to lead a fuller life, both in the economic and a larger social sense. In so far as the socialist State succeeds in achieving this aim it fulfils the highest object of its existence.

The fascist State may interfere on behalf of the worker in a labour dispute. Strikes being illegal in a fascist regime, the State must safeguard the interests of the worker, and it does so by virtue of the power that it exercises over all economic matters. The socialist State assumes the function of the employer. The welfare of the worker thus becomes its direct concern, and it can take direct action to raise wages and improve the general conditions of life and work. In this respect the difference between fascism and socialism is this: fascism acts through intermediaries to secure its object, and socialism directly. It will be admitted that the socialist State is a much better instrument for promoting the material welfare of workers than the fascist State.

The fascist State has to constantly assert its authority, as it preserves all the elements which make for economic war in a country. It is necessary to remind labour and capital, tenant and landlord, constantly that the State exists as their over-lord, and that is strong enough to punish the offender. That is how industrial peace is maintained under fascism. The socialist State is the people themselves organised as producers and consumers. There are no economic conflicts as under capitalism or fascism, because the antagonism of classes has been removed. The State is there all the time—as the supreme authority that makes laws, rewards and punishes, maintains internal peace, protects the country against foreign aggression, 'plans' production, guides the execution of its plans and, above all, instructs and educates the people. The socialist State is also a strong and sovereign State, but its awe-inspiring aspects are of less importance than its beneficent aspects.

Fascism and Democracy

Mussolini does not believe in Parliamentarism. The

Italian Parliament of the old regime was not worthy of respect. Writing in his Journal *Il Popolo d'Italia* under the caption "Down with the Parliament" in May 1915, Mussolini said that he was more and more firmly convinced that for the good of Italy it would be necessary to shoot in the back some dozens of deputees. He regarded the Italian Parliament as a pestilential bubo which poisoned the blood of the nation. It was necessary to extirpate it[30].

Italy at present is not governed by Parliament. The form of Government is dictatorship, with all power concentrated in the hands of Mussolini himself. What is Mussolini's justification of dictatorship?

"Dictatorship is in the facts, that is, in the necessity for unity of command; in the force, political, moral (and) intellectual of the man who exercises it; in the aims to be realised"[31].

All the threads of power are in Mussolini's hands. Mussolini is like one of our Great Moghuls—a despot with unlimited power. Every great movement, he once said, must have a representative man who suffers all the passion of the movement and carries all its fire. Mussolini is the representative of fascism. He is Fascism.

"Well then, Comrades", he once said in the course of a public address, "return to your land which I love, and shout with a loud voice and firm belief that the banner of the fascist revolution has been entrusted to my hands, and I will defend it against any one, even at the cost of my blood"[32].

One of his characteristic utterances may be quoted here as it gives us an insight into Mussolini's own character, and the character of the fascist government:

"It is not for nothing that I have chosen as the motto of my life 'Live dangerously', and say to you like the old warrior;

[30] *Diuturna*, p. 18.
[31] *Discorsi* 1929. p. 267.
[32] *Discorsi* 1925. p. 118.

If I advance, follow me; if I turn back, kill me; If I die, avenge me"[33].

The whole political life of Italy centres round Mussolini, the Dictator, the head of the Government, the General of the Fascist State. He leads and others follow. The Black Shirts have to swear fealty, not only to the King (who counts for little), to Italy, to Fascism, but to Mussolini personally.

Mussolini is indispensable to Fascism and Italy, at any rate, for many years to come. And speaking in 1927 Mussolini said that his successor had not yet been born[34].

Like a despot of old, the Italian Dictator has to be vigilant. He has to know all. "Let no one delude himself into thinking that I do not know what happens in the country, even in the farthest Italian village. I may know it a little later, but in the end I know it"[35]. On another occasion, referring again to the vigilance of the Government, (that is himself) Mussolini said:

"The Government is vigilant and nothing escapes it. Let no one imagine that the last little sheet which issues from the remotest parish is not known, at a certain moment, to Mussolini"[36].

Of course Mussolini's power is derived from the Party which he leads. He claims that the fascist regime rests on a Party of one million individuals, on another million of youths, and on "millions and millions of Italians who are perfecting themselves and organizing themselves"[37]. In this sense fascism may be based on the will of the Italian people. But the form of Government is not popular.

Mussolini thinks that the Parliamentary system has outgrown its utility. Liberalism, he explains, arose when nations were much smaller than the States of the present day. Their affairs could, therefore, be managed by a small class of

[33] *Discorsi* 1926. p. 123.
[34] *Discorsi* 1927. p. 143.
[35] *Discorsi* 1927. p. 135.
[36] *Discorsi* 1929. p. 182.
[37] *Discorsi* 1927. p. 142.

politicians recruited from a small number of aristocratic families. But conditions have changed—"The people cannot afford to wait; they are assailed by their problems, driven by their necessities"[38]. The struggle for life is harder, and international conflicts more terrible. Assemblies can talk; they are unable to arrive at quick decisions, and are therefore of little use in the modern world which is moving forward at break-neck speed. "A battle is either won by one general only, or lost by an assembly of generals"[39].

In these times of stress, therefore, a strong executive is a necessity. Fascism gives the greatest importance to executive power, for it is the power that declares war or concludes peace, which directs the complex machinery of the State, and solves the political, economic and other problems which arise from day to day. The Executive power takes the first place in the Italian constitution, and this is the cardinal feature of the political creed of fascism[40].

Mussolini as the head of the Executive power is assisted in the administration of the country by a well-disciplined hierarchy of officials. The Italian bureaucracy is an integral part of the State. "The bureaucracy", as Mussolini says, "is the State"[41]. Bureaucracy, which is so much criticised in India, has been raised by the Italian Government to the highest plane.

Under the Italian system of government, His Majesty's opposition would be of little use and might become a source of weakness. In fact the Opposition does not exist in Italy. The fascist State came into existence in Italy on January 3, 1925. Between October 28, 1922 and January 3, 1925 the fascists governed Italy with the collaboration of other parties. Gradually the other parties were eliminated, and the fascists alone took charge of the administration. The Government

[38] *Ibid*, p. 208.
[39] *Ibid*, p. 208.
[40] *Ibid*, p. 248.
[41] *Ibid*, p. 114.

of Italy between October 1922 and January 1925 was a coalition government. The non-fascists were thus represented in the government; they disappeared after January 3, 1925.

There was of course opposition in the country. This was completely suppressed in 1927. All those suspected of anti-Fascism, or who had shown any counter-revolutionary activity, were deported; all groups or associations, which were anti-fascist, or suspected of anti-fascism, were dissolved, and all anti-fascist newspapers and journals suppressed.

Thus in Italy there is no Opposition, either within the Government or outside.

Under a Parliamentary system the Opposition has a constitutional right to exist, and it discharges an important function. The two principal parties in a parliamentary system have been compared to the fore and hind legs of a stag —they run in the same direction, the hind legs following the fore-legs. The analogy, of course, is not complete. The hind legs of a stag must follow its fore-legs. But it is possible for two political parties to pull in opposite directions. And there may be more than two parties, and they may so much disagree as to make stable government impossible, as was the case in Italy before the rise of fascism.

In any case fascism has no use for an Opposition." The Opposition" Mussolini says, "is not necessary to the functioning of a healthy political regime". The Opposition may exist when the country can spare time for academic discussions. But in the first place we are now living in critical times, and, in the second place, the whole of Italy has turned fascist. Under such conditions, the Opposition in Italy would be "stupid, superflous"[42].

But there is another kind of Opposition which always exists and which has to be overcome. This is Opposition in a metaphysical sense:—

"But we have Opposition in ourselves, dear sirs, we are not old jades who require to be goaded. We control ourselves

[42] *Discorsi* 1927, pp. 122-23.

severely. We find opposition, above all, in things, in objective difficulties, in life, which provides a high mountain of difficulties, which might exhaust spirits even superior to my own. Therefore let no one hope after this discourse that anti-fascist journals will reappear—no—or that the resurrection of anti-fascist groups will be permitted—not that either"[43].

In the same speech, delivered on May 26, 1927, Mussolini also solemnly buried 'the lie of the universal democratic suffrage." He is unable to understand why the vote should be given to a citizen simply because he has completed 21 years. How can a question of chronology or civil condition become the criterion of the capacity of a citizen? In the course of an interview granted to a representative of a French newspaper, Mussolini said:

"I consider it absurd that a man should have the right to vote conferred on him solely because he has attained the age of 21 years.

"Only those should participate in the direction and administration of the State who work and produce, and offer their co-operation to the State with the product of their individual work"[44].

As for women, Mussolini regrets that Capitalism should have drawn millions of them from the domestic hearth into factories and offices. In his judgment women do not possess great powers of synthesis and are therefore incapable of creating great spiritual values. And he said in 1925 that he had never yet met any woman who asked him for the right of vote. "That does credit to the Italian woman" he added[45].

Mussolini's condemnation of the Parliamentary system is unequivocal and unqualified. Other fascist leaders, *e.g.*, Alfredo Rocco, admit the success of the democratic-liberal

[43] *Ibid*, pp. 122-23.
[44] *Il Fascismo*, p. 129.
[45] *Discorsi* 1925, p. 65.

State in France and Anglo-Saxon countries. These countries have great national traditions, and the idea of the State there grew and became strong in the course of a long political struggle from which the State emerged as victor, affirming its power and authority. In England, in addition, individualism is kept in check by a rigorous moral education, which, while theoretically justifying the maximum of individual liberty as against the State, permits the State, in fact, to limit it spontaneously[46].

Italy had no such traditions. The political anarchy of the Middle Ages and foreign domination had created among the people distrust and suspicion of the State. After Italy became independent, a democratic-liberal regime came into being, which lasted for 62 years (1860-1922). That this regime lasted so long, and that independence was not followed by anarchy, Rocco finds surprising. The conclusion of the War, however, found the Italian State weak and unable to control rival factions and parties which threatened to plunge Italy into a sanguinary civil war. Such were the conditions under which fascism arose.

It is obvious that representative Government presupposes a certain degree of responsibility, culture and discipline among those who enjoy the right to vote. Where these mental qualities are lacking, representative government must fail. The application of the principle of democracy to municipal administration in the Punjab, and probably also other parts of India, has not been attended with desirable results. Nor has democracy succeeded in education. As regards Provincial Councils and the Assembly, it may be doubted if the great majority of the elected legislators in the Provinces and in the Central government are in any sense fit to legislate. This, however, is no condemnation of democracy.

A strong, centralised bureaucratic government is better than confusion. That is the experience of Italy.

[46] *La Transformatione dello Stato* by Alfredo Rocco, p. 14.

The State must be strong and powerful, centralised and unitary. It is a citadel "in which there can be no antitheses, neither of individuals nor of groups"[47]. The State must control all bodies and organisations, and it is subject to none.

Ethics and Religion

Both the socialist and the fascist States have a clearly definite attitude towards religion. The socialist State is frankly atheist, and it carries on an active propaganda against religion. The reason for this anti-religious propaganda was thus explained by Stalin in September 1927 in the course of an interview with the First American Labour Delegation to Russia:

"The Party cannot be neutral towards religion, and it does conduct anti-religious propaganda against all and every religious prejudice because it stands for science while religious prejudices run counter to science, because all religion is something opposite to science"[48].

Here is then a State whose outlook is founded on science and which not only has no religion but is definitely hostile to religion.

From the very beginning the attitude of fascism towards the Church has been friendly. "Fascism", said Mussolini in 1921 "neither preaches nor practises anti-clericalism"[49]. And in the same speech he asked the Socialist Deputies of Parliament to bear witness that he had never been a Positivist, nor even when he belonged to their Party. Mussolini's religious philosophy is of special interest to us, as it is akin to an ancient school of Indian philosophy.

"Not only does the dualism of matter and spirit not exist for us, but we have abolished this antithesis in the synthesis of the spirit. The spirit alone exists: neither you,

[47] *Discorsi* 1925, p. 295.
[48] *Leninism*, Vol. II. p. 70.
[49] *Discorsi dal Banco di Deputato*, p. 47.

nor this hall, nor things and objects which appear on the fantastic cinema screen of the universe. The universe exists so far as I think of it, only in my thought, not independently of my thought"[50].

This is Mussolini's personal conviction. The fascist State, however, is not based on a view of reality which would make the State appear or disappear according as one did or did not choose to think of it. The ethical and religious character of the fascist State is founded on less idealistic philosophy.

The war against religion in Russia had attracted Mussolini's attention in 1920. He wrote in January 1920 that two religions, the black and the red, were contending against each other in the region of the spirit and in the world. He did not believe in either of them—for him the fight was everything. But he wondered which of the two religions would win in the end. "Will Galileo of the red hair (meaning Jesus Christ) win again?" He asked. "Or will the Mongolian Galileo of Kremlin win?"[51]. We know now that Galileo of the red hair has won in Italy and Galileo of Kremlin has won in Russia. The fascist State is as definitely religious as the socialist State is anti-religious.

The fascist State is described as "the ethical State". The ethical character of the fascist State is said to be one of its most important distinguishing features. What is the essence of this ethical character? The authoritative pronouncement of the founder of fascism is as follows:

"The moral character of the fascist State cannot be denied, for I should feel ashamed of talking from this tribune if I did not feel that I represented the moral and spiritual power of the State. What thing would the State be if it did not have its own spirit, its own morality, which gives force to its law, and by which it succeeds in getting itself obeyed by its citizens? A miserable thing, against which the citizens would have the right of revolt, or which they

[50] *Ibid*, pp. 123-24.
[51] *Diuturna*, p. 224.

would despise. The fascist State completely upholds its ethical character: it is Catholic but fascist, above all exclusively and essentially fascist. The Catholic faith integrates it—and we openly declare it—but let no one be led by specious philosophy or metaphysics to change the cards on the table"[52].

By 'changing the cards on the table' Mussolini meant reversing the order of importance of fascism and the Catholic church. Fascism comes first and religion next—the Church is within the fascist State, and the State is not subordinate to it. This is a point of some importance.

Another authoritative declaration is that of Alfred Rocco, Keeper of the Seals:

"From the social point of view the fascist State has its own aims, that is, its own function and its own mission. The fascist State is not agnostic, like the Liberal State, in every sphere of communal life; on the contrary in every sphere it has its function and its purpose.

"The fascist State has its morality, its religion, its political mission in the world, its function of social justice, in short, its economic duty. And therefore the fascist State must protect and propagate morality among the people; must concern itself with religious problems, and therefore profess and protect the true religion, that is the Catholic religion. . . ."[53].

Let us first consider the moral aspect of fascism. The State has its own notions of right and wrong which it propagates among the people. The question of the form of Government—whether the State expresses the general Will of the people, or only the Will of a select aristocracy, or elite of the community, which has been discussed at great length by Major Barnes, is irrelevant[54]. The main point is that the fascist State, in whatever manner it may be

[52] *Discorsi* 1929, pp. 182-83.

[53] Rocco,loc. cit., p. 17.

[54] *Fascism by Major Barnes* (Home University Library) See chapter entitled "The Ethical State".

constituted, endeavours to educate the people on questions of morality. The sphere of morals is not excluded from its jurisdiction. We agree with Mussolini that the State would be a miserable thing if it did not possess a moral character.

But is there any State in the world which does not possess a moral character in this sense? The State in India is neither religious, like the fascist State, nor anti-religious like the socialist State in Russia. It is frankly non-religious. But it possesses a moral character. It suppressed the evil practice of Suttee about a hundred years ago. That meant intervention in the moral and religious sphere. Recently it has prohibited child marriages. This is again interference with the moral and religious customs of the people. The action of the State is resented in orthodox circles, and probably the law is not being enforced rigorously, but the mere fact that such a law exists has an educative effect and shows the moral purpose of legislation. We have also a regular department for the reform of criminal tribes. The reclamation of born criminals and their transformation into law-abiding citizens is ethical action in the highest sense. Apart from special activities mentioned above, like all countries we have a penal code for punishing offenders. The penal code is a concrete expression of the moral opinions of the State. Cheating, theft, arson and murder are punished in every civilized country. The State enforces the law of contract, and adopts other measures to promote business honesty. Civilised life would be impossible without laws for punishing what offends the moral sense of the community. A State may be non-religious, but it cannot be non-moral. That would mean anarchy.

Under certain conditions a State cannot have a religious character. The Italian State has a religion, the true religion, Catholicism. This is the religion that fascism professes and protects in Italy. If an 'ethical State' in the fascist sense were to be established in India, which religion would the State profess and protect? The enforcement of a Moral Law which owed its inspiration to one religion, say

Catholicism, would plunge the whole country into sanguinary religious strife and endanger the very existence of the State. Where the subjects profess a multiplicity of religious creeds, the State cannot identify itself with any religion, but as we have seen, that does not mean that it becomes non-moral or immoral.

Let us now consider the position of the socialist State, which is anti-religious. Why should it not have its morality, its political mission in the world, its function of social justice, its economic duty? The economic functions of the socialist State far transcend in importance those of the fascist State. The socialist State has also its own ideas of social justice, which it enforces with all its authority. These consist in the elimination of the exploiter, equal treatment of the sexes, and the provision of equal opportunities for all. The socialist ideal of social justice is not inferior to that of fascism. Then Socialists—they may be misguided—also believe in their political mission in the world, like fascists.

If the fascist State is 'ethical' because it has its own aims and because of its morality, its conception of social justice, its economic functions, and its mission in the world, the socialist State must also be 'ethical' precisely in the same sense.

What are the peculiar features of fascist ethics, which raise the fascist State above the socialist State?

The answer is Religion.

"It (fascism) proclaims God, in fine, as the supreme sovereign, and the State as God's temporal vicar, responsible to God for the people's good government. This is the meaning of the fascist ethical State, which is accordingly also the authoritative and unitary State, with a definite, indivisible ethical purpose and a definite ethical justification"[55].

If for the 'State' we substitute the 'King' as God's temporal vicar, we should have a philosophy of the 'ethical' State little different from the "Divine Right of Kings". The

[55] Major Barnes, loc. cit. p. 116.

evolution of the 'ethical State' does not mark any advance in the history of political thought. In fact, as Major Barnes says, the fascist State recognizes God as the supreme sovereign "as in the Middle Ages"[56].

Major Barnes also explains why *vox Populi* is not *vox Dei*. Fascism definitely rejects majority government, or popular sovereignty. In theory fascism is government by an aristocracy of merit; in actual practice it is a Dictatorship. The Dictator thus becomes God's temporal vicar, responsible, not to the people, but to God for the people's good government!

All this is thoroughly absurd.

What has God to do with the State? The State is a historical growth. It is a human, not Divine institution. Those who govern are responsible to the governed and to no one else. Responsibility to God just means nothing—it is an excuse for irresponsibility.

Fascism assumes that the Moral Law has a supernatural sanction, or that God is the source of the Moral Law. But morality is independent of religion.

If the Moral Law is God's Law, God must have endowed us with the power to distinguish right from wrong, virtue from vice. It is in fact claimed that conscience is that power in us—it is the still small voice of God within us always telling us to do what is right. In the political sphere it is claimed that "this voice of conscience is a constant force operating in favour of good government"[57] though conscience may be atrophied by 'rationalistic habits of thought' or other equally condemnable habits or practices! If this is really the philosophy of the 'ethical State', it betrays a profound ignorance of some of the most elementary sociological facts.

Like the State, conscience is a historical growth.

The notions of right and wrong prevalent among

[56] *Ibid*, p. 122.

[57] *Ibid*, p. 107.

different peoples are not always the same, and the ethical standards of the same people change from time to time.

Savages certainly have a conscience, Mr. New says of the Wainka (an African tribe): "Conscience lives in them as the vicegerent of Almighty God, and is ever excusing or else accusing them". But it is difficult to understand why the vicegerent of Almighty God should tell primitive races to do things from which the civilised man turns back in horror and disgust.

Human sacrifice is practised by many savage races. The Patagonians bury the dying before they expire—from motives of pity and kindness. In Fiji it was regarded as a sign of filial affection to put an aged parent to death[59].

India is a land of ancient civilisation, but our law, as expressing our social conscience, does not punish bigamy. Europe is civilised, but adultery is no crime there. If A runs away with B's wife, in India A would be condemned to several years' penal servitude, in Europe only to civil damages.

The moral law everywhere is the product of a long growth, social, political and economic. And as conditions of social, political and economic development have not been the same in all countries, the social conscience of different peoples is different.

Conscience grows and develops so that notions of right and wrong change. The conscience of the civilised man does not approve of the sale of human beings like chattel, and slavery, in civilised countries, has been abolished by law. But the still small voice of God did not condemn slavery in the early ages. Martyrs then possessed slaves, and also abbots, bishops, Popes, monastries and churches.

These are undeniable facts, and their significance is perfectly clear to all except those who mislead the ignorant in the name of God.

[58] *Origin and Development of the Moral Ideas* by Westermarck, Vol. I. p. 391.
[59] *Ibid*, pp. 389-90.

If the Moral Law is a human law, it follows that even an atheistic State may be an ethical State in the fullest sense of the word. What makes a State an ethical State is not assertion of belief in God but the use of the power and authority of the State to inculcate the moral virtues of truth, honesty, kindness, charity, courage and sacrifice among the people. The ethical State existed in India in the time of Asoka Mauriya, more than two thousand years before its discovery in Italy in the third decade of the 20th century.[80]

It would be only fair to state that Mussolini himself, so far as the present writer is aware, has never claimed that as the acknowledged leader of fascism he is God's temporal vicar. He carries the banner of the fascist State, he suffers the whole passion of the fascist movement, and he embodies in his person the moral and spiritual forces of the Italian people. But as such he does not claim to be God's temporal vicar. Neither has he ever said, so far as the present writer is aware, that the fascist State is God's temporal vicar and therefore responsible to God for the people's good government. Mussolini is intelligent enough to know that the State, as a political institution, has nothing whatever to do with God. He has accepted the alliance of the State with the Catholic Church, but only on the condition that the State is not subordinated to the Church. The State comes first, the church next—and Mussolini would not permit this relation to be reversed. There was a struggle between the Church and fascism before the conclusion of the Treaty of Laterano. Mussolini dealt with the situation firmly—never acknowledging the right of the Pope to interfere in temporal matters. And every one knows what Mussolini would do if the Pope adopted a policy or measures tending to undermine the fascist State, or weaken fascism.

Italy is a Catholic country and Mussolini, with the true insight of a statesman, has used the Church to strengthen the State. A war between the church and the State would have

[80] *Ibid*, 695.

weakened fascism—hence Mussolini's anxiety to obtain the blessings of the Church. It may be recalled that Mussolini is a great admirer of Macchiavelli. In the preface, contributed by him to a new edition of Macchiavelli's works he bestows high praise on this great political philosopher who lived 400 years ago. Mussolini calls Macchiavelli's *The Prince* "*Vade-mel'um per cuomo di governo*" (Guide-book for Rulers). He holds that Macchiavelli's teaching is as true today as it was 400 years ago since the nature of the individual or the people has not fundamentally changed—nor is it likely to change, we may add.

Now Macchiavelli did not believe in religion as the ordinary religious man does. To Macchiavelli, as to Mussolini, the State is all-in-all. It is something infinitely superior to all things human and all interests of life and society. Macchiavelli valued religion, but not more than the State. Religion appeared to him merely as a purely political means (*un puro mezzo politico*) by which uncultured people may be guided. Prayer and religious ceremonies are necessary, he said, because they create harmony and order among the people. "For him religion is an instrument that helps to keep in check human passions, and to get the people to obey the orders given—that is all; of the satisfaction of an intimate need there is not a single trace"[61].

Fascist leaders may be thoroughly and sincerely religious. In that case they do not know anything of modern science, which is definitely anti-religious. If fascist leaders are not utter strangers to the scientific point of view, their homage to religion must be of the Macchiavellian type. The level of mass intelligence in every country is low. A devout Catholic is not unlike a devout Hindu, or a devout Mussalman. He believes in a personal God because this faith is comforting. He will not give up his cherished beliefs and the faith of his fore-fathers, whether science knows a God of Love or not. To preach rationalism, therefore, is to initiate a religious war,

[61] *Storia della Letteratura Italiana* by Vittorio Rossi, Vol. II, Part II, p. 15.

which must create civil discord and strife. This is precisely what fascist leaders would avoid, particularly at a time like this when the exhibition of national strength as against other countries is the only means of satisfying Italy's political aspirations. Truth may, therefore, be sacrificed to expediency. This is probably all the significance of the "ethical State" so far as the fascist State derives its ethical character from its alliance with the Church.

Ethics of Fascism

What are the moral virtues which fascism inculcates?

We have seen that fascism derives its inspiration and strength from nationalism. Its chief aim is to make Italy great. Fascism therefore exalts the fighting virtues, the virtues with the greatest military value—order, discipline, courage and self-sacrifice. Mussolini has re-organised the economic and political life of Italy on a military basis.

"I consider the Italian nation in a state of permanent war", said Mussolini in 1925. He does not believe in "peace lasting for centuries". Therefore, while with one eye he is looking for "the dove of peace which might arise in a distant horizon", he is regarding with the other eye "the concrete necessities of life, or history, which is not contained in any treaty"[62].

Italy must, therefore, be prepared for war. This preparation is two-fold: material and spiritual. As regards the material equipment of war, Mussolini wants to be able to mobilise, at a given moment, 5 millions of armed men; he wants a strong navy; and he wants aircrafts which are so numerous and so powerful that the noise of their motors should drown all other noise in the peninsula, and whose wings should hide the sun from Italy[63].

But in augmenting "to the limit of human possibility" the war-efficiency of the nation[64], the preparation of the

[62] *Discorsi* 1925, pp. 229-30.
[63] *Discorsi* 1927, p. 148.
[64] *Discorsi* 1925, p. 32.

spirit is of vital importance. This is the supreme purpose served by the ethics of fascism.

Rome, in the old days, was the centre of a vast Empire. Rome is to be restored to her old glory.

Mussolini has taught the whole nation to think Imperially.

To realise her aims Italy must become united. The war of classes must end. The enforced collaboration of labour and capital has not only an economic but political significance. It is part of the ethics of fascism.

Mussolini has aroused a war-like spirit in the whole population. The Black Shirts are a military organization. Through various other organisations Mussolini is teaching military discipline to all. The young and the old all must obey Il Duce without asking questions. The whole nation seems to be waiting for the supreme moment—the outbreak of war.

It is impossible for Rome to regain her old glory. However, the ideal of old Rome furnishes the inspiration for militarising the population.

The ethics of fascism is the ethics of war. It will be tested in war, which may not be long in coming. Should Italy emerge as victor from the next war, fascism will grow stronger. Defeat would lead to the collapse of the whole system, for it does not contain elements of permanence.

Transient State

The fascist State is a State created by and meant for an emergency. It is a transient form of State, and in this respect it is inferior to the democratic-liberal State which fascism despises and the socialist State which it refuses to recognise.

Opposition, as we have seen, has no place in the fascist State. But so long as there is a conflict of class interests in a society, opposition must exist. The voice of the opposition may be silenced, as Mussolini has done in Italy, but the conflict of interests is not removed thereby.

The opposition will grow if (a) the authority of the State weakens, and (b) if the fascist State is unable to fulfil its promises.

Under a form of Government which is in essence Dictatorship or the rule of one man, the strength of the Government is the strength of the Dictator. Despotic rule may also be strong and efficient, as was the case in India under Akbar. The downfall of the Moghul Empire was in no small measure due to the weakness of Aurangzeb's successors.

Mussolini has succeeded in imposing his will on the Italian people. Is his successor born yet? He himself does not think so.

Secondly, the opposing factions may be held together for a time by fervent appeals to patriotic sentiment, backed by promises of victory in war, conquest and colonial expansion. But suppose the prospects of a successful war do not materialise? An impossible situation will arise both in Italy and Germany in the course of a generation. As we have seen, both these countries are densly populated, and yet, in both countries, vigorous measures are being adopted to encourage the growth of numbers for military reasons. A growing population wants room for expansion which only colonies can provide. Failing to acquire new territory through a successful war, the fascist State must break up. The growth of numbers will lead to a fall in the standard of living of the masses and sharpen class antagonisms. In a democratic-liberal State a constitutional remedy exists for the ventilation of grievances and their redress. The dissatisfied groups are permitted to organise, increase their strength and even capture the machinery of administration. Labour was in power in England before the formation of the National Government. There is, constitutionally, nothing to prevent the return of labour to power. The government, in a democratic-liberal regime, may change without a revolution. This is impossible under fascism. The fascist government is not responsible to the people. A change of Government, therefore, means a revolution and break-up of fascism. The much despised democratic-liberal government possesses a safety valve against political and economic discontent; the fascist government possesses none.

There are no higher and lower classes in the Socialist State. There is no opposition in the socialist State, because the grounds of opposition have been removed. A socialist State may exist for ever and ever. Further, a number of socialist States may live in peace and harmony with one another. The wider the scope of planning the greater the stability of prices, trade and income.

But it is impossible to think of the world as divided into a number of strong fascist States, each State pursuing its ends selfishly, each State desiring to expand at the expense of others. Universal fascism is a contradiction in terms.

The Corporate State

The economic constitution of fascist Italy consists of four elements: syndicates, which may be called primary cells of the economic organism; federations, which are unions of syndicates; confederations, composed of federations as members; and Corporations, which are central unifying organisations. Above all, supervising the working of the whole economic hierarchy, is the Council of Corporations, constituted in 1930, with Mussolini as President, and Government Minister of Corporation as Vice-President.

Syndicates

A syndicate is an association of employers or employees recognised by the State. It is not necessary for an association to seek legal recognition. Association may exist as "*associazione de fatto*", or *de facto* associations, in accordance with existing legislation. Officially recognised associations, or syndicates, however, enjoy certain privileges and are under the control of the State. Only legally recognised associations may name representatives of employers or employees to councils, organisations etc., for which this representation is provided by law. According to article 3 of the Charter of Labour, only a syndicate or trade association which is legally recognised, and is under the control of the State, has the right of legally representing all the catagories of employers or labourers constituting it; of protecting their interests as against the State and other trade associations; of negotiating collective labour contracts binding on all those comprised in its categories; and of levying contributions and of exercising in respect of them the public functions assigned to it. The syndicates guarantee legal equality between employers and employees, maintain discipline in production, and endeavour to make it more efficient (Article 6 of the Charter of Labour). The Government recognises only one syndicate in a particular category in a given area. Multiplicity of syndicates would make it difficult for the State to control them.

Syndicates are recognised by the Government by means of a royal decree. Certain conditions must be satisfied before recognition is granted:

1. The employers who wish to form a syndicate must employ at least one-tenth of the total number of workers engaged in the business for which the association is formed. Similarly the employees who seek recognition as a syndicate must represent at least one-tenth of the total number of workers of the category for which the association is formed in a given area. Such employers or employees come together voluntarily for forming a syndicate.

Walter Heinrich tells us that the requirement of 10 per cent voluntary members was not a too easy condition, in view of the Italian worker's lack of interest in associations. He estimates that at present the syndicates comprise 30 per cent of Italian employers and employees[65].

2. The associations seeking legal recognition must include among their aims, besides protection of the economic and moral interests of their members, the education of their members, and promotion of their welfare.

[65] *Der Faschismus, Munich* 1932, p. 50.

3. The leader or head of the association must give proof of his competence, good moral conduct, and patriotism (dependability from the national point of view).

The syndicates are not permitted to form connections with associations in other countries. Their activities, as we have seen, are of a manifold character: social, educative, cultural, economic and political. The constitution of a syndicate must clearly state its aim, the method of appointing administrative officials and conditions of membership. One of these conditions is good political conduct from the national point of view. A member (whether employer or employee) must have attained the age of 18 years.

Non-Italians may become members after a stay in Italy of 10 years, but they are not permitted to become leaders or heads of syndicates.

The following classes are not permitted to form associations: officers, non-commissioned officers, and soldiers of the Royal Italian Army, Royal Navy, Royal Air-Force and of the other armed corps of the State, provinces and municipalities; magistrates, professors of secondary and higher institutions, officers and employees of the Ministers of the Interior, foreign affairs and colonies.

A syndicate, while it has a legal existence, is not a State organ. It is called "*ente autarchica*", an autonomous body. It may be considered 'autarchica' only in so far as associations are formed voluntarily. Otherwise the Syndicates are under stringent Government control.

The heads of syndicates are fascists, and under the direction of the Fascist Party.

The recognition of syndicates depends on the State in the sense that the State has the power of with-holding recognition. That alone shows the complete dependence of syndicates on the State.

Further; the State, through the Minister of Corporations, may veto the resolutions of a syndicate. The Minister of Corporations may also dissolve the board of directors of a syndicate and concentrate all the powers in the President, or

Secretary of a syndicate for a certain period (not exceeding one year). In serious cases he may appoint a commissioner to look after the administration during the emergency.

The Syndicates have to pay 10 per cent of their subscriptions to the State, which is credited to a special fund under the control of the Minister of Corporations.

Federations and Confederations

Federations are associations of the second degree, syndicates being associations of primary or first degree. A federation may be municipal, provincial or national according to the syndicates of a given area which it federates. An association of federations is a Confederation, which is called an association of the third degree. Federations and Confederations may be legally recognised. Their duty is to supervise the working of their member associations.

There are 6 Confederations of employers and 6 of employees. A thirteenth Confederation is that of Liberal Professions and Arts:

The associations of employers are the following:

1. National Fascist Confederation of Agriculturists.
2. National Fascist Confederation of Italian Industry.
3. National Fascist Confederation of Traders.
4. National Fascist Confederation of Internal Transport and Navigation.
5. General Confederation of Fascist Bankers.
6. National Fascist Confederation of Maritime and Aerial Transport.

The associations of workers are the following:

1. National Confederation of Fascist Syndicates of Agriculture.
2. National Confederation of Fascist Syndicates of Commerce.
3. National Confederation of Fascist Syndicates of Internal Transport and Navigation.
4. National Confederation of Fascist Syndicates of Industry.

5. National Confederation of Fascist Syndicates of Bank Employees.

6. National Confederation of Fascist Syndicates of Maritime and Aerial Transport Workers.

7. National Confederation of Fascist Syndicates of Intellectuals.

Employees of State railways, posts and telegraphs and certain others form 9 National authorised associations (*Associazioni autorizzate*), and in addition there are two general associations of employees of the State and other public bodies. All these associations are under the control of the General Secretary of the Fascist Party.

The total number of legally recognised associations of all kinds in 1930 was 5,432 with over 4 millions members.

Italy has also a Federation of hand-workers, which is included in the Confederation of Italian Industry.

The National Confederation of Agriculturists consist of Provincial Federations of Agriculturists. Each Provincial Federation consists of three syndicates: (*a*) syndicates of cultivating agriculturists, (*b*) syndicate of non-cultivating agriculturists, and (*c*) syndicate of lessors (proprietors of land given on rent—*proprietari di terre affitate*). Those paying rent in kind form part of the syndicate of labourers.

CORPORATIONS.

A syndicate, as we have seen, is formed by the voluntary association of employers or employees; a corporation is created by the State. A syndicate is a juridical body, but a Corporation is a State organ; it is not a juridical body.

The number of Corporations is 22. The first eight are concerned with the utilisation of agricultural products: (1) food-grains (2) fruits and vegetables, (3) wines, (4) oils, (5) sugar, (6) cattle and fish, (7) wood, (8) textiles. The next eight are concerned with industrial operations: (1) Metals and machines, (2) chemicals, (3) clothing, (4) paper and printing, (5) building and building materials, (6) water, gas and electrical energy, (7) mining and (8) glass and earthen-ware. The remaining 6 Corporations deal with (1) insurance and credit, (2) liberal professions and arts, (3) sea and air transport, (4) land transport, (5) theatres, and (6) hotels.

A Corporation includes all businesses which are concerned with the production, manufacture and sale of a group of related products. For example, the Corporation of sugar was formed by taking the National Syndicate of cane-growers from the Confederation of Agriculture, sugar-manufacturers from the Confederation of Industry, sugar-dealers from the Federation of trade, and the corresponding labour organisations from their respective federations or confederations[66].

The Corporations, as we have said above, are unifying bodies, representing both labour and capital. They are empowered to frame rules for the regulation of conditions of work and also for the co-ordination of production through member associations.

The President of a Corporation is appointed by the Minister of Corporations. Each Corporation has a Committee consisting of representatives of the associations which form the corporation.

As we have seen, each Corporation consists of associations of employers and employees; on the committee the number of employers' representatives is equal to that of representatives of labour, including under labour both intellectual and hand-workers.

Council of Corporations.

This Council builds the top and pinnacle of the whole system. It has 150 members and is divided into 7 sections: (1) Liberal Professions and Arts, (2) Industry and Handwork, (3) Agriculture, (4) Trade, (5) Sea and Air Transport, (6) Land Transport and Internal Navigation and (7) Banks.

[66] See report on Italy by Dr. Max Biehl in *W. D.* for 25th May, 1934.

Mussolini thus defined the position of the Council in the course of his inaugural address on April 22, 1930: "The National Council of Corporations is in the Italian economic system what the General Staff is in the Army: the thinking brain which plans and co-ordinates (*il cervello pensante che prepara e coordina*[67]. The object of the Council of Corporations is "to augment the power and welfare of the Italian people."[68]

Such is the economic structure of the fascist State in Italy.

Italy is known as the Corporate State, as the economic life of Italy is organised through Corporations.

ITALIAN SYNDICALISM.

Other writers identify the Italian State, not with Corporations, but with Syndicates, the unit of the economic administration of Italy. Panunzio says: "It is not sufficient to say: The Fascist State is a Sovereign State; It is necessary to add: "A sovereign State over society organised in syndicates"[69]. Panunzio speaks of identification (*immed esimazione*) of the State with the syndicates, of a synthesis of the two. The Italian State is thus composed not of individuals or persons in a physical sense, but of syndicates, which are 'judicial persons'. But while the State is composed of syndicates, it is at the same time above the syndicates. *Panunzio* makes it clear that the syndicates are not autonomous entities (*enti autonomi*) but institutions of the State which controls them and uses them for its own ends"[70].

It is clear that Italian Syndicalism is essentially different from the French variety. "I am a syndicalist, fascist syndicalist", says Mussolini[71]. French syndicalism preaches class-war. Italian syndicalism, on the other hand "unites all the

[67] *Discorsi* 1930, p. 41.
[68] *Ibid*, p. 51.
[69] *Panunzio, Loc. cit.* p. 151.
[70] *Ibid*, p. 134.
[71] *Discorsi* 1925, p. 181.

factors of production and puts them on the same plane, which is the nation"[72]. This means that labour and capital must work together in the interests of the nation.

Fascism respects and upholds the right of private property. Mussolini has made this quite clear. In explaining the difference between fascist and red syndicalism he said in 1925:

"There is a fundamental difference between our and red syndicalism, and it consists in this that it does not aim at abolishing the right of property. When an employer finds himself confronting a red syndicate he has before him a syndicate that fights incidentally for increase in wages, while its final, distant aim is a revoluntionary change, namely the abolition of the right of property"[73].

Italian syndicalism repudiates class-war. The identification of the Syndicates (or Corporations) with the State is meant to show the unity of workers and employers on the one hand, and their subordination to the interests of the nation on the other. The first article of the Charter of Labour declares the Italian nation to be an organism and a unity in the moral, political and economic sense. It is emphasized that the aims of the State are superior to those of separate individuals, or groups composing it. This view of the State having been accepted, it follows that labour is a 'social duty' and that there must be no strikes or lock-outs.

While fascism cannot plan, its economic hierarchy represents an attempt to organise economic life, or to introduce order and discipline where, under a system of free competition, there is conflict and confusion of individual interests.

Secondly, there is close co-operation between government and the business world. Fascism maintains individual responsibility, but under rigid Government control. As an economic system it may be described as a compromise between

[72] *Ibid*, p. 181.
[73] *Ibid*, p. 281.

individualism and socialism. It is neither of the two completely, but it is something of both in parts.

The Anti-Strike Law

Labourers who go on strike in groups of three or more are punishable in fascist Italy by a fine from 100 to 1,000 lire. Employers who close their factories with the object of compelling workers to modify existing labour contracts are punishable by fines from 10,000 to 100,000 lire.

The organisers of strikes or lock-outs are punishable by imprisonment for not less than one and not exceeding two years, in addition to the fines mentioned above.

State employees and others employed in public utility-services are punishable for striking work by solitary confinement from one to six months, and the organisers of such strikes by solitary confinement from six months to two years.

The administrators of public services and businesses of public utility are punishable by solitary confinement from six months to a year and by a fine from 5,000 to 10,000 lire for suspending work without justification.

Failure to carry out the decisions of a labour magistrate also entails punishment by a fine and imprisonment, both for employers and employees.

Labour Courts

The Labour Court is the organ through which the State settles labour disputes, whether concerning the observance of existing rules and agreements or the determination of new condition of work (Art. 5 of the Charter of Labour).

No labour dispute is referred to the Labour Court unless conciliation through syndicates, federations, confederations and corporations has failed. Art 10 of the Charter of Labour gives trade associations the right of offering their mediation in controversies concerning the interpretation of collective labour contracts. Article 68 of the Anti-Strike Law confers on syndicates and associations of a higher order the power to act in labour disputes. The public ministry has also the right to intervene when the interests of the public demand it.

The Labour Court is assisted by 2 unofficials assessors, possessing expert knowledge of production and labour.

In cases in which new conditions have to be fixed for labour, the Labour Court judges in accordance with equity, with the object of harmonising the interests of the employers with those of employees, and protecting the higher interests of production. When a Labour Court fixes new conditions for labour, the period of time during which the new conditions shall be in force must be specified.

The Labour Court gives its decision after hearing the verbal opinion of the public ministry. The Government, therefore, may influence the judgment of the Labour Court.

Will Fascism Come to Britain?

The story of the origin and growth of the British Fascist Party has been told by Mr. James Drennan and Mr. John Strachey[74] though the attitude of these two writers towards fascism is different—Mr. Drennan is an admirer of Sir Oswald Mosley, while Mr. Strachey writes as a socialist. Sir Oswald's views may also be known to Indian readers through the reports of his speeches published in Indian papers and his two books, *Greater Britain* and *A National Policy*.

Will fascism come to Britain? Mr. Strachey is certain of it: "The Fascist attempt—the attempt, that is, of the capitalists to preserve their system by violence—is bound to be made in Britain as elsewhere"[75]. The reason for the growth of fascism, according to Mr. Strachey, is not peculiar to any one country. He is therefore, looking forward to the rise of fascism "in each and every country in the world"[76] as

[74] *Oswald Mosley and British Fascism* by James Drennan (John Murray, 1934) and *The Menace of Fascism* by John Strachey (Gollancz, 1933).

[75] *Strachey,* loc cit. p. 181.

[76] *Ibid,* p. 171.

the inevitable consequence of the weakening of the labour movement.

Mr. G. D. H. Cole takes a different view. He does not believe in Britain's conversion to fascism: (*a*) Britain has no ruined middle class, (*b*) economic distress in Britain is not acute and (*c*) Britain is not suffering under the psychology of defeat[77].

Mr. Strachey attempts to answer Mr. Cole. Italy won the war. "It is true", Mr. Strachey adds, "that her victory did not bring her all the benefits which she expected. But is that not true of all the nations which took part in the war? Do the British people today think that 'the land fit for heroes to live in' has been realized at last?"[78].

Now this is no answer to Mr. Cole. Germany has lost the whole of her colonial empire. Italy is furious at being treated worse than Portugal at the Peace Conference. Both Italy and Germany want room for expansion because their population is rapidly growing. As for the British Empire, Mr. Strachey may think that it is not good enough for heroes to live in, but it is the greatest empire in history. Cunningham compares the British Empire with the Roman Empire, to the disadvantage of the latter[79]. Britain has every reason to be proud of her Empire.

There is a difference between the mentality of Germany and Italy on the one hand and that of Britain on the other. Britain won the War as well as the peace; Italy won the War but lost the peace and Germany lost both. As we have seen, both in Italy and Germany nationalism is the chief support of fascism, and this nationalism is the product of the dissatisfaction of both countries with the Treaty of Versailles. British fascism lacks this driving force.

Mr. Strachey admits that the British middle class is not yet ruined, but he thinks that it is "absolutely certain to be

[77] Quoted by Strachey, pp. 166-67.
[78] Strachey, p. 168.
[79] *Growth of English Industry and Commerce,* Vol. III, pp. 883-85.

first threatened (the process has begun) and then ruined"[80] He also takes an entirely pessimistic view of Britain's prospects of recovery from the economic crisis[81].

In considering the future of the British middle class and of British trade and industry it is important to remember that Britain's colonial empire is a source of immense economic strength to her. It provides a large and secure market for British goods. Capitalism may break down in other countries. Its position is much stronger in Britain. If fascism is to come to Britain when the British middle class is completely ruined, it is not coming to Britain at all—or, at any rate, not until the dissolution of the British Empire.

Sir Oswald Mosley knows the value of her colonial empire to Britain. He advocates the fullest development of the Empire according to plan. This he calls Imperial Planning. Imperial Planning is the chief article of faith of British fascists. As a policy of economic Imperialism it will find favour in Britain. But Imperial Planning and the Corporate State are two different things.

The Corporate State will not be acceptable even to British capitalists.

The fascist State cannot plan but it has the right of intervention in business affairs. British capitalism will welcome the co-operation of the State, but it would not take its orders from the State. It has grown up in a spirit of freedom and it is self-reliant.

It is well known that the Nazi movement in Germany was largely financed by the heavy industrialists of the Ruhr, and that strikes in the Ruhr led these industrialists to

[80] *Strachey*, loc. cit. p. 170.

[81] "If we could believe", says Strachey, "that the economic crisis would, permanently, depart, that, slowly but surely, we should continue to 'turn the corner', until a golden age of stable, peaceful, pleasant Capitalism stretched before the British middle class, then truly there would be no need to worry about Fascism. But then, in that case, there would be small opportunity to think of socialism either" (p. 169).

contribute more generously to the Nazi funds[82]. In Italy fascism emerged at a time when the growing menace of labour threatened the existence of the capitalist order of society (there occurred more than 2,000 strikes in Italy in 1920). No such state of things exists in Britain. The chances of a socialist up-rising in Britain are so small as to be negligible. If class-war suddenly sharpened in Britain and the struggle for power really began, British capitalism might seek to crush labour by fascist methods. But British labour is not revolutionary—it has come to believe in "the inevitability of gradualness". So long as labour willingly cooperates with capital, why should capitalism set up a repressive machinery to compel that co-operation? British socialism does not require to be crushed as Italian socialism did. To employ the drastic and violent methods of fascism to break British socialism would be to use a sledge hammer to kill a small fly. And the British socialist fly is not only small but harmless.

Further, a dictatorship is impossible in Britain. The British people are a liberty-loving people; the British Parliament is the mother of Parliaments. The 'Stato forte' (strong State) is good enough for Italy. Democracy has failed in Italy. But a well-disciplined people, with liberal-democratic traditions, want a higher type of State.

Nor would racial discrimination, as in Germany, or emphasis on the ethical and religious aspects of fascism, as in Italy, make any appeal to the British people. The persecution of Jews roused feelings of indignation in Britain. Then in every civilised country the ethical character of the State is taken for granted; it is not necessary to proclaim it from the house-tops. As for the responsibility of the fascist State to God the British people would have to forget all their past history and traditions before they accept unmitigated humbug as profound political philosophy.

[82] *Profits* and *Politics in the Post-War Period by* Charques and Ewen (Collancz, 1934) pp. 116-17.

No Corporate State is going to be established in Britain. But fascist propaganda will strengthen British Imperialism, and this is of some interest to us.

The idea of Imperial Planning is an attractive one. For British capital it means more profits, and for British labour less unemployment and higher wages.

The self-governing parts of the Empire will be left alone. They enter into the scheme of Imperial planning only so far as they may accept mutually beneficial trade agreements for developing Empire trade. But Imperial Planning will aim at directing the economic development of the non-self-governing parts of the British Empire. What will be the line of this development?

Writing in 1931 in *A National Policy* Sir Oswald Mosley was willing to provide for "the steady industrialisation of suitable areas" in the non-self-governing parts of the Empire[83]. This industrialisation would proceed according to a deliberate, well-considered plan, not hap-hazardly. Sir Oswald did not think that the industrial development of dependencies would injure British manufacturing industries. For many years to come dependencies would have to depend on Britain for "their more complicated and highly developed industrial needs"[84]. British industry would supply these needs and the very process of industrialisation of India (for example) might be expected to create a market for particular classes of British goods (*e.g.*, means of production).

Recently Sir Oswald seems to have modified his views. He now thinks that what India wants is an agricultural policy; he is not pleased with the progress of the Indian cotton mill industry which, he complains, is drawing the masses from the country into the towns and driving the Lancashire cotton textiles out of the market[85].

[83] *National Policy* (Macmillan, 1931). p. 26.

[84] *National Policy* (Macmillan, 1931). p. 26.

[85] Sir Oswald Mosley's speech at Stoke-on-Trent in April, 1934.

Sir Oswald has not yet disclosed his plan for the steady industrialisation of India. One may hope that it does not mean an agricultural policy alone and no industrialisation.

The objection to Imperial Planning from our point of view is that we shall not control our economic development. If others plan for us, our interests may be ignored, as they have been ignored in the past. Sir Oswald's utterances are anything but re-assuring. Sometime ago he declared that he was opposed to the White Paper policy root and branch.

That is how fascists may influence British policy. And they will be heard as under the new conditions of world trade it is difficult for British capitalists to re-capture the foreign markets they have lost. They will therefore cling all the more tenaciously to the Empire markets which they possess.

APPENDIX TO CHAPTER XI

THE CHARTER OF LABOUR

Granted on the evening of April 21, 1927

THE CORPORATE STATE AND ITS ORGANISATION

1. The Italian Nation is an Organism having aims, life and instruments of action more powerful and permanent than those of separate individuals or groups which compose it. It is a unity in the moral, political and economic sense which is realised integrally in the Fascist State.

2. Labour in all its organised and executive forms, whether intellectual, technical or manual, is a social duty. For this and this reason alone it is protected by the State.

The whole system of production is a unity from the national point of view; its objects are one, which may be briefly expressed as the well-being of individuals and the development of national power.

3. Organisation, whether by Syndicates or Trades, is free. But only a Syndicate which is legally recognised and is under the control of the State has the right of legally representing all the categories of employers or labourers constituting it; or protecting their interests as against the State and other Trade associations; of negotiating collective labour contracts binding on all those comprised in its categories; and of levying contributions from them and of exercising in respect of them public functions assigned to it.

4. The solidarity of various factors of production finds its concrete expression in the collective labour contract, through the reconciliation of conflicting interests of employers

and employees, and their subordination to the higher interests of production.

5. The Labour Court is the organ through which the State regulates labour disputes, whether concerning the observance of existing rules and agreements or the determination of new conditions of work.

6. Legally recognised trade associations guarantee legal equality between employers and employees, maintain discipline in production and in work and seek to make them more efficient.

The Corporations are unified organisations of production and represent all its interests.

In virtue of this complete representation, and since the interests of production are national interests, the Corporations are recognised as organs of the State.

The corporations representing the unified interests of production can frame compulsory rules for the regulation of conditions of work and also for the co-ordination of production whenever they are empowered to do so by the associations of which they are a union.

7. The Corporate State considers private initiative in the field of production as the most efficacious and useful instrument in the interests of the nation.

The private organisation of production being a function of national interest, the organisation of a business is responsible to the State for the direction of production. From the collaboration of productive forces is derived the reciprocity of rights and duties among them. The employee, whether a technician, clerk or workman is an active collaborator in the economic undertaking, whose direction is in the hands of the employer and who is responsible for it.

8. Trade associations of employers are under obligation to take every step to increase production, to make it more efficient and to reduce costs of production. Associations representing those who practise the liberal professions or

the arts, and associations of State employees, help in the protection of the interests of art, of science and of letters, in increasing the efficiency of production and in the realisation of the moral aims of the corporate organisation.

9. The State intervenes in the sphere of economic production only when private initiative is lacking or found insufficient or when the political interests of the State are involved. This intervention may assume the form of control, encouragement, or direct management.

10. In collective disputes of labour, legal action cannot be instituted before the corporate organ has first attempted conciliation.

In individual controversies concerning the interpretation and application of collective labour contracts, trade associations have the power of offering their mediation for conciliation.

Ordinary labour courts, with the addition of assessors nominated by the trade associations concerned, are competent to settle such disputes.

The Collective Labour Contract and Guarantees of Labour

11. Trade associations are under obligation to regulate, through collective contracts, the relations between employers and employees whom they represent.

The collective labour contract is made between associations of the primary grade under the guidance and control of central organisations, except when in cases provided by law and statutes, associations of a higher grade may take the place of the association of the primary grade.

Each collective labour contract, under penalty of nullity, should contain precise rules relating to discipline, period of trial, amount and method of wage payments and hours of work.

12. The action of the Syndicate, the conciliatory measures of corporate organisations and the decisions of

Labour Counts guarantee a wage confirming to the normal requirements of life, to the possibilities of production and to the productivity of labour.

The fixing of wages is withdrawn from any general rule and is entrusted to agreements between parties in the collective contracts.

13. Losses occasioned by crises of production and monetary changes must be equally shared by all factors of production.

Statistics issued by Government Departments, by the Central Institute of Statistics and by legally recognised Trade Associations, relating to the conditions of production and labour, the situation of the money-market and the standard of life of workers, co-ordinated and elaborated by the Minister of Corporations, will furnish the direction for harmonising the interests of various categories and classes as among themselves and with the higher interests of production.

14. The wage must be made to conform, in the most suitable manner, to the requirements of the labourers and the undertaking.

When wages are paid according to piece-work, and payment is made at intervals exceeding a fortnight, fortnightly and weekly accounts must be prepared.

Night work, not included in regular shifts, must be paid for at a rate higher than that for work during the day.

When wages are paid according to piece-work, the rate of wages should be determined in such a way as to allow a faithful worker, of normal working capacity, to earn a minimum in excess of the basic wage.

15. The employee is entitled to a weekly holiday coinciding with Sunday.

Collective contracts will apply this principle keeping in view existing laws and the technical requirements of the business, and within the limits of these requirements they will likewise respect civil and religious festivities according to local traditions. The employee must scrupulously and earnestly observe the hours of work.

16. After one year's uninterrupted service in a business which works throughout the year the worker is entitled to a period of rest with pay.

17. In a business which works throughout the year, a worker discharged without his fault is entitled to compensation proportionate to his years of service. Such compensation must be paid also in the event of the worker's death.

18. The transfer of ownership of a business working throughout the year does not terminate the labour contract, and its employees retain their rights as against the new proprietors.

Similarly, the illness of a worker, when it does not exceed a fixed period, does not terminate the labour contract. The call to arms, or service in the M. V. S. N. (*Milizia Volontaria per la Sicurezza Nozionale*=Fascist Voluntary Militia for National Defence) is not a cause for dismissal.

19. Infringements of discipline, and acts committed by employees disturbing the normal functioning of a business, are punished, according to the gravity of the offence, with fine, or suspension of work, and in the severest cases, with immediate dismissal without compensation.

The cases in which the employer can inflict fine, or punish with suspension or immediate dismissal without compensation shall be specified.

20. The new employee is subject to a period of trial during which there is a reciprocal right to terminate the contract with the payment of wages to the worker only for the period during which he actually worked.

21. The benefits and the discipline of the collective labour contract are extended also to home-workers. Special rules will be framed by the State to insure that home-work is done under clean and hygienic conditions.

Employment Bureaus

22. The State ascertains and controls the phenomena of employment and unemployment, which are good indices of the conditions of production and work.

23. Employment bureaus are formed on the basis of equality [*i.e.*, equal representation of employees and employers] under the control of corporate organisations of the State. Employers are under obligation to engage workers through these bureaus. They may make a selection out of the registered names, but preference is to be given to those belonging to the Fascist party and Fascist Syndicates, according to priority of registration.

24. Trade associations of workers are under obligation to practise selection among workers with the object of constantly improving their technical capacity and moral value.

25. The Corporate organisations see to it that the laws relating to the prevention of accidents and sanitation are observed by individuals who are placed under united associations.

Insurance, Assistance, Education and Instruction

26. Insurance is an important expression of the principle of collaboration. The employer and the employees must share its burdens proportionally. The State through the Corporate organisations and trade associations will endeavour to co-ordinate and unify, as far as possible, the system and institutions of insurance.

27. The Fascist State proposes:

(i) To improve accident insurance.

(ii) To improve and extend maternity insurance.

(iii) To introduce insurance against professional diseases and against tuberculosis as a beginning towards general insurance against all diseases.

(iv) To improve insurance against involuntary unemployment.

(v) To devise special forms of endowment insurance for young workers.

28. It is the duty of associations of workers to protect those they represent in administrative and legal matters relating to accident insurance and all forms of social insurance.

In collective labour contracts provision will be made, in cases in which this is technically possible, for the constitution of mutual funds, with contributions from employers and employees, to be administered by the representatives of both under the supervision of corporate organisations.

29. It is the right and duty of Trade associations to provide relief for those whom they represent, that is, for both members and non-members. Trade associations must directly exercise their functions of providing relief; these cannot be delegated to other organisations or institutions, except for objects of a general nature, which exceed the limits of individual categories [*i.e.*, the trade concerned].

30. Education and training, particularly professional training, of those they represent, whether members or non-members, is one of the principal duties of Trade associations. They must assist the work of national institutions concerned with *Dopolavaro* [Recreation after work], and other measures of education.

CHAPTER XII

EDUCATED UNEMPLOYMENT

Cultural planning may be regarded from two points of view: (*a*) adapting the system of education to the economic requirements of a country, and (*b*) using the system of education to raise the cultural level of the masses.

In regard to methods and aims of education India may learn even from Fascist Italy. Fascism has transformed Italian education. Fascism despises culture which is purely ornamental. It values that culture alone which "arms and fortifies the spirit for conquering new battles".[1] Fascist education is practical, not merely theoretical. Giovanni Gentile, whose name is associated with the reform of the Italian system of education, says:

"Fascism is a war against Intellectualism. The Fascist spirit is Will; it is not Intellect—Fascism fights, and should fight ceaselessly and pitilessly, not Intelligence, but Intellectualism, which is the disease of Intelligence." The distinction between Intellectualism and Intelligence is of some significance. Intellectualism is barren. It is mental training for its own sake. Intelligence consists in applying the intellect to the solution of problems of life.

In Russia education has been made wholly subservient to economics. Educational planning was a part of the First Five Year Plan. The success of the Plan in making Russia an industrial country, producing her own technical equipment, depended on the development of technical education.

[1] *Che Cosa é il Fascismo*, p. 98.

Everything was therefore done to spread technical knowledge. The country has been covered by a net-work of technical colleges and polytechnics. According to a critic of Bolshevism, "Education no longer aims at producing an educated man. Its object is to turn out an officer in the proletarian army, capable of taking an active part in the civil service, industry or finance."[2]

It cannot be said that the Indian system of education is aimless. "In its very inception", wrote a Director of Public Instruction, Punjab, "it was moulded with the special object of preparing boys for external examinations," the object being the training of boys "for clerical vacations which are now proclaimed to be over-stocked and which offer insufficient avenues of employment to the large throng of applicants"[3]. In this sense our system of education has survived its usefulness. The supply of clerks much exceeds the demand for them either in Government or in private offices.

The problem of educated unemployment was the subject of investigation by special committees, appointed in several Provinces. The University authorities in the Punjab took the view in 1927 that there was 'probably' some unemployment among graduates (especially those of inferior quality) and 'much' unemployment among matriculates and failed matriculates. The Punjab Committee was led by the evidence tendered before it to the conclusion that there was 'extensive' unemployment among educated classes, meaning by that term those who have received a purely literary Anglo-Vernacular education. The conclusion of the Madras Committee was the same. It found unemployment among graduates without professional qualifications, and more unemployment among Intermediates, S. S. L. C's and failed S. S. L. C's.

Since 1926-27, unemployment has increased on account of the progress of education.

[2] *Theory and Practise of Bolshevism*, by W. Gurean, p. 154.
[3] *Report of Punjab Committee on Unemployment*, p. xi.

Schools and Colleges in British India and Number of scholars attending them

	1916-17	1926-27	1930-31
Colleges:			
Arts and Science: Institutions ..	134	232	244
Scholars	47,135	71,968	71,639
Total, including professional Colleges: Institutions—Male ..	179	283	283
—Female ..	16	26	28
Scholars: —Male ..	57,617	87,641	88,815
—Female ..	1,022	2,278	3,213

The highest recorded figures for male scholars are for the year 1929-30: 94,025. The fall in 1930-31 (largely in Bengal) is explained by adverse economic conditions.

The number of scholars reading in high schools increased from 547,313 in 1916-17, to 744,444 in 1926-27 and 853,416 in 1930-31.

The following table shows the number of University Graduates, and Undergraduates in arts and science in certain years:

	Graduates			Undergraduates		
	1916-17	1926-27	1930-31	1916-17	1926-27	1930-31
Madras ..	1,243	1,027	2,101	9,625	11,566	17,041
Bombay ..	673	1,150	1,065	4,702	6,743	8,466
Bengal ..	2,233	2,243	3,069	17,866	24,382	17,235
U. P. ..	675	1,664	2,165	4,537	3,685	4,218
Punjab ..	612	894	1,273	1,362	7,037	9,842
Behar and Orissa ..	232	357	443	2,534	3,511	3,479
Total for all Provinces	5,934	7,887	10,950	43,538	62,050	66,379

These figures are significant, particularly as regards graduates. Between 1916-17 and 1930-31 the increase in the number of graduates in India was 84 per cent. In 5 years between 1926-27 and 1930-31, the percentage increase was 39. In Bengal there was a heavy fall in 1930-31 as compared with 1926-27, which accounts for the comparatively small increase in the number of under-graduates in India in 1930-31 as campared with 1926-27 (7 per cent).

In the year 1921, 37,292 candidates sat for the Matriculation examination in British India, of whom 23,904 were declared successful (64·09 per cent). In 1930-31, the number of candidates rose to 52,857, and of the successful candidates to 32,101 (pass percentage 60·73).

In view of the rapid growth in the number of matriculates, under-graduates and graduates, it is not surprising that educated unemployment has attained serious dimensions. Striking examples of keen competition for jobs are given in the report of the Madras Committee on unemployment. A test advertisement in the newspapers for a clerk's post under the Government carrying a salary of Rs. 35 per mensem brought in 666 applications (including 30 from graduates). No less than 787 applications were received in response to a similar test advertisement for a clerk's post in a commercial firm in Madras.

Certain professions (notably that of law), are overcrowded. While the number of law graduates has rapidly increased, litigation, on account of the depression, has decreased. Sometime ago, 500 vakils from the Mofussil and the City of Madras applied for the post of bench clerk in the High Court of Madras.

Bengal

Bengal was the first Province to appoint a committee to examine the problem of unemployment. This committee was appointed in 1922 and its report was published in 1924. It dealt both with the general problem of unemployment, and with educated unemployment.

The Committee found that the increase in the number of educated men seeking employment in Bengal was due to the following causes:

1. The rise in the standard of living.
2. The rise in the cost of living.
3. The absorption of numbers from lower classes resulting from natural aspirations and also an effort among those lower classes to surmount the financial effects of both (1) and (2).
4. Decay of industries owing to the failure to adopt progressive methods of production to meet foreign competition.

Since 1922 the cost of living has fallen. In 1922 a middle-class man was faced with the difficulties of rising prices, a desire for a higher standard of living, and an income which he did not find it easy to increase. At the present time, owing to the contraction of income, it has become difficult to maintain old standards of living. The depression has, however, increased the desire of agricultural classes and 'lower classes' to earn a living through Government or private service. Educational facilities have increased, and the number of educated persons seeking employment has, as we have seen, considerably increased.

The Bengal Committee points out that in former days the middle-class Bengalees were supported largely from income derived from land. Now it is found necessary to supplement this income from other sources. "This has been one of the main causes of the breakdown of the joint-family system and of the gradual flow of the educated middle-classes from villages to the town" (p.11). The cause of the trek into towns may be the desire for a higher standard of living, the attractions of town life, or the growing pressure of population on the soil, but the fact remains that those who have left the villages for towns, will gain very little by returning to the villages now.

Nor is it possible to check immigration from lower classes into the Bhadralok class. "For a period", explains the

Committee, "the educated middle class Bengali doubtless flourished." Other classes wished to emulate him. They arrived late and have missed the rise, but they will take the downward swing lower than it might otherwise have gone.

The Committee expressed their dissatisfaction with the system of education. It leads to one end only: the M.A., M.Sc., or B. L. examination. "It is like a bamboo, each joint being an examination and the diameter remaining practically the same size from the root to very near the top. It has no branches and the crowning top covers a very small area". By this simile the Committee meant to illustrate the very limited objective of the system of education, and its dead uniformity. In introducing the system of education Lord Macaulay had written that "We must at present do our best to form a class who may be interpreters between us and the millions we govern, a class of persons, Indian in blood and colour, but English in taste, in opinions, in morals and in intellect". This class of interpreters duly came into existence, but they are fit to do little else than interpreting. Further, our universities continue to produce the class of interpreters even when there is not enough interpreters' work for all members of the class. As the Committee wrote: "And the most depressing thought of all is that the process is still going on and any modification even in the near future will not become effective for many years to come" (p. 15).

The Committee admitted the charges commonly brought against the system of education: it bears no relation to the everyday life of the student; it destroys his adaptability; it leads from one examination to another offering on the way no points of natural divergences; and, finally, in the case of a large proportion of students, it does not lead to any means of earning a livelihood.

The recommendations of the Committee covered a wide field. It laid emphasis on the need for encouraging the economic development of the country: "The mere provision of facilities for technical training may help for a little time, but it will not solve the problem unless at the same time an economic development takes place, be it spontaneously or with external assistance" (p. 15).

With this necessary qualification the Committee favoured the immediate adoption of a comprehensive scheme of technical education with the object of producing industrial workers of various classes, such as managers, foremen, supervisors and workmen. A Board of Technical Education was to be established for the control of training, both theoretical and practical, for industry and commerce. Among other things the Board was to undertake the duties of estimating and publishing the prospects of employment in various occupations, prescribing courses of training to be followed to enter such occupations, and furnishing assistance to trained men in finding employment through the establishment of an employment bureau for those who had been trained according to the prescribed standards.

The Committee considered that ordinary high school education in the last two years should be divided into two groups, (1) literary, and (2) scientific, and that each student should make a definite selection. When the students arrived at the University Matriculation stage, all were not to take that examination. Some from the literary side could take the examination of the Board of Control of Technical Education referred to above and, if successful, pursue a training leading to employment in commerce; some from the scientific side could take the appropriate examinations of the Board and proceed to a technical training leading to employment in industry.

For those who left off before the high school stage was reached, the Committee recommended training in the mufassil in special trade schools. These were to be small technical schools with workshops attached to them. Here young men could be taught to handle tools and machinery. "It is obvious", wrote the Committee "that the development of rural industries, the application of modern labour-saving machinery such as pumping plant, timber-sawing machines, mechanical workshops for the repair and maintenance of motor cars, tractors, piping installations, etc. throughout Bengal would absorb a large number of young men of the Bhadralok class, equipped with a will to apply themselves to this object" (p. 19).

In regard to the economic development of the country the Committee pointed out that agriculture was the main support of the population. "In our opinion," they wrote, "what is required therefore is the intensive development of agriculture and of the industries associated with agriculture" (p. 22). They recommended agriculture as a profession for the Bengali Bhadralok. It was also desirable to make experiments in cattle-breeding, dairy-farming, poultry farming etc., as occupations for Bengal Bhadralok (among other things, the Punjab Committee on unemployment recommended rose-growing and tobacco-cultivation as new occupations for Punjabi Bhadralok). Further, the Committee recommended the expansion of cooperative activities in directions other than the provision of credit: provision of seed, manure, implements, irrigation, water, cattle, yarn, looms and power. Co-operative production and sale were also to be encouraged.

Finally the Committee concluded:

"In our opinion the solution lies in the intensive economic development of the country, in the entrance of the Bengali Bhadralok into the industry, trade, (including marine trade) and commerce of the country and in the immediate acceleration of the development of schemes which will train the Bhadralok to effect this entrance" (p. 25).

United Provinces

In the United Provinces Legislative Council, when, in August 1929, a resolution was moved recommending the appointment of a Committee to suggest ways and means to alleviate unemployment among the educated middle-classes, the Government opposed the motion on the ground that the "appointment of a Committee was unnecessary in view of various measures for provincial development which they had taken". Eventually the resolution was accepted by the

Government, and the matter referred to the provincial Development Board. The Board was "greatly impressed" by the magnitude and complexity of the problem, and recommended the appointment of a special Committee to deal with the question. A departmental Committee was finally appointed in November 1927.

The Committee found that the causes of educated unemployment were "not one but various", having their roots in the social and economic system of the Province, or arising from its physical characteristics and its past history, or "due to errors of policy in the past". Some of the causes were connected with the period of "change and rapid transition" through which the country was passing. But one thing was clear: the supply of educated men was greater than the supply of suitable posts. Government service and the legal profession were the main occupations of the educated classes. The legal profession was over-crowded, and as for Government service, it could not absorb more than about one in five of those who passed the high-school examination.

Can more jobs be created for educated men? The Committee made two suggestions. First, educated young men should be induced to take up trades and occupations which they have so far neglected, and assisted to create new ones. Secondly, measures may be adopted to expand the prosperity and productive power of old occupations. "One process starts with the man, we may call it 'tuition'. The other starts with the occupation, we may call it 'development'; but they are really opposite aspects of the same thing. Development means increased production, and so more to divide, and higher earnings for the educated man" (p. 7).

The two direct sources of wealth production are agriculture and industry. The Committee took the view that no solution of the problem could be found in attempts to settle educated men, unconnected with agriculture, on the land. Already three out of four of the inhabitants of the United Provinces were dependent on agriculture for their livelihood. The Province "is already one of the most closely cultivated regions in the world". Excepting jungly areas, every square yard of land which was capable of cultivation was already tilled. However the Committee recommended that efforts should be made to keep the educated young zamindar or prosperous tenant's son on the land. This may be done by showing him how he can make agriculture more profitable, by imparting an agricultural bias to the education given in rural areas, by improving the amenities of village life (both cultural and hygienic), and by developing new sources of livelihood in the collection and sale of agricultural products, upkeep of machinery (*i.e.*, power-driven tube-wells, cane-crushers etc.) and in the better organisation of rural Co-operative effort.

It appears that agriculture of the United Provinces cannot provide much room for the educated unemployed. It is desirable to keep the sons of zamindars on the land, provided they can earn something for themselves there. But even in 1927, that is before the catastrophic fall of prices, agriculture had ceased to be a remunerative profession for educated young men:

"A boy of the cultivating classes no sooner gets a little education than he is off to the town to try to get a job as a clerk on Rs. 15 or Rs. 20 per mensem. The reason is sometimes a faulty kind of education. But it must quite as often be the fact that such a post gives him in pay as well as in amenities what his ancestral holding could never give him even though he were to apply to it all the latest devices and methods, and farm it with the utmost skill" (p. 6).

Considering the existing heavy pressure on the land and the recent fall in agricultural income it would be still more difficult to induce the sons of agriculturists to stay on the land.

What are the chances of increased employment of educated men in industries?

It has been estimated that an investment of a crore of rupees in factory industries creates employment for about 500 men for direction and supervision. In this sense jobs for educated men depend on the amount of capital available for investment in industry (assuming, among other things, that adequate supplies of skilled and unskilled labour are available). There is capital in the United Provinces, labour is cheap and abundant, and raw material for manufactures, based on agricultural or forest produce, is not lacking. But the Province is handicapped by the complete absence of coal, oil, or other mineral wealth. The introduction of cheap hydro-electric power into the Western districts of the Province may remove this handicap.

Under existing conditions factory industries in the United Provinces offer no hope of increased employment to educated men. "The existing posts are already filled, and it is only wastage that has to be provided for" (p. 14).

The cottage industries, in which there is some room at present are: tailoring, laundry work and dry-cleaning, tomato-canning, and bee-keeping, and the manufacture of wooden and leather goods, matches (as a cottage industry), candles, cane basket-ware, woollen blankets (hand-loom), card-board boxes, pen-nibs and other small metal articles, hosiery, envelopes, buttons, jams, lac-varnishes and dyes, glue, and confectionery. But educated men taking to these occupations will have first to compete with more skilled professional artisans, and secondly, to face the competition of machinery. The market for the products of these industries is not very extensive, and as machine competition increases, it must shrink. Technical education in industrial schools, whose object is to train hand-workers for cottage industries, wrote the Committee, "is not the panacea for the unemployment problem which it is often alleged to be"—a sound observation. It follows that cottage industries provide no solution of our problem, but only relief for a very short period, and on a very limited scale.

The Committee recommended the establishment of employment bureaus in a few centres with the following chief objects, (*a*) to maintain a register of middle-class students wanting jobs, (*b*) to ascertain openings for employment for them, (*c*) to bring them into touch with employers, and (*d*) to give advice and information to parents about careers for boys.

Punjab and Madras

The aim of education in the Punjab, as in other Provinces, is Government service. Very few care for knowledge for its own sake. Government service is preferred for various reasons: (*a*) emoluments of Government servants, (*b*) prestige or *izzat* of officials, (*c*) security and regular promotion in Government service "and no particular need for efficiency".[4] Another interesting reason was mentioned by a witness in his evidence before the Punjab Committee: "At present an average zamindar thinks rightly or wrongly that he can save himself from every-day insults heaped upon him by Government officials by taking some sort of Government service and leaving his ancestral profession".[5] Finally, Government service is the principal source of employment for educated young men; other avenues of employment are few.

It is obvious that the ranks of the unemployed are swelled by half-educated boys and young men drawn from many classes whose ancestral occupation is different. It is stated that education renders boys unfit for their ancestral occupation, *e.g.*, agriculture and cottage industries. There is a growing aversion from manual labour among certain classes. Having attended school or college, the son of a zamindar considers it beneath his dignity to touch a spade or a plough.

Among special causes of unemployment the Madras Committee mentions caste, early marriage, joint family and communal inequalities or social disabilities. Early marriage burdens a young man with responsibilities at an immature age. Caste restrictions interfere with the mobility of labour: a caste Hindu may not follow certain occupations. The joint-family encourages laziness and parasitism.

[4] *Report of the Punjab Committee on Unemployment*, p. 17.
[5] *Ibid*, p. 17.

These causes are of little importance. The age of marriage is rising, but by itself it will have little effect in reducing unemployment or increasing the number of jobs. Nor would unemployment be much reduced by caste-Hindus taking to 'untouchable' occupations. The joint-family as a defensive economic organisation is of great value in times of hardship. The abolition of the joint-family would in no way contribute to the solution of our problem.

If educated unemployment is chiefly due to the rapid growth of education, a remedy for the evil may be found in reducing educational facilities, or making it more difficult to obtain degrees and diplomas. The Punjab Committee recommended this step, at the same time insisting that educational qualifications required for certain Government appointments should be lowered. They admitted that whatever standards were adapted, the number of youths to be recruited for the public services would not be affected. The supply of candidates for Government service would exceed the demand even then, but it is desirable that the requirements of Government service should not unduly lengthen the period of education.

Education must be related to life. "The pupils in the ordinary schools", wrote the Punjab Committee, "should be encouraged to appreciate the dignity of labour, to make good use of their spare time and to acquire an earnest spirit of service".[6]

The provision of increasing facilities for technical and industrial education, it is next argued, will enable young men to earn an independent living as producers. The existence of large numbers of trained young men will give an impetus to the development of industries at present non-existent in the Punjab. The Punjab Committee recommended the extension of professional education in certain directions: architecture, pharmacy and conveyancing. Architects will help not only in improving the appearance of buildings, but also in ameliorating health conditions in towns. We also want more

[6] *Ibid*, p. 23.

trained pharmacists. The drafting of legal documents by competent and trained conveyancers will save a considerable amount of litigation due to inefficient drafting and conveyances.

The Madras Committee saw a general remedy for unemployment in the extension of primary education. If, for example, compulsory primary education were introduced, an enormous demand for teachers would be created. But where is the money for compulsory primary education, or even for a wide extension of primary education to come from?

Both Committees devote much space to a discussion of agriculture in relation to education. The Punjab Committee recommended that small holdings should be provided for educated young men for certain purposes. But it is evident that only a very limited amount of land is available for such a purpose. Some time ago Principals of Arts colleges at Lahore were asked to recommend six students each for the grant of land for model farming. This is not a solution of educated unemployment, admitting, for the sake of argument, that farms managed by educated young men may serve as a source of inspiration to uneducated cultivators. The Punjab Committee insisted that education should not make a boy unfit for agriculture or create in him a distaste for the life of an agriculturist. From this point of view the Committee emphasized the importance of village 'uplift' work and of encouraging rural sports and pastimes.

The Madras Committee recommended that village life should be made more attractive by starting social clubs and libraries. In rural schools, agriculture should be made the centre of study, and, where possible, a farm should be attached to the High School. The boys must be taught to value agriculture: the idea that agriculture is inferior to the occupation of a clerk, or the profession of a lawyer or teacher must be eradicated. "The example of the King-Emperor and of the present Viceroy (Lord Irwin) should inspire the zamindars of this country to take up farming, cattle and sheep-breeding, and improvement of crops more seriously. The Ministers in

South Africa and the leaders of the Opposition are several of them farmers by profession and a majority of them spend their leisure on their own farms".[7] The Madras Committee makes it absolutely clear that the Government cannot provide jobs for all educated unemployed: "No Government in the world could be expected to furnish all those who come out of schools and colleges with appointments, and in India of the present day, when the educational output is so large and there is a legitimate cry of retrenchment, such an expectation is unreasonable as well as unjust to the tax-payer."[8] The Committee admitted that no 'heroic remedy' for unemployment existed. No such remedy for abolishing or reducing unemployment was brought to the notice of the Committee or was independently discovered by the Committee.

The work of these Committees has shown both the complexity and gravity of the problem of educated unemployment.

In a sense the solution is easy. If the supply of graduates exceeds the demand, by raising the cost of obtaining Degrees, the number of graduates may be easily reduced. Equilibrium between supply and demand will be thus restored.

If matriculates are unemployed because they have left their ancestral callings, let them return to their ancestral calling. Let them realise the dignity of labour and learn to love agriculture.

But why do young men seek to earn a living through education? Why do they leave their ancestral callings?

The increasing competition of machine-made goods has, in each successive decade, reduced the proportion of the population dependent on 'Industry'. Industry supported a higher percentage of the population in 1921 than in 1931, in 1911 than in 1921, and in 1901 than in 1911. The development of factory industries has created more unemployment than employment. For ten hand-workers who have lost their

[7] *Report of Madras Committee on Unemployment*, p. 25.
[8] *Ibid*, p. 24.

occupation on account of growth of imports or Indian machine competition, perhaps one or two have found work in factories. This tendency cannot be reversed by preaching sermons on 'the dignity of labour', or by the opening of industrial schools or technical institutions where hand-workers are trained.

Sons of zamindars and others connected with the land seek education in the hope of entering a more lucrative profession. With the decline of industries the proportion of the population dependent on the land has steadily increased. Agriculture is already supporting too many people, and unless methods of agriculture are radically changed, enabling the yield of land to be enormously increased (which is impossible under the existing system of land-ownership) little is to be gained by increasing the pressure on agricultural resources by settling the educated unemployed on the land.

Further, over large parts of the country agriculture has ceased to be remunerative. At the present time, in the Punjab, which is agriculturally more advanced than other provinces, the peasant does not earn more than 75 rupees a year from cultivation; probably he earns much less. Sons of zamindars seek Government employment because it is better to be a peon than a peasant.

It would be foolish not to follow the example of Ministers of South Africa and leaders of the Opposition, if one possessed estates of 500 acres or more. But when the average amount of land per cultivator is a little more than six acres, and net income per acre 10 or 12 rupees, the agriculturist is compelled by dire necessity to seek non-agricultural means of livelihood. No solution of the problem of unemployment is therefore to be found in such devices (however commendable in themselves) as giving a rural bias to education, nature study in villages, development of rural games and pastimes, or increasing the attraction of village life by the provisions of social amenities in the shape of clubs and libraries.

The Madras Committee were aware of the limitations of

their recommendations. Hence the confession of their inability to suggest a solution.

We are confronted with a hopeless situation. Year after year we are adding to the number of unemployed matriculates and graduates, destined to lead a life of misery and starvation. Year after year this waste of money and effort must continue. We are presenting to the world the unedifying spectacle of a huge waste of productive power, which, if properly organized and directed, might enrich the country.

There is one and only one solution of the problem of educated unemployment: economic planning. The existing situation is entirely due to *laissez faire* in education.

It may be argued that education is concerned with the formation of character and that it has nothing to do with economic aims or policies.

Even if the chief aim of education is the moral or intellectual perfection of the youth of a country, this aim is not realised by the present educational system. Unemployment degrades young men both morally and intellectually.

In a poor country education cannot be an end-in-itself. Educational ideals suitable for British universities are of little use here.

It is recognized by every one that the present literary education has failed. The advantages of technical education were emphasized by all the Committees on unemployment.

But planless technical education will not reduce the numbers of the unemployed—it may increase them. Before creating technicians, we must create the industries which will employ them. How are these industries to be created?

It may be argued that our industrial output is expanding. In course of time the existing industries will grow bigger and new industries will be established. The problem of unemployment will thus be automatically solved.

This is an argument for doing nothing at all.

A planned economy for India will aim at industrialising India within a given period. There is at least one example of a country which achieved a miracle in this sense.

Educational planning must necessarily form an integral part of economic planning. Its object will be to use education as a means for augmenting the production of wealth.

The problem of unemployment is easy of solution when the authorities who direct the economic development of a country also control the quantity and quality of technically skilled labour. They know what goods are to be produced and the means of producing them. If the supplies of trained labour are inadequate, they train more labour. Supply is thus adjusted to demand. There can be no unemployment unless mistakes are made in estimating demand, and more labour is trained than is actually needed.

CHAPTER XIII

CULTURAL PLANNING

Cultural planning may be used as an instrument to augment production. It achieves its aim by making education subservient to economics, or by adapting the system of education to the economic needs of the country.

Not less important than this is the moral aim of cultural planning.

As in education, so in the sphere of religion, our present policy is that of *laissez faire*. This policy, in recent years, has produced violent communal conflicts.

The Government is not identified with any religious creed, and its general policy is to leave every one free in the exercise of his or her faith.

It will be said that religion is a person's own private affair. And where there is a multiplicity of creeds, what else can the State do except to follow a policy of strict neutrality?

But religion in India is not merely an intellectual faith in a Prime Cause or Creator of the Universe. It is life itself. In the case of a Hindu, from the moment of birth to the moment of death, life is governed by religious injunctions, which are very often based on the crudest superstitions.

Further, with the advent of political reforms, communal differences, which had always existed, have become unduly emphasized. India, at the present time, is divided into a number of religious communities, distrusting one another, hating one another and at war with one another.

Can the development of such a situation be a matter of indifference to the State?

It is argued that faith in a personal God is necessary for enforcing the Moral Law. But in India this faith threatens to subvert the moral order and produce chaos.

In the interests of communal peace and national progress and prosperity, a view of life which does not derive its inspiration from any religious code or 'revealed' book, must be found.

We have already seen that morality is independent of religion. Cultural planning will aim at building up a society in which the moral virtues will be practised as necessary social virtues, not because of the supposed religious sanction behind them.

Another, and not less important task of cultural planning will be to promote an impersonal view of life and the universe.

A Law-governed Universe

The earthquake in Bihar gave rise to an interesting controversy between Mahatma Gandhi and Poet Tagore. Mahatma Gandhi connected the earthquake with the 'sin of untouchability', while Rabindra Nath Tagore attributed earthquakes and other natural catastrophies to laws "in the working of which God himself never interferes".

If natural calamities which visit us are punishment for our 'sinfulness', India must indeed be the abode of sinners.

"*Har Bala-i kaz asman ayad,*
Khana-i Hindyan talash kunad".

Apart from famines and floods, which are recurrent calamities, the influenza epidemic of 1918-19 carried off about 22 millions of people. It was a world-wide epidemic, but in no part of the world did it exact a heavier toll of mortality than in India.

Has Providence chosen India as the dumping ground for wicked souls? The older theologians used to defend the biblical account of the Flood as a singular event of supernatural character, and spoke of it as '*das Strafgericht der Suendfluth*' (punishment for sin). But it is now admitted that Noah's flood was only a partial and local inundation, and no universal calamity, after which the world was re-peopled from Mount Arrarat as centre. The biblical account of the Flood and the attempt to link it with the sinfulness of man is opposed alike to science and commonsense.

According to Mahatma Gandhi the earthquake in Bihar was an expression of 'Divine wrath' for the 'sin of untouchability'. The year 1555-56, the year of Akbar's accession to the throne, was marked by a severe famine. "As a date for that year," says the historian Badaoni, "*Khasham-i-Ezad*" (Divine Wrath) was invented. The Dutch factor Van Twist, who has given us a horrible description of the famine which devastated Gujrat in 1630, regarded the famine as an expression of 'the righteous indignation' (*rechtvaerdighen Toorn*) of the 'Most High'.

In the economics class room, however, famines are regarded as a normal feature of a certain type of economic organisation. They are not linked with 'sinfulness'.

As regards earthquakes, it would seem that untouchability is not the only form of sin that produces them, for they visit other countries also where 'untouchability' does not exist.

The earthquake of Lisbon on November 1, 1755 killed 60,000 persons in six minutes and ruined the whole city. An earthquake on February 5, 1783 killed 30,000 persons in Calabria and North Eastern Sicily, and in two minutes threw down houses and buildings in hundreds of cities. The Tokyo earthquake of September 1923 cost approximately 100,000 lives; the loss of property was estimated at 1,100 crores of rupees. Japan is most favoured by earthquakes. The records show an average of 1,447 shocks per year, or a daily average of 4.

There was a volcanic outburst in Karakatao (an island in the Straits of Sunda, which separate Java from Sumatra) on August 26, 1883, followed by a tidal wave which washed away towns and villages and drowned 36,000 people. It is stated that the noise of the eruption was heard in places even 3,000 miles away, and that the greatest of the vertical explosions attained a height of no less than 17 miles. The tidal wave, when it met the land, was about 100 feet high, and it was measurable even in the English Channel, after traversing more than 14,000 miles of sea. It will be ridiculous to suggest that God caused the valcano to explode and the tidal wave to arise with a moral object in view.

Natural calamities such as famines, floods and earthquakes, are governed by physical laws. They must be withdrawn from God's jurisdiction. God's omnipotence is thereby limited, but not to limit it in this manner would imply that human ethics was superior to Divine ethics. For saints and sinners, men and women, the young and the old, suffer indiscriminately in natural calamities. We are forced to admit that natural calamities are due to the mechanical working of natural forces which have nothing to do with the moral or spiritual condition of human beings. Their action may be described as 'mechanical' as it is devoid of intelligence.

This argument may be further developed. The evolution of the universe, the evolution of life itself, is found to be governed by laws which have no ethical significance.

There is no Will of God behind famines, floods and earthquakes. Similarly there is no Will of God behind the process of evolution. It is neither a righteous nor an intelligent process. The Devil can claim a large share of credit in evolution, if evolution has a purpose.

There is progress in evolution—a constant striving towards something better, which has resulted in man. But there is degeneration also, and degeneration is a far commoner phenomenon than progress. "If we consider any given evolutionary level, we generally find one or two lines leading up to it and dozens leading down."[1]

Evolution has produced the rose, and also the tapeworm, the cholera germ, the plague germ, and the germs of other diseases. There are wonderful adaptations in nature. The most common phenomena of life and growth seem to suggest

[1] *The Causes of Evolution*, by J. B. S. Haldane, p. 153 (Longmans, 1932)

intelligent and beneficent design: the unthinking cells of our body are ceaselessly busy assimilating what the system requires and rejecting what is useless. But adaptation in nature is both good and evil. We serve as hosts for many parasites. The malarial parasite feeds on our red cells. The tetanus (lock-jaw) bacillus, once it has entered our body, begins to shed its poison into the blood, which is so deadly that one-three-hundredth-thousands of an ounce is enough to kill a man. The wonderful adaptations which enable disease germs to feed on us cannot have been purposely designed by a beneficent Creator. Further, man has been described as 'a veritable museum of antiquities'. We have vestigal organs, or historical documents, which prove our evolution from lower forms by the method of trial and error. The vermiform appendix is not only useless but sometimes a death-trap. Regarded as pieces of machinery we are marvellously constructed, but at the same time we are full of imperfections.

Biological phenomena of life and growth are governed by laws working mechanically. That is alone how we can account for degeneration, ugliness and parasitism. The method of evolution itself—over-production, the resulting struggle for survival, and elimination of the weak, shows lack of intelligent, not to speak of beneficent purpose. Prof. Woodruff in his experimental study of Paramecum found that there were 3,029 generations in five years. Protoplasm was produced in this period equal to ten thousand times the volume of the earth. It has been estimated that at the end of the 9000th generation the mass would exceed the confines of the known universe, and the rate of growth would be extending into space with the velocity of light (186,000 miles per second)! Nature produces millions to preserve one. The necessary result of this fearful over-production is fearful slaughter of the weak, or elimination of the unfit. And 'fitness' is not to be understood in a moral sense. It does not mean righteousness.

The study of evolution is a study of laws of cause and effect, without any reference to the Will of God.

The same law of cause and effect is found working in human history. History shows a gigantic conflict of human passions and forces. The rise and downfall of empires is an impressive phenomenon, but devoid of any ethical significance.

From the ethical standpoint India never had any ruler greater than Asoka (272 B.C. to 232 or 231 B.C.). Asoka endeavoured to make India the 'Kingdom of Righteousness' and vigorous official propaganda was carried on during his reign for the moral uplift of the people. Asoka inculcated the virtues of reverence, compassion, truthfulness and sympathy; he condemned irreverence, cruelty, falsehood and intolerance. "The preacher was no mere sermon-writer. He was a man of affairs, versed in the arts of peace and war, the capable ruler of an immense Empire, a great man and a great king."[2] Asoka's propaganda was successful. One may even say that in certain respects it left a permanent impress on Hindu character. But the Hindu failed to develop qualities which give victory in the struggle for life. These are the militant virtues. Nature is warlike. And Nature knows no pity.

We see that not only natural catastrophies, but evolution and human history must be excluded from God's jurisdiction, unless we wish to make God responsible for all the undesirable features of the evolutionary process, and all the injustice, oppression and cruelty in which the history of nations abounds.

Is it possible to interpret economic phenomena in a spiritual sense? Can we connect them with the Will of God?

Some earlier economists saw the hand of God in the working of the economic machine. But the modern point of view is different. Adam Smith thought that the individual, in seeking his own advantage, was 'led by an invisible hand' to promote the good of the society. But such harmony of

[2] *Early History of India*, by V. A. Smith, p. 170.

interests does not actually exist. As List wrote[3], robbers, thieves, smugglers and swindlers know what promotes their interests, and pursue their trades with zeal and industry, but in the interests of the whole body of the people the State has to limit their activities. Or take another example. The world is pleased with our exports of gold. But the Moghul Kings 300 years ago used to cut off the heads of bullion exporters, as they considered such export disadvantageous from the national point of view. When, within a country the interests of particular individuals or groups frequently clash with those of other individuals, groups or the country as a whole, international or universal harmony of interests would be still more difficult to find. The World Economic Conference of 1933 broke up in confusion because of international clash of interests. Dollar depreciation suited the United States but not the Gold Block. We heavily tax imports of cotton goods from Japan, but that does not suit Japan.

The support of religion was invoked by the advocates of free trade in England in their campaign against the Corn Laws and anti-Corn Law sermons played as large a part in that agitation as anti-Corn Law lectures[4]. Cobden himself ingeniously turned Christ's teaching 'Do ye to all men as ye would do unto you' into an argument for free trade.[5] Even if free trade was a Divine institution 75 years ago, it has entirely lost that character now. There is not a single country at the present time which strictly upholds the ideals of free trade. The change from free trade to protection is due to causes which can be explained in material terms.

Have trusts or combinations a Divine sanction? Not more than cheats and cut-throats, you will say. But the secretary of an international trust for manufacturing reaping machines, a Mr. Wood, claimed in 1912 that the formation of trusts was in harmony with the Divine world order![6]

[3] *Das Nationale System der pol. Oek,* (Jena 1920), p. 258.
[4] and [5] *Theoretische Nationaloekonomie,* by K. Diehl (Jena 1922), p. 378.
[6] *Diehl* loc. cit. p. 378.

The institution of property is considered Divine, but its origin is human, 'all too human'. There was a time when the wicked institution of slavery was supposed to be an expression of Divine reason! Can anything be more absurd?

Next consider economic laws. Has the law of Demand and Supply any religious significance? Marginal utility explains the princely salaries of cinema stars and also the extraordinary cheapness of our graduates, without reference to their moral qualities. The Law of Comparative Costs explains how India may give to foreign countries the products of two days' labour in exchange for goods which represent only half a day's labour. Under a given type of economic organisation labour may be subjected to fearful exploitation, and capital may earn a reward out of all proportion to its services in production. Again, under a primitive system of production, the amount of wealth produced annually is small and per capita income is consequently small. That means a low standard of living, low vitality and disease-resisting power of the population, inefficiency in production and great mortality in epidemics. Can we substitute the Divine Will for the economic causes of the trade depression, or unemployment?

Western sciences are taught in all Indian universities, and in most of our colleges some time is devoted daily to the study of 'theology' or religion. We are not aware that traditional religion and science teach us totally different and mutually contradictory views of life. In the 'theology' period the professor expounds to his pupils a philosophy of the relation of God to the universe which is not the harmony with their work in other classes. Science is impersonal—it seeks to explain the unknown in terms of the known. Its broad concern is Causality—the relation of cause and effect, as determined by the action of physical, biological and other laws. It starts with the assumption that all earthly phenomena are governed by laws; and the scientific explanation is complete when causes have been projected forward to their effects and effects traced back to their causes. Religion substitutes the Will of

God for causality. And when the workings of the Divine Will are difficult to understand, we are taught to connect its manifestations (as in the case of the Bihar earthquake) with sinfulness!

It is not clear how far Rabindra Nath Tagore is prepared to go in limiting the Omnipotence of God. If the whole universe is governed by laws, and God never interferes in the working of His laws, the Will of God as a determinant of earthly phenomena, whether of a physical or other order, entirely disappears. God becomes Law. In his reply to Tagore Mahatma Gandhi admitted that God was Law, but qualified his statement by declaring that God was also Truth, Love and a million other things. Law is Truth, in the sense that the action of natural laws is reliable. Law is trustworthy, as a truthful person is trustworthy. But Law is not Love. Laws neither love nor hate. They are impersonal.

Causality

All laws are statements of what tends to happen under given conditions. They are statements of Causality.

The admission of Causality is the negation of a personal God, and of religion based on the conception of a personal God. This explains why the discovery of the principle of Indeterminacy was hailed in 1927 as the discovery of religion. Religion, says Eddington, "first became possible for a reasonable scientific man about the year 1927".[7]

Considering the profound implications of Causality, no apology is needed for the following brief discussion of the subject.

Matter does not consist of hard little lumps. Matter is electrical. Instead of atoms of matter, physicists now talk of atoms of electricity. The electrical constitution of matter is shown by simple experiments, as electrolysis, or when an electric discharge is sent through a glass tube from which all

[7] *The Nature of the Physical World*, by Sir Arthur Eddington, 1931. p. 350.

possible air has been expelled. The glass wall of the
struck by electrons, and begins to emit a lovely gree

The electron is a very tiny thing. Its m
·0,000,000,000,000,000,000,000,000,009 gram. The e
moves at a tremendous speed. In the study of electron
cities above 161,000 miles per second are actually encou

Now it is found that an electron does not behav
deterministic fashion, whether it is regarded as a particle or as a wave (it has both aspects). Heisenberg has shown that we may choose either to determine the place of a flying electron or to ascertain its speed with precision. Position and velocity cannot be fixed at once with the maximum accuracy. This is the famous Principle of Indeterminacy or Uncertainty. No experiment can be devised which would enable the observer to fix the position and speed of an electron at the same time with as high accuracy as he may desire. We cannot see the electron without some kind of light, and the light drives it away.

Important philosophical conclusions have been drawn by certain leading physicists from the Uncertainty Principle.

Eddington says: "If the atom has indeterminacy, surely the human mind will have an equal indeterminacy; for we can scarcely accept a theory which makes out the mind to be more mechanistic than the atom".[8]

Reichenbach agrees with Eddington. If it is impossible to compute the electron's future path with arbitrary exactness, the conclusion is inevitable, argues Reichenbach, that Nature is not completely determined. "It (Nature) is not to be compared to the precise functioning of a machine, for choice rules in small dimensions; and it is only in the large that the numberless separate atomic events combine in processes of such great probability that we can treat them in practice as certain".[9] Reichenbach speaks in terms of 'probability', not mathematical certainty. The view of Jeans is

[8] *Ibid*, p. 295.
[9] *Atom and Cosmos* by Prof. Hans Reichenbach, London, 1930, p. 278.

Conceived as a particle, he says, the electron shows ninism, and just because the wave-mechanics of the 'deals only with probabilities and statistical assemb- apparent determinism may be only another way of ng the law of averages".[10] The old, exact, mathe- conception of natural laws disappears. "It is not at ie", says Reichenbach, "that we ever find strict laws ure".[11] The idea of probability thus enters the formu- of all laws of nature.

e student of economics is familiar with statistical laws, ws of averages. If a rupee were tossed 100,000 times, d tail would turn up about 50,000 times each. An g illustration of statistical regularity is provided by matches between England and Australia. Harold n *'Body-line?'* says:—

> true it is that the luck in cricket is very evenly etween two old and very regular opponents, is he fact that over the whole series of tests we have s 65 times to Australia's 64, while both sides have 51 matches each" (p. 171).

The winning of equal number of matches by the two sides in a long series of tests presupposes that they are evenly balanced.

The law of statistical regularity applies to births, deaths, crimes, suicides and marriages. The excess of males over females at birth is a well-known phenomenon, which is true of all countries. Mortality at different ages obeys the law of averages, which makes it possible to estimate the rate at which the risk of death increases as age rises, and to express it in the form of rupees and fractions of a rupee. For example, for an assurance of Rs. 1000 payable at death whenever it may happen an insurance company of Lahore demands a single premium of Rs. 564-2 at age 42, and Rs. 387-12 at age 21.

[10] *The New Background of Science,* by Sir James Jeans, 1933, pp. 250-57.
[11] *Reichenbach,* loc. cit. p. 275.

In the Punjab about one-fifth of the children born living die before completing the age of one year. The rate of infant mortality is much lower in Europe—in the Canton of Zurich in Switzerland it is as low as 3 per cent. Under certain conditions infant mortality is high, and so long as these conditions remain unchanged, the average rate of infant mortality will remain about the same.

In India marriage is universal. In Europe it is by free choice, but it is subject to the law of statistical regularity. As Adolf Wagner wrote long ago: "Those who marry and seek divorce think they are acting according to their free will, and yet they only fulfil the law".

Statistical regularity indicates orderliness in the universe. It has even been invested with a Divine character. The old German statistician Suessmilch regarded it as an expression of '*goetlichen Ordnung*', or 'Divine order', which reveals itself in the events and phenomena of human life.[12]

The law of averages gives reliable results on the whole. It gives practical certainty when we are dealing with large numbers, but there is no certainty in regard to individuals composing a class. For example, we know that under existing conditions, one-fifth of the children born living in the Punjab are destined to die before the age of one year, but we do not know which unfortunate infants have been marked down by the Angel of Death. There is individual uncertainty in the midst of aggregate uniformity.

This uncertainty has led Eddington to say that 'there is no strict causal behaviour anywhere'. He finds in it reasons for 'dropping causality in the external world".[13] "There is no more reason", he says, "to believe that the universe is governed by causation than to believe that the moon is made of green cheese".[14]

[12] *Lehrbuch der Statistik* by Al. Kaufmann (Tuebingen, 1913), p. 162 and *La Methode Statistique* by Alfredo Niceforo (Paris, 1925), p. 15.

[13] *Eddington*, loc. cit. p. 309.

[14] Eddington quoted in an article entitled "*Cause, Effect and Prof. Eddington*" by the Rt. Hon'ble Herbert Samuel in the Nineteenth Century and *After*, for April, 1933, p. 471.

This position is untenable. Max Planck, the author of quantum mechanics, says:

"In point of fact, statistical laws are dependent upon the assumption of the strict law of causality functioning in each particular case. And the non-fulfilment of the statistical rule in particular cases is not therefore due to the fact that the law of causality is not fulfilled, but rather to the fact that our observations are not sufficiently delicate and accurate to put the law of causality to a direct test in each case. If it were possible for us to follow the movement of each individual molecule in this very intricate labyrinth of processes, then we should find in each case an exact fulfilment of the dynamical laws."[15]

Eddington quotes Planck in his support in the *Nineteenth Century and After* for June 1933, and mis-interprets him:

" 'Is it perfectly certain and necessary for human thought that for every event in every instance there must be a corresponding cause?...... Of course the answer is in the negative' (Planck). If it is not necessary for every event in every instance to have a corresponding cause, there may be uncaused events, due to pure chance. Planck seems to abandon causality, while maintaining elsewhere in the same book that physical science, together with astronomy and chemistry and mineralogy, are all based on the strict and universal validity of the principle of causality" (p. 147).

As a matter of fact he does not. The passage, from which Eddington has quoted a couple of sentences, is reproduced below:

"Would the thought involve a logical contradiction that in this or that case the event has absolutely happened of itself, and has no causal relation to any other event? Of course the answer is in the negative; for it is very easy to think of an event as having no explanatory cause whatsoever".

[15] *Whither is Science Going?* by Max Planck (London, 1933), p. 145.

"In such cases", Planck continues, "we speak of miracles and wonders and magic...... We can think of the Niagra Falls, for instance, as shooting upwards, though this would be impossible in the world of reality. I can think of the door of my room in which I am now writing as opening of its own accord. And I can think of historical personages as entering the room and standing beside my table".

It is in this sense that 'the concept of strict causality is not an inherent necessity of human thought.' One may think of a human nose as three feet long, of our University Hall as rising in the air and flying round the world like a mammoth aeroplane, etc. etc. This is not thinking but imagining.

It would appear that science is based on the assumption of strict and universal causality. The jumps of the electron seem to be due to chance, but as Sir Oliver Lodge says, "There must be a cause for each of those jumps".[16] And the cause is being sought by eminent physicists.

When a coin is tossed, we are not able to predict whether head or tail will turn up. The result seems to be due to chance. But we should be able to predict it if we knew all the forces acting on the coin: position at rest, initial velocity, acceleration, resistance of the air, etc. Each child born in the Punjab or elsewhere is subject to the law of cause and effect, and again, if we had full knowledge of all the relevant factors, we should be able to predict how many and which children out of a given number will die and which will live. We do not know all, but that is no argument for supposing that human affairs are not governed by strict causation. A supernatural fiat, independent of Causality, governing the universe explains nothing. It is a confession of ignorance, and has no place in a rational system of thought.

It is curious that while all sciences are taught in our Universities, the message of science is ignored by us. To a

[16] *Beyond Physics*, by Sir Oliver Lodge, London, 1930, p. 147.

people torn by religious strife, science brings the message of peace and unity.

That is how we may use modern knowledge to fight ignorance and superstition and raise the cultural level of the masses.

APPENDIX TO CHAPTERS XII AND XIII

THE CONCEPT OF GOD AS LAW, OR THE IDEA OF AN IMPERSONAL GOD

Common religion is founded on a personal God, in India as in other countries. But it is remarkable that, comparatively speaking, theism in this sense occupies an unimportant place in Hindu philosophy.

Samkhya, Niyaya and Vaisheshika are realistic systems of philosophy. Realism has no need for a Creator; it regards matter as eternal and subject to evolution by its own laws.

The Samkhya philosophers had no explanation to offer of the origin of species, and their account of creation by the combination of the three *gunas* will not bear scientific examination. But they boldly stated their conviction that life was governed by natural laws which worked mechanically. This is illustrated by the following Samkhya aphorisms.

"Though she be unintelligent, yet Nature acts; like milk" (III 59). The idea is that Nature acts spontaneously, as milk turns into curd.

"Or as is the case with the acts (or on-goings)—for we see them—of Time etc". (III 60).[1]

A commentator explains this aphorism as follows: "Or as is the case with the acts (or on-goings) of Time etc., the spontaneous action of Nature is proved from what is seen. The action of Time, for example, takes place spontaneously, in the shape of one season's now departing and another's coming on: let the behaviour of Nature also be thus: for the supposition conforms to observed facts: such is the meaning."

[1] *The Samkhya Aphorisms of Kapila* by J. R. Ballantyne.

"From her own nature she acts, not from thought; like a servant (III 61)."

The illustration is curious, but the meaning is plain: Nature works unconsciously and mechanically.

Realistic philosophy has no God. Pantheism has a God, but it is not the God of the theist. Pantheism identifies God with the universe, while the God of the theist is a Being possessing various attributes, who, standing apart from the universe, guides and controls it.

The teaching of the Upanishads is more pantheistic than theistic. The Bhagwad Gita itself presents to us a pantheistic view of the universe which it seeks to reconcile with theism.

The Bhagwad Gita

The great German Orientalist Garbe is led by *Wiedersprueche* or 'inconsistencies' in the Bhagwad Gita to suppose that there are many interpolations in this work. These inconsistencies have attracted the attention of many European writers. Gita presents to us, so wrote Holtzmann, "on the one hand, the pantheistic Universal Soul which is thoroughly impersonal and, on the other hand, the highly personal and realistic Krishna-Vishnu incarnation as man, and we are asked to believe that these two are the same".[2] Garbe agrees with Holtzmann. But while Holtzmann held the view that the original Gita was pantheistic, the personal conception of God being a later addition, Garbe maintains that the original Gita was composed at a time when Krishna-Vishnu was worshipped as God, the indentification of Krishna with Brahman in the pantheistic sense coming later[3]. Of the 700 verses of the Gita Garbe excludes 146 which are pantheistic.[4]

[2] Quoted by Garbe in his *Bhagwadgita* (Haesel Leipzig, 1921), p. 14.

[3] Garbe *loc. cit.* p. 16.

[4] Not including the first 19 verses and the concluding five verses of the Gita. Another writer, M. Winternitz, agrees with Garbe about the exclusion of 170 verses suggested by Garbe and would himself exclude another 200. The old and original *Bhagwad Gita* according to this writer, was thus about half of its present size. Garbe, p. 25.

The identification of Krishna-Vishnu with Brahman, according to Garbe, took place gradually. In the beginning Shri Krishna was simply the founder of a sect. The first period in the history of the Bhagwata religion came to a close about 300 years before Christ. This period saw the development of monotheism, the strengthening of the religious feeling through *bhakti*, and the transformation of the founder of the religion into God.[5]

In the second period began the assimilation of the new sect by Brahminism. This cannot have proceeded without difficulty, as Shri Krishna's views regarding the authority of the Vedas and sacrifice were not those of the Brahmins. But Shri Krishna was already worshipped as God by a growing sect, and the Brahmins, who were then engaged in fighting Buddhism, thought it prudent to recognise him as the *avatar* of Vishnu. In the Gita Arjuna refers to Shri Krishna as Vishnu in XI, 3, 24, and in X, 21 the Lord declares that of Adityas He is Vishnu. When Megasthenes visited India (302 B.C.) Shri Krishna and Vishnu had become one. The second period in the history of the Bhagwata religion extends from about 300 B.C. to the beginning of the Christian era. Garbe believes that the original Gita (without pantheistic interpolations) was composed in this period.

The third period, which began with the Christian era and lasted till the middle of the 11th century, saw the transformation of the personal God Krishna-Vishnu into the impersonal Brahman. "There remain preserved, however," adds Garbe, "in spite of the Vedantic interpretation of Krishnaism, the old Samkhya-Yoga elements. The Bhagawad Gita was re-written in the earlier part of this period".[6]

It is natural that Garbe should not regard the Gita as a work of art, or the product of creative genius. It is to him

[5] Garbe, pp. 45-50.

[6] "Verses from the Upanishads have been reproduced word for word in the Bhagwad Gita, which no truly inspired Prose would have done". Garbe, p. 16.

a work prepared to propagate certain religious and philosophical doctrines.[7]

Garbe's views have found little acceptance among more recent writers. Hill calls his criticism 'drastic and superficial' and endeavours to prove that 'the poem is less a medley than a reconciliation of beliefs'.[8] The 'inconsistencies' are more apparent than real, and are due to 'a misapprehension of their significance'. Lamotte shows that most of the verses which Garbe excludes as interpolations 'suitably occupy their place in the context, and fit in perfectly with the doctrines developed elsewhere in the poem'.[9] Lamotte accepts the Gita as a homogeneous work, and is convinced of its unity of composition. He rejects Garbe's chronology of religious sentiments.

Most of us will be inclined to agree with Hill and Lamotte in regarding the Gita as a homogeneous work. And yet theism and pantheism are mutually irreconcilable. They represent two essentially different conceptions of the relation of God to the universe. God cannot both be personal and impersonal. A personal God loves and is loved; He is the source of the Moral Law; He is good, intelligent and forgiving. The impersonal God of pantheism is completely identified with Natural Laws, which possess neither intelligence nor any moral significance.

Impersonal God of the Gita

Let us consider the Impersonal God of the Bhagwad Gita. He is imperishable and eternal (XI, 18), unborn and immutable (IV, 6) all-pervading (VI, 30) and unmanifest (VIII, 21). In the 11th Adhyaya the Lord shows His Vishvrupa to Arjuna. Arjuna saw concentrated in the body of

[7] Garbe, p. 18.

[8] *The Bhagwad Gita* by W. Douglas P. Hill (Oxford University Press. 1928). p. 15.

[9] *Notes sur la Bhagwad Gita* by Etienne Lamotte (Paul Guethner, Paris. 1929) p. 8.

the Lord the whole universe (XI, 13). The Lord had many arms, bellies, mouths and eyes (XI, 16), thighs and feet (XI, 23). He filled the earth, Heaven and the inter-spaces of Heaven and earth. Arjuna saw him licking up all the worlds around, devouring them with flaming mouths (XI, 30). According to this view, God is not something apart from the universe. He is the universe itself. He embodies in His own person the laws of birth and growth, as well as those of decay, dissolution and death.

The conception of God as the All or the universe is not easy. How can a person have every where hands and feet eyes, heads and mouths? How can a person be all-hearing, and how can he dwell in the world enveloping all (XIII, 13)? In this sense the Lord is incomprehensible—*mam tu ved na kashchana* (no one knows me, VII, 26). He who is everywhere is necessarily *achintya,* (unthinkable, XII, 3), of *achintyarupa,* or of inconceivable form (VIII, 9).

UPANISHADS

We next turn to the Upanishads. Deussen calls the Svetasvatara the leading example of the theistic teaching of the Upanishads,[10] but idealism and pantheism exist side by side even in this Upanishad. "Hence it follows," says Deussen, "that Svetasvatara is a work brimful of contradictions".[11]

The impersonal nature of the Brahman of the Upanishads may be illustrated by a few examples.

(*a*) The symbols used for Brahman are *prana,* vayu and akasha. Prana is the breath of life pervading both the human body and the entire universe. Brahman is *akasavat sarvgatashcha nitya* (omnipresent like space and eternal).[12] *Brihadaranyaka* 5. 1. 1. says: 'Om! the firmament is Brahman, the permanent air-filled firmament' (*Om kham Brahma,*

[10] *Philosophy of the Upanishads* by Deussen, p. 177.
[11] *Ibid*, p. 178.
[12] *Ibid*, p. 112.

kham puranam, vayuram kham). God as a Person is not conceived as breath, air or firmament.

(*b*) Brahman is Being and Not-Being (*sat and asat*), Reality and not-Reality (*satyam* and *asatyam*). Similarly in the Bhagwad Gita the Lord says: 'Being and Not Being am I, O Arjuna' (IX, 19, XI, 37 and XIII, 12) Brahman, conceived thus, is indefinable. It is neither thick nor thin, neither short nor long, neither red (like fire) nor fluid (like water), neither shadowy nor dark, neither wind nor ether (space), not adhesive (like gum), without taste or smell, without eye or ear, without speech, without understanding (*amana*), without vital force and without breath, without mouth or size, without inner or outer; never consuming anything nor consumed by any (*Brihad*, 3. 8. 8.). *Neti, neti* (it is not so, it is not so) expresses the impossibility of knowing Brahman.

Like the Vedantist the Sufi exclaims:

An zaman ko ra 'ayan joi nihan
Van zaman ko ra nihan joi 'ayan
Gar 'ayan joi nihan angeh buad
Van nihan joi 'ayan angeh buad.

How can one describe in words such an elusive being? The best course to follow, therefore, is silence:—

Chun mago chun dar isharat naydat
Dam mazan chun dar 'ibarat nayadat
Na 'ibarat me pazirad ne bayan
Na kase zan 'ilm darad ne bayan

(*Attar, Mantaq-ut-Tair*)

When Vashkali said to Bhava: 'Teach me, most reverent sir, the nature of Brahman,' Bhava remained silent. But when the question was put for the second or third time he answered: 'I teach you indeed, but you do no understand; the Atman is silence'. A beautiful story, which emphasizes the unknowableness of Brahman.[18]

[18] *Deussen, loc. cit.* p. 156.

(*c*) The complete identification of God with the universe is taught in *Brihad*. 1. 4. 7. which declares that the Atman has entered into the universe 'up to the finger-nails, (*a nakhagrebhya*), as a razor is hidden in its sheath, or the all-sustaining fire in the fire-preserving (wood)'. Another illustration used to bring out the same idea is that of salt dissolved in water (*Brihad* 2. 4. 12.). It would be easy to multiply such instances.

From pantheism to idealism is but a step. The great Maulana Rum says:

Jumla m'ashuq ast o 'ashaq parda-e,
Zinda m'ashuq ast o 'ashaq murda-e.

This is the famous doctrine of *vahdat-ul-vajud* or *hama ost* which does not find favour with the orthodox Mussalman. There is little difference between *hama ost* and *Vasudeva sarvam* or *idam sarvam Brahma* of Vedanta.

Science supports idealistic philosophy. If we are governed by laws, and not by the fiat of a Personal God, every thing is pre-determined by the relation of cause and effect (Determinism). The illusion of freedom is preserved, but it is an illusion. Things and events, which we take to be real, are not more real than things and events on the screen.

Jehan ra nest hasti juz majazi
Sarasar kar-i-o lehv ast o bazi.

(*Gulshan-i-raz*)

We are told in the Bhagwad Gita that 'The Lord, by His *maya*, causes all things to revolve, as if set on a machine' (XVIII, 61). Science calls this machine causality. The Gita again declares: "All actions are wrought by Prakirti's gunas, but the Self deluded by *ahamkara* thinketh 'I am the doer' "—words of infinite wisdom. The message of *modern* science is summarised in this single verse though it was composed about 2,000 years ago.

The existence of the crudest theism in our sacred books side by side with the highest idealism can only be explained by supposing that our ancient teachers thought that everyone was incapable of understanding Truth and Reality. The result of this has been that the intellectual level of our masses has not only not risen but is probably lower to-day than two or three thousand years ago. The message of science is for all. It is the message of the Rishis; the only difference is that, being founded on observation and experiment, it carries its verification with it. And this message creates unity, instead of disunity and discord created by common religion.

INDEX

A

B

C

D

I

J

K

L

M